The Merchant of Venice

ARDEN SHAKESPEARE STATE OF PLAY SERIES

General Editors: Lena Cowen Orlin and Ann Thompson

Elizabethan Narrative Poems: The State of Play, edited by Lynn Enterline
Macbeth: The State of Play, edited by Ann Thompson
Othello: The State of Play, edited by Lena Cowen Orlin
The Revenger's Tragedy: The State of Play, edited by Gretchen E. Minton
The Sonnets: The State of Play, edited by Hannah Crawforth, Elizabeth Scott-Baumann and Clare Whitehead
Titus Andronicus: The State of Play, edited by Farah Karim-Cooper

Forthcoming titles:
Hamlet: The State of Play, edited by Sonia Massai and Lucy Munro
The Taming of the Shrew: The State of Play, edited by Heather C. Easterling and Jennifer Flaherty

The Merchant of Venice
The State of Play

Edited by
M. Lindsay Kaplan

THE ARDEN SHAKESPEARE
LONDON • NEW YORK • OXFORD • NEW DELHI • SYDNEY

THE ARDEN SHAKESPEARE
Bloomsbury Publishing Plc
50 Bedford Square, London, WC1B 3DP, UK
1385 Broadway, New York, NY 10018, USA
29 Earlsfort Terrace, Dublin 2, Ireland

BLOOMSBURY, THE ARDEN SHAKESPEARE and the Arden Shakespeare
logo are trademarks of Bloomsbury Publishing Plc

First published in Great Britain 2020
This paperback edition published in 2022

Copyright © M. Lindsay Kaplan and contributors, 2020

M. Lindsay Kaplan and contributors have asserted their right under
the Copyright, Designs and Patents Act, 1988, to be identified as
the authors of this work.

Cover image © Shutterstock

All rights reserved. No part of this publication may be reproduced or
transmitted in any form or by any means, electronic or mechanical,
including photocopying, recording, or any information storage or retrieval
system, without prior permission in writing from the publishers.

Bloomsbury Publishing Plc does not have any control over, or responsibility
for, any third-party websites referred to or in this book. All internet
addresses given in this book were correct at the time of going to
press. The author and publisher regret any inconvenience caused if
addresses have changed or sites have ceased to exist, but can accept no
responsibility for any such changes.

A catalogue record for this book is available from the British Library.

A catalog record for this book is available from the Library of Congress.

ISBN:	HB:	978-1-3501-1022-9
	PB:	978-1-3502-4662-1
	ePDF:	978-1-3501-1024-3
	eBook:	978-1-3501-1023-6

Series: Arden Shakespeare The State of Play

Typeset by Integra Software Services Pvt. Ltd.

To find out more about our authors and books visit www.bloomsbury.com
and sign up for our newsletters.

CONTENTS

List of Illustrations vii
Notes on Contributors viii
Series Preface xi

Introduction: Recent Trends in *Merchant of Venice* Criticism M. *Lindsay Kaplan* 1

1 'Lend it rather to thine enemy': Accentuating Difference in *The Merchant of Venice*
Miriam Gilbert 17

2 Dangerous Border Crossings: Nicolas Stemann's *Merchant* in Munich *Benjamin Fowler* 43

3 Thomas Jordan's 'The Forfeiture': A Mercantilist Rewriting of Shakespeare
Katherine Romack 69

4 Jessica, Women's Activism and Maurice Schwartz's 1947 *Shayloks Tochter*
Sara Coodin 89

5 'Woolly Breeders': Animal Generation and Economies of Knowledge in *The Merchant of Venice*
James Kearney 113

6 'The means whereby I live': Deep Play in *The Merchant of Venice*
   Jeanette Nguyen Tran 135

7 'Qualities of Breeding': Race, Class and Conduct in *The Merchant of Venice*
   Patricia Akhimie 153

8 Jessica, Sarra, Ruth: Jewish Women in Shakespeare's Venice *Shaul Bassi* 173

9 'Marvellously Changed': Shakespeare's Repurposing of Fiorentino's Doting Godfather in *The Merchant of Venice*
   Thomas Cartelli 195

10 Balthazar's Beard: Looking (Again) Into the Merchant's Closet *A. Eliza Greenstadt* 217

Works Cited 243
Index 264

LIST OF ILLUSTRATIONS

1 Patrick Stewart as Shylock, in his office, in the 2011 Royal Shakespeare Company production, directed by Rupert Goold 22

2 Patrick Stewart as Shylock, at the trial, in the 2011 Royal Shakespeare Company production, directed by Rupert Goold 24

3 Susannah Fielding as Portia, with blonde wig, in 1.2, in the 2011 Royal Shakespeare Company production, directed by Rupert Goold 31

4 Susannah Fielding, a disappointed Portia, without her wig, in the final scene of the 2011 Royal Shakespeare Company production, directed by Rupert Goold 33

5 Lily Rabe (Portia), Al Pacino (Shylock) and Byron Jennings (Antonio) in the trial scene of the 2010 New York production, directed by Daniel Sullivan 35

6 Phoebe Pryce as Jessica, in the 2015 Shakespeare's Globe production, directed by Jonathan Munby 38

NOTES ON CONTRIBUTORS

Patricia Akhimie is Associate Professor of English at Rutgers University-Newark, where she teaches Shakespeare, Renaissance drama and early modern women's travel writing. She is the author of *Shakespeare and the Cultivation of Difference: Race and Conduct in the Early Modern World* (2018). She is co-editor, with Bernadette Andrea, of *Travel and Travail: Early Modern Women, English Drama, and the Wider World* (2019). Her research has been supported by the Folger Shakespeare Library, the National Endowment for the Humanities, the Ford Foundation, and the John Carter Brown Library.

Shaul Bassi is Associate Professor of English and director of the International Center for Humanities and Social Change at Ca' Foscari University of Venice. His publications include *Visions of Venice in Shakespeare* (with Laura Tosi, 2011) and *Shakespeare's Italy and Italy's Shakespeare. Place, 'Race', and Politics* (2016). He is the co-founder and former director of Venice's international literary festival *Incroci di civiltà*. He was the coordinator of the cultural projects related to the 500th anniversary of the Ghetto of Venice (1516–2016). He is the scientific director of the Creative Europe project 'Shakespeare In and Beyond the Ghetto' (2016–19).

Thomas Cartelli is Professor of English and Film Studies at Muhlenberg College. He is the author of *Marlowe, Shakespeare, and the Economy of Theatrical Experience* (1991), *Repositioning Shakespeare* (1999) and *Reenacting Shakespeare in the Shakespeare Aftermath* (2019); co-author (with Katherine Rowe) of *New Wave Shakespeare on Screen* (2007); and editor of the Norton Critical Edition of Shakespeare's *Richard III* (2009) and of two additional single-text editions of *Richard III* for *The Norton Shakespeare 3* (2015).

Sara Coodin is Associate Professor of English in the Department of Classics and Letters at the University of Oklahoma. She is the author of *Is Shylock Jewish?: Citing Scripture and the Moral Agency of Shakespeare's Jews* (2017).

Benjamin Fowler is a Lecturer in Drama, Theatre and Performance at the University of Sussex. His research focuses on directing and dramaturgy in contemporary European theatre.

Miriam Gilbert is Professor Emerita of English at the University of Iowa, where she taught from 1969 to 2013. Her publications include *Shakespeare in Performance: Love's Labour's Lost* (1993) and *Shakespeare at Stratford: The Merchant of Venice* (The Arden Shakespeare, 2002), as well as articles on teaching Shakespeare through performance. With Carl Klaus, she co-edited *Modern and Contemporary Drama* (1994) and *Stages of Drama* (1995–2002). She has taught eight seminars for the National Endowment for the Humanities, and from 2005 to 2013 taught for the Bread Loaf School of English at Lincoln College, Oxford University.

A. Eliza Greenstadt is Professor of Film at Portland State University, where she teaches courses on Shakespeare and popular culture. Her book *Rape and the Rise of the Author: Gendering Intention in Early Modern England* came out in 2009. She is currently working on two monographs: one, provisionally titled *Beyond the Closet: Inexpressible Desires in Premodern England*, analyses representational codes surrounding same-sex eroticism; the other, *Pricked Out: Genital Alienation and the Birth of Human Equality*, considers how liberal notions of personhood involved reimagining gendered bodies. Greenstadt has previously published essays on *The Merchant of Venice* in the journal *ELH* and the collection *Queer Shakespeare* (Arden Shakespeare, 2017).

M. Lindsay Kaplan is Professor of English at Georgetown University. She authored *The Culture of Slander in Early Modern England* (1997, 2006) and *Figuring Racism in Medieval*

Christianity (2019); edited *The Merchant of Venice: Texts and Contexts* (2002); and co-edited, along with Valerie Traub and Dympna Callaghan, *Emerging Subjects: Feminist Readings of Early Modern Culture* (1996). Her next monograph, *Medieval Merchant of Venice*, will consider the play's engagement with medieval discourses about Jews in the post-Reformation context.

James Kearney is Associate Professor of English at the University of California, Santa Barbara. He is the author of *The Incarnate Text: Imagining the Book in Reformation England* (2009) and co-editor of a special issue of the journal *Criticism* on 'Shakespeare and Phenomenology'. He is currently working on a research project that addresses ethical experience in Shakespeare's late plays. His work has appeared in a variety of journals and collections, including *ELR*, *Shakespeare Studies*, *Criticism*, *JMEMS*, *the Oxford Handbook of Shakespeare*, *The Cambridge Guide to the Worlds of Shakespeare*, *Shakespeare and Hospitality* and *Cultural Reformations*.

Katherine Romack is an Associate Professor of English at the University of West Florida. Romack is the co-editor, with James Fitzmaurice, of *Cavendish and Shakespeare, Interconnections*. Her work on seventeenth-century women and culture includes essays on early modern tropes of monstrous maternity and early Quaker performance. Other research interests include Milton, the poetics of religious enthusiasm, and women's troubled relationship to the metaphysical tradition. She is currently at work on a monograph documenting the seventeenth-century reception of Shakespeare, and a project with Robert Yeager charting the Protestant reception of John Gower.

Jeanette Nguyen Tran is an Assistant Professor in the Department of English at Drake University.

SERIES PREFACE

The Arden Shakespeare
State of Play
Series editors: Lena Cowen Orlin and Ann Thompson

This series represents a collaboration between King's College London and Georgetown University. King's is the home of the London Shakespeare Centre and Georgetown is the home of the Shakespeare Association of America (SAA). Each volume in the series is an expedition to discover the 'state of play' with respect to specific works by Shakespeare. Our method is to convene a seminar at the annual convention of the SAA and see what it is that preoccupies scholars now. SAA seminars are enrolled through an open registration process that brings together academics from all stages of their careers. Participants prepare short papers that are circulated in advance and then discussed when the seminar convenes on conference weekend. From the papers submitted, the seminar leader selects a group for inclusion in a collection that aims to include fresh work by emerging voices and established scholars both. The general editors are grateful for the further collaboration of Bloomsbury Publishing, and especially our commissioning editors Margaret Bartley and Mark Dudgeon.

Introduction: Recent Trends in *Merchant of Venice* Criticism

M. Lindsay Kaplan

While many of Shakespeare's dramatic works enjoy sustained interest across the centuries – inspiring performance, adaptation and literary criticism that reinterpret the plays' relevance in light of differing contemporary moments – *The Merchant of Venice* has acquired a particularly controversial status in the wake of the Holocaust. However, as recent criticism demonstrates, the play's provocations lie not only in its representation of Jews and Judaism, but also in its representations of gender, blackness, Islam and queerness. Several methodological forays into early modern studies that emerged in the past several decades – gender studies, historicism, critical race theory, queer theory, animal studies and religious studies – developed and advanced their theoretical approaches through interpretation of the play's representation of these discourses and their intersection. At the beginning of the third decade of the twenty-first century, we bear witness to various forms of violent hostility to peoples of colour, to women, to Muslims, to immigrants, to the LGBTQ+ community and to Jews in America and across the globe; this is perhaps less evidence of an intensification in feeling than a bolder articulation of an already-existing hatred. As the study of the play across its history demonstrates, these animosities are not so much new as renewed – in fact, they predate the composition of the play – but their current iterations make the play's content and its reception even more salient today.

A brief introduction cannot usefully account for the full range of current critical engagement with *The Merchant of Venice*. A perennial question, and one raised to greater or lesser extents by the authors of this volume's essays, is how to understand *The Merchant of Venice*'s representation of Jews and Judaism. In the context of rising rates of racist discourse and violence against non-Christians, including Jews, this question has taken on a new urgency. I therefore devote the first part of this introduction to a consideration of the methodological trends – historicist, critical race studies and religion studies – that have profoundly shaped attempts in the recent critical conversation to answer this question. James Shapiro's *Shakespeare and the Jews* effectively inaugurated the New Historicist approach to *Merchant*, putting it into productive conversation with a wide range of contemporary ideas about Jews (1996). His analysis transformed the study of the play, moving it beyond Christian supersessionist or topical historical readings to explore the larger religious, political, racial and cultural meanings of Jews in early modern England. While Emma Smith challenged this line of inquiry by provocatively calling into question Shylock's Jewish identity (2013), a scholarly consensus investigates the play's engagement with early modern ideas of Jews and Judaism; some important recent books in this field include Adelman 2008; Biberman 2004; Bovilsky 2008; Coodin 2017; Harris 2006; Lupton 2005; Shoulson 2013; and Yaffe 1998.

Critical race studies similarly transformed how we understand Jews through the play's coordination of their portrayals in relation to gender, race and Islam. Kim Hall cogently argued for the need to attend to the racial and gender identities of black and brown characters in the play, the Negro or Moor woman and the Prince of Morocco, in addition to Jewish characters (1992). Subsequent work on the play has explored early modern discourses on Jewish race, its inflection by gender and/or anti-black/Muslim racism (Adelman 2008; Andreas 2002; Bovilsky 2008, 2010; Britton 2014; Chakravarty 2018; Harris 2010; Hirsch 2006, 2009; Jajja 2014; Kaplan 2002, 2007; Lampert 2004; Loomba 2002; Metzger 1998; Shapiro 1996; I. Smith 2016; and Spiller 1998). In particular, Loomba (2002) has helped delineate the multiple 'vocabularies' that contribute to the construction of race in early modernity: lineage, faith/nation, gender/sexuality, class and colour. *The Merchant of Venice* incorporates all of these discourses in a rich interrogation of racial difference through or adjacent to Jews.

The turn to religion in early modern scholarship has also produced new perspectives on the play's representation of Jews, not only in relation to other infidels such as Muslims (Andreas 2002; Charry 2008; and Jajja 2014), but also in the context of post-Reformation intra-Christian polemic. While medieval Christianity classified Jews and Muslims as enemies of the faith, the religious schism within the Church produced new, more threatening Christian adversaries. A number of scholars have explored the play through the lenses of various Christian preoccupations with illuminating results. Lampert (2004) productively employed Jeremy Cohen's concept of the 'hermeneutic Jew [...], an ideological construction created not as a reflection of actual reality but as a tool of Christian theology', in her intersectional analysis of gender and Judaism in medieval literature and *Merchant* (2004: 9). Work along these lines considers Jews as figures or other means of working through difficult theological problems within Christianity (Britton 2014; Freinkel 2002; Harris 2007; Hirschfeld 2005, 2006, 2010; Lupton 2005; Nirenberg 2010; and Shoulson 2013). Other critics explore various biblical and liturgical texts or contexts to develop new readings, not only on the place of Jews in Christian theology, but on the play's multifarious engagement with Christianity itself (a partial list of essays includes Conti 2015; Ephraim 2005, 2008; Espinosa 2009; Kaplan 2019a; Kietzman 2017; Mcadam 2015; and Stockton 2017). Imaginative considerations of a Jewish perspective on the play are suggested in Kaplan 2002, but more widely investigated by Coodin 2017 and in Nahshon and Shapiro 2017.

Future analyses of the representation of Jews in the play might fruitfully combine all three of these approaches with periodization, a methodology that questions the imposition of disjunctions between historical periods in favour of exploring continuities. While many early modern ideas about Jews pre-date the sixteenth century, no one has systematically analysed *The Merchant of Venice* to determine the extent to which it offers unchanged iterations of medieval discourses, adapts earlier concepts or presents new ideas in the wake of the Reformation (although see Loomba 2007, who calls for the analysis of the longer history of race, and Lampert 2004). Such an approach would rely heavily on historicist and religious studies models in tracing reformers' reception of Catholic ideas about Jews. To what extent do Protestants continue to circulate medieval Catholic antisemitism or formulate new, and possibly more positive, ways for thinking about Jews? Critical race studies would also make a vital contribution to this investigation. As I have recently argued, medieval Christianity gave rise to a racist construction of Jewish identity in the form of hereditary servitude through the deployment of typology and canon law (Kaplan 2019b). Did the emerging trade in enslaved Africans, which intensifies discourses identifying blackness as a sign of inherent inferiority, effectively decrease the racialization of Jews in the period?[1]

Medieval ideas about Jews clearly persist in *The Merchant of Venice*. The construction of Jews as enemies to the true faith finds powerful and dangerous articulation in the association of Jews with the devil. As I have argued elsewhere, in the wake of the Reformation, the devil and Antichrist are increasingly associated with Christian adversaries (Kaplan 2013). However,

Shakespeare advances an older view of demonic Jews expressed in medieval theology and art, an example of which can be found in Stratford's Trinity Church in the form of a fifteenth-century misericord carving depicting two Jews with a devil. While the play correlates the devil with Christians, as well as Muslims, it associates or equates Shylock, Tubal or other male Jews with the demonic more frequently. The foolishness of Launcelot's internal debate over whether he should heed the actual devil and flee Shylock or remain does not undermine the servant's sinister conclusion that his Jewish master, the 'devil incarnation', is effectively worse than the devil himself.

The link between Jews and the devil helps bring into focus an attendant medieval conception: the coordination of Jews and Muslims. As Jeremy Cohen has argued, 'during the early Middle Ages, the Jews invariably presented Christendom with a paradigm for the evaluation and classification of the Muslim "other," a springboard for formulating a deliberate response to him and his faith' (1999: 161). As the original challengers to the truth of Christianity, the Jews' role of enemy of the faith shaped and was subsequently shaped by attitudes towards Islam. Loomba notes the intersection of blackness and the demonic with representations of Muslims and Jews in medieval and early modern religious and literary texts (2002: 27). Readings of the play tend to look at its depiction of blackness and Islam separately from the portrayal of Jews (however, see Andreas 2002; Britton 2014; and Jajja 2014). An analysis that undertakes a related reading of Muslims and Jews in the context of the longer history of their representation can reveal what persists and what new understandings are formed.

Given the centrality of theology for medieval forms of racism, the Jewish-black-Muslim coordination could also offer a fuller understanding of the play's representation of race. In spite of Loomba's demonstration of the intersection of the identities of Jews and Muslims, no one has fully explored the play's representations of race for both the Jews and Muslims/Africans in the play (some initial considerations include Andreas 2002; Bassi 2011; Hall 1992; and Lupton 2011).

As my recent work demonstrates, the medieval articulation of a racist Jewish identity through the concept of hereditary servitude employs the biblical figures of Cain, Ham and Ishmael as proof-texts. The plasticity of typology enables its reapplication to other peoples; the same types that prove Jewish inferiority also serve to degrade and racialize Muslims and Africans. Many early modern literary representations that focus on Jews also include Muslims, and vice versa. A wider interrogation of Jewish and Muslim race that takes blackness into consideration could produce new readings of the play and contribute to the larger field of early modern critical race studies.

Scholarship on early modern race, and on *Merchant* in particular, has attended to the intersection of race with gender (Adelman 2008; Britton 2014; Hall 1992; Hirsch 2006, 2009; Kaplan 2007; Lampert 2004; Loomba 2002; and Metzger 1998). However, most of this work has overlooked the medieval antecedents of the figure of a compliant, 'whitened' female infidel convert to Christianity. While critics of medieval literature have considered the coincidences and divergences in representations of Jewish and Muslim women (Mirrer 1996; Kruger 1997, 2006), few have compared early modern dramatic representations of Jewish and Muslim women (Britton 2014 and Landau 2006 are exceptions). Early modern scholars unfamiliar with the medieval context tend to read the two groups of women as representing entirely different faiths, ethnicities or even races. However, a number of sixteenth- and seventeenth-century texts represent infidel women with the shared characteristics of whiteness, beauty, wealth, sexual allure, sexual receptivity and openness to conversion. Medieval literature initially develops these tropes with regard to Muslim women, but extends them in several instances to portrayals of Jewish women. A consideration of medieval coordination of Muslim and Jewish women converts could provide a clarifying lens through which to understand *Merchant*'s adjacent depiction of Jessica and the Moor-Negro woman.

However, the play doesn't simply confirm or adapt medieval ideas; it also calls them into question. The concept of hereditary servitude established in medieval theology and law subtends the construction of an embodied Jewish difference. While referencing the discourse of servile Jewish inferiority, the play nevertheless rejects this status as resulting from an inherent physical trait by instead demonstrating its construction in secular law. Although medieval concepts of Jewish embodied inferiority continue to circulate in early modernity, they are increasingly discredited, including in *The Merchant of Venice*. Jewish somatic difference was formulated by means of and in conjunction with medieval theological and legal discourses that identified a divine curse as effecting the spiritual, physical, social and economic subordination of Jews to Christians. Given the expulsion of Jews from most of Western Europe by the beginning of the early modern period, this combined effort can be judged a success. The play might seem to advance a more tolerant view of Jews in de-emphasizing their physical difference and omitting earlier discourses alleging a degrading, divinely imposed, Jewish bleeding disease that renders them inferior to Christians. Although Portia's triumph in court seems to turn on a distinction between Christian and Jewish blood, her citation of law rather than medical discourses essentially invalidates the notion of Jewish inferiority as inherently embodied. However, the legal discourse she employs is no less effective in forcefully delivering Shylock and his wealth into the power of Christians. If medieval Christian racial discourses emerged in an attempt to impose an inferior status on Jews, by the early modern period, the legal and political accomplishment of this aim may render the earlier concepts obsolete. Precisely because both Shylock and Jessica have been successfully subordinated to – if not incorporated in – Christian society, there is no need to emphasize earlier discourses of Jewish servitude and somatic inferiority.

Viewing *Merchant* in its historical contexts has the paradoxical effect of demonstrating its continuing relevance today. While Jewish, Muslim, black, immigrant, feminist and

LGBTQ+ groups sometimes perceive their interests at odds with each other, white supremacists recognize and redeploy historical discourses that coordinate the demonization and degradation of these identities. The circulation of subordinating falsehoods demonstrates the interconnected victimizing effects across these groups and demands the creation of stronger coalitions between them to challenge these damaging stereotypes. It also requires us to re-read *The Merchant of Venice* in our current moment to better understand these shared histories in order to chart a new direction forward.

The essays in the collection include and move beyond Jewish questions, reflecting something of the breadth of contemporary scholarship in their consideration or reconsideration of the play from various perspectives: performance history, adaptation, the status of humans, risk, race, gender and queerness. In Chapters 1 and 2, respectively, Miriam Gilbert and Benjamin Fowler examine how performances of *The Merchant of Venice* in the wake of the Holocaust emphasize the play's conflicts in ways that preclude an easy comic resolution and reflect on contemporary social and political unease. In '"Lend it rather to thine enemy": Accentuating Difference in *The Merchant of Venice*', Gilbert focuses on representative and influential post-Second World War productions to demonstrate their embrace of the challenges in Shakespeare's controversial comedy. During this period, stage performances and film versions in England and America have generally moved towards reflecting the play's difficulties, making the audience feel unsettled, jostled even horrified. Through the use of extended pre-shows that set up particular social and cultural situations, the interpolation of extra text (in Yiddish, Hebrew and even Latin), the choice of settings that clearly emphasize religious (and social) difference, and, throughout, by portraying the contradictory impulses in all of the characters (so that there are no easy 'heroes' or 'villains'), the various productions heighten the audience's uncertainty, even discomfort. Choices about the final scene are particularly crucial, since the play's ending seems to move in the direction of reconciliation, but performance has often stressed the fragility and/or irony of such a conciliatory conclusion.

While Gilbert explores a number of English and American productions across several decades, Fowler's 'Dangerous Border Crossings: Nicolas Stemann's *Merchant* in Munich' argues that the strategies of the 2015 Kammerspiele production transformed the play into an echo chamber for contemporary moral and intellectual situations. It drew on a series of global and local contexts – including the contemporary refugee crisis – to intensify debates over stereotypes, difference and tolerance in German society. Using suspended screens from which the actors read a German translation of Shakespeare's text throughout, the performance forced critical distance between the play and its contemporary enunciation, creating an elaborate counterpoint that caused multiple forms of exclusion to resonate (not least in the sections that presented Shylock as a Muslim figure). Comparing Stemann's theatrical strategies with other directors' attempts to resist the play's textual antisemitism from within, Fowler explores the questions raised by a production that put Shakespeare's 'comedy' itself on trial. He demonstrates how Stemann's approach to the text doubled as an interrogation of the role of the classics in reacting to contemporary political crises, particularly in the context of the highly subsidized German state theatre.

Adaptations of the play, like performance history, similarly rework the play's elements in order to intervene in and respond to contemporary religious, social and economic concerns. Chapter 3, Katherine Romack's 'Thomas Jordan's "The Forfeiture": A Mercantilist Rewriting of Shakespeare', situates *The Merchant of Venice* in the context of the Jewish resettlement debates of the 1650s and 1660s.[2] She identifies Thomas Jordan's ballad as the first expressly antisemitic adaptation of Shakespeare's play. Significantly, the poet was not driven by residual medieval antisemitism that provided the backdrop of much of the literature about Jews in this period, nor by religious disputes between millenarians and their opponents that dominated the readmission controversy.

Instead, the ballad's negative representation of Jews likely resulted from Jordan's sympathy with loyalist London merchants, who feared that formal readmission might result in effective competition from their Jewish counterparts. In its portrayal of the 'deformed' Jew who grows wealthy through usury, 'The Forfeiture' displaces negative values associated with economic gain by presenting deceptiveness as an *essential* attribute of the Jewish 'race'. The replacement of Portia by the Jewish daughter operates similarly; it elides the questions Shakespeare raised about the fairness of Christian courts (and commercial adjudication more generally) by relocating the manipulation of the law to a Jew. Providing ideological cover for contemporary mercantile activity by eliminating any trace of questionable Christian business ethics, Jordan's ballad converts Shakespeare's economic realism into romance.

In Chapter 4, 'Jessica, Women's Activism and Maurice Schwartz's 1947 *Shayloks Tochter*', Sara Coodin expands on her earlier consideration of the play (Coodin 2017), analysing a radically different adaptation produced by an American Jew writing in the context of the Second World War. The critically acclaimed Yiddish-language play preserves the early modern Venetian setting established by Shakespeare, but focuses the action on Shylock's social-activist daughter whose departure from her traditional Jewish household ends tragically as a result of the pressures exerted by both Christian and Jewish religious communities. Coodin's reading intervenes in the critical conversation on the play as an example of post-Holocaust literature by focusing on Jessica's identification with her Jewish heritage through activist work. The most innovative features of Schwartz's adaptation of Jessica's character trace a series of definitive shifts in Jewish women's lives, paralleling the long history of women's participation in North American labour activism that prompted new modes of social organization both inside and outside the Jewish community. Coodin considers Jessica as a figure whose turn towards activism powerfully reflects the lived experiences of Schwartz's Jewish-American audience, including their own history of participation in factory work and labour activism. *Shayloks Tochter* transforms key elements of Shakespeare's play in its inquiry into the bonds of Jewish social solidarity and its exploration of new sources of Jewish community that moves away from esoteric scholarly study, instead emphasizing active modes of advancing social justice.

In addition to fascinating new work on performances and adaptations, *The Merchant of Venice* continues to generate important literary criticism that engages with a range of established and novel theoretical approaches. Animal studies, a methodology whose early modern iteration emerged over the last twenty years, found an early articulation in Bruce Boehrer's essay on *Merchant* (Boehrer 1999); scholars working in this field have continued to investigate the play's multifarious animal portrayals. James Kearney's '"Woolly Breeders": Animal Generation and Economies of Knowledge in *The Merchant of Venice*' enters into this conversation through the discussion of Laban's sheep to interrogate the weight that is placed on the animals' reproductive capacities and accomplishments. Animal generation is a crucial area of concern for early modern economic thought, especially with regard to risk management. Early moderns locate the contingent in the realm of the divine, thus beyond human knowledge and economic calculation. In late medieval and early modern controversies on usury specifically and economics generally, one key area of dispute focuses on the proper domains of influence and action: when and where must one acknowledge the limits of human knowledge and influence? This desire to establish these boundaries dovetails in striking ways with the ongoing contemporary critique of an anthropocentric modernity that colonizes the alterity of animal materialities through the instruments of scientific knowledge and economic calculation. The animal tropes in *The Merchant of Venice* breed and figure many things, especially an 'unknowability' or creaturely opacity that generates epistemological humility in relation to the familiar alterity of the natural world.

If Kearney uses the play's engagement with animal reproduction to explore early modern questions about the limits of cognition and the management of risk, Jeanette Nguyen Tran takes up similar inquiries from a philosophical perspective, an established approach that has enjoyed a recent renewed interest in Shakespeare studies. Chapter 6, '"The means whereby I live": Deep Play in *The Merchant of Venice*', makes an innovative contribution to the critical conversation by appropriating from the early nineteenth-century philosopher Jeremy Bentham the concept of 'deep play', a situation in which the marginal utility of what one stands to gain is less than the marginal disutility of what one stands to lose. This idea makes legible two moments of deep play in *Merchant*: the sealing of the bond between Shylock and Antonio, and the casket game. Both Antonio and Bassanio risk self-destruction by wilfully participating in deep play; their responses to their predicaments shed light on how the credit and legal system exposes individuals to a host of financial, emotional and physical risks which demand the development of new instruments to manage them. Antonio and Bassanio both actively overlook the likely adverse consequences of their actions, highlighting the power and necessity of illusory self-determinacy in an emerging mercantile economy where individual profit and security are prioritized, but are also progressively riskier and elusive. The play's representation of deep play ultimately illustrates how an attitude – a fitness or adaptation that responds to a change in the environment, stimulus or stress – can be understood as a kind of instrument, like insurance, to manage risk. Though all individuals are perpetually at-risk, the play also reveals how the ability to own risk is shaped by gender and race.

The study of race in early modernity emerged in the last thirty years in part through critical engagement with *Merchant*. Kim Hall's foundational work on the intersection of race and gender in early modern English culture found an early articulation in her essay demonstrating the importance of the largely ignored 'Negro' or 'Moor' woman mentioned in the play (Hall 1992). Subsequent scholarship explored the racial status of religious others in the play, not only Jews but the Muslim Prince of Morocco; gender also frequently figures in this work. The understanding that the construction of race in early modern discourse includes not only skin colour but also religious identity has moved the exploration of racial formation into the area of culture. A recent contributor to this phase of early modern critical race studies, Patricia Akhimie, has argued for the complex interaction between acquired and inherited traits in *Merchant*'s representation of the Prince of Morocco (2018). In Chapter 7, '"Qualities of Breeding": Race, Class and Conduct in *The Merchant of Venice*', she focuses on Shylock to demonstrate how the multiple meanings of 'quality' in the play triangulate a new mode of social differentiation, one which locates racialism at the nexus of ideas about shared *ability*, shared *nature* and shared *belief* or *rank*. The concept of relative 'quality' is used to distinguish between groups on the basis of attributes that are inherent or inherited, and those that are learned, providing a reasoning for existing inequalities of access and opportunity. *The Merchant of Venice* features competing vocabularies of valuation as measured by worldly wealth, moral worth and good conduct. Shylock enters this minefield of contradictory valuation with a great deal of capital, as one capable of funding, and thus fulfilling, the aspirations of others to improve and to rise in the world, but he finds that his own aspirations are repeatedly thwarted, that people 'like him' are despised. He discovers that where undesirable persons seem to possess worldly wealth, measures of moral worth and good conduct may be deployed to exclude them on other grounds. The contradictions inherent in the overlapping models for measuring relative value in the play reveal an underlying ideology of racial differentiation, a belief in the existence of innate differences between groups.

Feminist and gender scholarship has also explored widely the play's portrayal of women; as Coodin's and Gilbert's essays demonstrate, Jessica's character has attracted writers and directors, as well as critics interested in the complex and competing aspects of her portrayal as a Jewish woman who converts to Christianity. Shaul Bassi interrogates Jessica's representation through the lens of a seventeenth-century Venetian Jewish woman navigating the early modern juncture of gender and religious identity. In Chapter 8, 'Jessica, Sarra, Ruth: Jewish Women in Shakespeare's Venice', he juxtaposes and compares the character of Jessica and the historical figure of Sarra Copia Sulam, an early modern intellectual living in the Ghetto of Venice. He deploys this association to explore the entanglements and tensions between liberal, Jewish and feminist interpretations of *The Merchant of Venice*. Working against the grain of inquiries that try to establish parallels between the actual history of the Jews of Venice and the text and contexts of this 'Jewish' play, he argues for understanding the Ghetto of Venice as a place in which fact and fiction collide and merge, and for the special role played by the Jewish women and poets who occupy it. If their liminality ultimately condemns Jessica and Sarra to silence, Bassi reads Supreme Court Justice Ruth Bader Ginsburg as effecting a remediation, by means of her voice and authority, in her displacement of Portia in a retrial and acquittal of Shylock, staged in the Ghetto in 2016.

As with the other critical methodologies that emerged in the early 1990s, foundational explorations of sexuality and queer theory in early modern culture identified *Merchant* as a key text (see especially Sinfield 1996). In his contribution to this important body of scholarship in Chapter 9, '"Marvelously Changed": Shakespeare's Repurposing of Fiorentino's Doting Godfather in *The Merchant of Venice*', Thomas Cartelli employs source-study as a means to chart the play's articulation of Antonio's queer attachment to Bassanio. Cartelli demonstrates Shakespeare's radical alteration of the configurations of character and relationship he found in his likeliest primary source: Fiorentino's late fourteenth-century *Il Pecorone*. Shakespeare repurposes the story of a callow youth's successful pursuit of a wealthy widow into the considerably darker face-off between a contentious Jewish moneylender who hates Christians and a closeted Christian merchant who hates Jews. The pointed substitution of Antonio's melancholy, self-loathing, antisemitism and desire to sacrifice all for a handsome gentleman differs so decidedly from the warm-hearted paternalism of Fiorentino's doting Ansaldo as to prompt renewed attention to what is effectively unsourced and thus unique and purposive in the play. In this respect, the source becomes a crucial resource for isolating exactly what the playwright has chosen to add, subtract, intensify, suppress or transform and for speculating about why such choices may have been made in the first place.

A. Eliza Greenstadt continues her sustained consideration of the play's queerness in Chapter 10, 'Balthazar's Beard: Looking (Again) Into the Merchant's Closet'. Ever since Alan Sinfield's influential essay, critics have interpreted the rivalry between Antonio and Portia in terms of a historical shift in erotic epistemology. Portia is 'ahead of her time' as the enforcer of an emergent heteronormative regime in which the institution of friendship would no longer legitimize male-male *amor*. Scholarship following Sinfield views the merchant as tragically poised to step into a closet that is first being constructed at this very moment in history. While it is certainly true that the institution of friendship permitted physical and verbal expressions of love between men that would become increasingly taboo in succeeding centuries, the notion that during the time period in which Shakespeare was writing this play same-sex passion did not attract 'much attention' requires further investigation. In what ways is this *not* a version of concealment? Greenstadt examines how Shakespeare's play calls on its characters and audience to be complicit in an ideology of friendship that wilfully ignores its erotic manifestations. Since much recent discussion in queer historiography has turned on Foucault's distinction between early modern 'sodomy' and modern 'homosexuality' as *disciplinary* regimes, what do we gain by fine-tuning our analysis of the varying textures of silence that characterize a historical trajectory from the sin 'not to be named among Christians' to the love that 'dare not speak its name'?

While this collection of essays does not attempt to exhaust the range of methodologies applied in contemporary criticism on the play, it offers some significant current readings as well as demonstrates the important ways in which *The Merchant of Venice* has contributed to the history, and might contribute to the future, of various theoretical approaches.

Notes

1 Jonathan Schorsch (2004) has argued that Jewish whiteness was invented in the seventeenth century.
2 The Jews were expelled from England in 1290 and permitted to return in 1656 (Shapiro 1996: 43–62).

1

'Lend it rather to thine enemy': Accentuating Difference in *The Merchant of Venice*

Miriam Gilbert

A canal in Venice, a gondola with a monk who glares menacingly, a brief scenic location, 'Venice, 1596', a torch burning a Hebrew book and scroll and then a series of informative and interpretative statements:

> Intolerance of the Jews was a fact of 16th Century life even in Venice, the most powerful and liberal city state in Europe.
>
> By law the Jews were forced to live in the old walled foundry or 'Geto' area of the city. After sundown the gate was locked and guarded by Christians.
>
> In the daytime any man leaving the ghetto had to wear a red hat to mark him as a Jew.

> The Jews were forbidden to own property. So they practiced usury, the lending of money at interest. This was against Christian law.

And intercut with each screen, an illustrative visual: a lock slamming shut, a young red-hatted man attacked, a coin dropped into a hand. Al Pacino (Shylock), wearing a red hat, makes his way through a crowd of people on and around the Rialto bridge, while the monk in the gondola rails against usury and the crowd responds by throwing a man off the bridge into the canal. Another recognizable figure, Jeremy Irons, bumps into Pacino, who says 'Antonio'; and Irons spits in his face, then walks away through the crowd. As Pacino wipes his face, the screen shot turns into the burning of holy Hebrew texts. The music, which at the beginning, featured a solo male voice in a Hebrew prayer, now turns to a Latin text, invoking '*Dominus*', and in the next shot, we see Irons kneeling, crossing himself.

This extended opening sequence of the 2004 film directed by Michael Radford represents a series of tendencies in post-Second World War productions of *The Merchant of Venice*: the foregrounding of religious prejudice, the clear differentiation between Christians and Jews, the overt hostility (spitting has become a sadly familiar cliché), and beginning not with the words of the play but with a pre-show sequence that creates a particular world. These choices and the concomitant rethinking of Antonio, Portia and Jessica, as well as the deliberate unease that the opening generates, are features not only of the film but have also dominated major stage productions of the last seventy years.

Take, for example, the Royal Shakespeare Company's (RSC) 1987 production, directed by Bill Alexander. There, on a stage of wooden planks, as if near a mooring for a Venetian gondola, and with a large yellow Mogen David scrawled on the back wall (as well as an elegantly Byzantine golden icon of the Virgin), two young men spat at a Jew, identified as such because of the yellow Mogen David on his shoulder. He hadn't done anything to them, and so the very casualness of the gesture was noticeable. As the production went on, the attacks became more pointed, with a trio labelled in the prompt book as 'freaks' (the programme called them 'citizens of Venice') popping up to harass Shylock, even throwing stones at him, and, in the trial scene, alternating cheers at Gratiano's attacks and jeers of 'Jew, Jew'.

Both the Radford film's beginning and the RSC production's pre-show couldn't come as a surprise to the audience, whether in the cinema or in the theatre; the warnings, on screen, or with the contrasting motifs on the upstage wall, were clear. By contrast, the 2015 production at Shakespeare's Globe, directed by Jonathan Munby, gained much of its power through surprise. Musicians and singers in Renaissance costumes strode onto the Globe stage. Such an opening is certainly a familiar, even conventional, way for Globe productions to open. Actors wearing leather commedia-style masks appeared, and a white-and-gold-clad Cupid bounded onto a small white platform stage in the middle of the Globe's larger stage, so we seemed to have 'street theatre', a small masque for Venice's carnival time. The appearance of two more masked figures, also in white – a man and a woman (the lovers 'shot' by Cupid with his golden bow) – turned the first group of Globe musicians and dancers into Venetians enjoying the carnival, singing, dancing and creating an atmosphere of fun. When a man walked in, pulled off his mask, paused and walked off, as if unwilling to participate, no one on stage paid any attention (although, no surprise, he turned out to be Antonio) and the dancing continued. But when two other men marked as Jews, with distinctive red hats, and a small yellow circle on their gowns, came in and tried to cross the stage, each found himself blocked, and then attacked, pushed to the ground; one was viciously kneed and kicked, then spat upon. And then, as one of the Jews helped his companion to stand up, and both exited through the crowd standing in the Globe's audience, the dancing and singing continued. By sending a variety of conflicting signals, the Globe's production shocked its viewers by destabilizing them. The light-hearted, even stylized, comedy first shown became deeply disturbing, in part because it started in the audience's 'world' before moving into the world of the play, in part because the dancing and singing continued even after the gratuitous violence.

Of course, not every production has an extended pre-show, but many productions have wanted to create a specific world for the play, especially those that choose a setting other than Renaissance Italy. That setting can be as minimal as the columns, archways and walls in the BBC Shakespeare (Bulman 1991: 10–11), where we come to know characters through their costumes, particularly the opulent fabrics worn by the Venetians as contrasted with the black robe of Shylock. One familiar opening for the play has been a table and chairs, whether in the bare space of The Other Place in Stratford (RSC, 1978; directed by John Barton) as Antonio, Salerio and Solanio met to talk, or in the elegant café (specified as Café Florian) for the National Theatre's 1970 production directed by Jonathan Miller, where the white tablecloths, elaborate coffee service and an obsequious waiter made clear that these men had plenty of money to spend. Indeed, when the pre-show or the set doesn't insist on religious prejudice, it usually creates a world of wealth and privilege. In the 1993 RSC production in Stratford (dir. David Thacker), the table and chairs for the play's opening conversation were downstage left, but a huge metallic structure of poles and staircases dominated the upstage area, with desks and computer work-stations visible. We saw a contemporary work-place, stylized and elegant, but clearly signifying a world focusing on business concerns. Similarly, in the 1997 RSC production in Stratford (dir. Gregory Doran), the opening moments featured commercial ventures. On a dark Renaissance Venetian wharf, merchants and potential customers looked at one of the huge wrapped objects on stage, while a prostitute solicited customers. That production's most vivid moment also threw – literally – money on stage, as Bassanio emptied a chest with 3,000 ducats; later, Philip Voss's kneeling Shylock kept slipping on those coins as he tried to rise and leave the courtroom, his physical embarrassment embodying his emotional defeat.

Perhaps the most extended pre-show of recent times came in 2011 in Stratford's newly redesigned Royal Shakespeare Theatre, where director Rupert Goold set the play in Las Vegas, and the opening scene in a casino. Here Antonio played cards, tourists in wildly awful clothes (from tacky flowered shirts to a long fur coat) sashayed around, and cocktail waitresses in high heels, short skirts and almost-backless tops served drinks and flirted with the customers. Chorus girls on the two curved staircases upstage heralded the arrival of an Elvis Presley impersonator, wearing a white suit studded with sequins, thrusting his hips, singing 'Viva Las Vegas' – the central roulette table rose up to become 'Elvis's' stage. When Shakespeare's lines finally were heard, they were spoken with American accents. Everything and almost everyone on stage seemed casual, careless, caught up in the meaningless glitz of the casino; Scott Handy's pale Antonio, dressed in a blue blazer and blue trousers, was the least flashy person on stage, and in that way attracted our attention.

Such an elaborate opening raises the question: what is the point of a pre-show? I would contend that, like the interpretative screens at the beginning of the Radford film, the pre-show sequence offers the director a way to explain to the audience the context in which the actions of the play – if not justifiable – will, at least, make sense. Thus, the overt violence shown towards Jews at the beginning of the productions in 1987 and 2015 immediately let the audience know that these worlds divided people into abusers and victims, insiders and outsiders. Both of these productions chose time periods roughly contemporary with the play's writing, just as the Radford film announced itself as set in Venice, 1596. By contrast, productions set in more recent time periods, especially those with nineteenth- and twentieth-century settings, seem less likely to stress overt antisemitism. Such productions – and here I think primarily of the 1970 National Theatre production and the 1993 RSC production, both of which showed Shylock as a prosperous banker – may gradually reveal antisemitic behaviour, but often that comes as a surprise to Shylock, as well as to the audience.

The Las Vegas setting might seem unrelated, certainly to antisemitism, and to the play; indeed, a number of reviewers felt that Rupert Goold's choices were flashy and incoherent. Charles Spencer, in the *Daily Telegraph*, spoke of 'director's theatre run riot' (2011), and Michael Billington, in *The Guardian*, began by admitting that he had 'difficulty working out the logic of the setting: why, in particular, should Patrick Stewart's multi-millionaire property-owning, semi-assimilated Shylock feel an "ancient grudge" towards the local Christians? And could we really believe they would void their spittle upon him in the wide streets of the US gambling capital?' (2011). But Billington moved beyond his initial question to the idea that 'wealth is no barrier against ingrained anti-semitism and Stewart's Shylock, however comfortable he may seem, is secretly despised and he is reduced, presumably because denied access to the golf clubs, to trying a few putting shots in

FIGURE 1 *Patrick Stewart as Shylock, in his office, in the 2011 Royal Shakespeare Company production, directed by Rupert Goold. Photo by Ellie Kurttz © RSC.*

his office. And, the greater his sense of isolation, the more he (Shylock) reverts to his ancestral religion' (2011: 530). Perhaps Stewart's Shylock was isolated, but he was also elegant and confident, in a three-piece grey suit (subdued pinstripes), a silk tie, his neatly trimmed beard and glasses making him seem almost grandfatherly (see Figure 1). When he goes out to dinner he wears evening dress, first removing the yarmulke that he seems to wear when he's not doing business.

But after Jessica's elopement, we see the emotional strain reflected, albeit minimally, in Shylock's costume for 3.1; the bow tie that Jessica had tied for him is now undone. By the trial scene, not only does he wear a dark suit, but also a yarmulke, while the fringes of the *tallit katan* (small tallit) are visible under his jacket. Moreover, as he prepares to attack Antonio, he puts on a larger blue-and-white striped tallit, and we can hear a murmured prayer in Hebrew (see Figure 2). The costume change emphasizes Shylock's new perspective, and the seemingly incongruous Las Vegas setting becomes a useful background. For this Shylock at first does not really understand that being Jewish means to live, always, in a society that quietly, or overtly, hates him. He may not perceive himself as hiding, but perhaps as superior – the only grown-up in a world of games, including the games available in the casino he owns. But when that game-world intrudes, he finally realizes the hatred. The moment is quietly nasty: Salerio and Solanio are seated at a table down left; when Shylock enters, and moves to a table up right, Solanio makes a hissing sound, and a gesture of 'turning on the gas'. The audience doesn't know if Shylock has or hasn't heard this not-very-subtle allusion to the Holocaust, but a few minutes later, as Shylock confronts the two men, asking, 'If you prick us, do we not bleed?' (3.1.58), he hisses 'usss' in a way that makes clear he *did* hear.

So, too, in 1993, David Calder's Shylock looked supremely comfortable in the business world that dominated the stage; his office was on the main stage (unlike the upstage 'office' where Bassanio seemed to work, along with Gratiano), he wore a well-cut suit, and his assimilation into the financial

FIGURE 2 *Patrick Stewart as Shylock, at the trial, in the 2011 Royal Shakespeare Company production, directed by Rupert Goold. Photo by Ellie Kurttz © RSC.*

world was underscored by the presence in that office of a noticeably foreign-looking Tubal. Textually, Tubal doesn't enter the play until 3.1, when he comes to tell Shylock that attempts to find Jessica have not succeeded. However, in the 1993 RSC production, Tubal, in a long dark coat, a yarmulke and side curls, made his presence felt in 1.3, when he came over to whisper in Shylock's ear, so that the hesitation about lending money to Bassanio could be ended, with a reference to Tubal, 'a wealthy Hebrew of my tribe' (1.3.53), as the source of that large sum. When we saw Calder's Shylock on his own, he wore a luxurious smoking-jacket, listened to Brahms and gazed at a framed photograph of (we assumed) his late wife. And again, the loss of Jessica seemed to send Shylock back to his Jewish identity. When Calder's Shylock complained to Tubal, 'The curse never fell upon our nation till now. I never felt it till now' (3.1.77–8), the line came with a bitter sense of realization that he could not escape from being Jewish, no matter how much money he had or what clothes he wore. Indeed, when he appeared in the courtroom, he now wore the kind of long dark coat that we had seen Tubal wearing, and his appearance was no longer that of the merchant banker but of the outsider Jew.

Both of these productions (1993 and 2011) were developments of the crucially revealing production of the second half of the twentieth century, at the National Theatre in 1970, directed by Jonathan Miller, with Laurence Olivier as Shylock. I am not alone in this judgment (Bulman 1991: 75–100; Drakakis 2011: 131–2), but let me suggest the choices that have been most influential, starting with the notion that Shylock is, in Olivier's terms, not Fagin but Disraeli (Gilbert 2017: 291–316). 'I was determined to maintain dignity and not stoop physically and mentally to Victorian villainy', wrote Olivier (Olivier 1986: 119), and that choice, filtered through and refined by Jonathan Miller, was central. Portia famously asks, 'Which is the merchant here, and which the Jew?' (4.1.170), and Olivier's performance and costume made that question not simply plausible but integral to seeing Shylock as an insider, not an outsider, as a wealthy banker, not a scruffy loanshark. The nineteenth-century setting was particularly useful, since 'allowing Shylock to appear as one among many businessmen, scarcely distinguishable from them, ... made sense of his claim that, apart from his customs, a Jew is like everyone else' (Miller 1986: 155).

The line from Olivier to David Suchet's jovial smiling Shylock wearing an expensive fur-trimmed coat (RSC, 1981) to David Calder to Patrick Stewart is clear, and was echoed in the United States by Al Pacino in 2010 (first in Central Park, then on Broadway). Pacino, like these others, was a wealthy and prosperous Shylock; though he wore a yarmulke and glasses, he sported a three-piece suit and seemed similar in class status to Antonio (Byron Jennings). But Antonio was noticeably reluctant to shake Shylock's hand; there was an uncomfortable silence after 'Your worship was the last man in our mouths' (1.3.56), as Antonio looked at Shylock's outstretched hand and finally made the briefest move he could, clearly not wanting to touch him.

In addition to establishing the possibility of playing Shylock as a would-be insider, the National Theatre's 1970 Miller-Olivier production also raised, albeit subtly, the notion of a homosexual relationship between Antonio and Bassanio, something that the RSC had done in 1965 (dir. Clifford Williams), with Brewster Mason and Peter McEnery. Some reviewers pointed explicitly to that relationship in 1965, while others did not, just as in 1971 (dir. Terry Hands), where the subtlety of Tony Church's performance as Antonio suggested an unrequited love for Bassanio without being obvious. For the National Theatre's 1970 production, Miller clearly thought of Antonio and Bassanio in terms of 'the relationship between Oscar Wilde and Bosie where a sad old queen regrets the opportunistic hetero-sexual love of a person whom he adored' (Miller 1986: 107), and again one sees how the nineteenth-century setting both allowed and suggested this emphasis.

Later productions have made the Antonio/Bassanio relationship even more clearly one of homosexual affection, usually repressed by Antonio, though felt by Bassanio, and sometimes exploited. In 1987 (and with a Renaissance setting), John Carlisle's Antonio replied to the suggestion that he (Antonio) was in love with a noticeably curt 'Fie, fie' (1.1.46), was clearly sad as Bassanio described Portia, and then responded to Bassanio's 'thank-you' hug with a kiss on the lips. In this production, Nicholas Farrell's Bassanio was aware of Antonio's feelings, staying physically close to Antonio, touching his shoulders while speaking of Portia; and if Antonio initiated the kiss in 1.1, in 1.3, once the loan was secured, Bassanio kissed Antonio. Moreover, the production featured another homosexual couple in Salerio (Michael Cadman) and Solanio (Gregory Doran), in part to find a way to make them more than ciphers, but also because their lines point to the Antonio/Bassanio relationship, as when Solanio comments about Antonio, 'I think he only loves the world for him' (2.8.50) (Gilbert 2002: 56; Doran 1993: 68–76). The word 'love' reverberates through the play, especially when Antonio bids farewell to Bassanio:

> Commend me to your honourable wife;
> Say how I loved you, speak me fair in death,
> And, when the tale is told, bid her be judge
> Whether Bassanio had not once a love.
>
> (4.1.269–72)

This context invites us to see Antonio as a 'rival lover' to Portia (Hyman 1970). Indeed, in 1997, Julian Curry's Antonio held Bassanio (Scott Handy) throughout the farewell speech, stroking his back. In 2011, with Scott Handy now playing Antonio, the orange jump suit he wore as a prisoner (shades of Guantànamo) was pulled down so that he was naked from the waist up, and Bassanio's hug was inescapably sexual. And 'love' becomes almost a term of blackmail at the end of the trial scene when Antonio insists that Bassanio should give away the ring to the lawyer: 'Let his deservings and my love withal / Be valued 'gainst your wife's commandement' (4.1.446–7). Here again, the text sets up a clear opposition between Antonio and Portia, so much so that playing Antonio as a potential sexual partner for Bassanio makes sense.

If the text allows or invites such readings, it's fair to ask why they have become so much more prominent and frequent. Are such interpretations merely an anachronistic response to the text, reflecting contemporary interests and sensibilities? In part, the understanding that homosexual feelings are not only real, but even normal, has become more accepted in the past fifty years. But I think that reading Antonio as someone whose sadness is not really so mysterious, but grows out of the pain of seeing that the man he loves wishes to marry a woman, also reflects the sense that the play's polarities are less than absolute. Not only can one see Shylock as, at moments, wishing to be accepted by, respected by, the Christian community, one can also question the values and behaviour of that Christian community. The audience's feelings about homosexual relationships may well be conflicted (Bulman 1991: 126–8) and that very conflict is what performance seeks to evoke. No longer can one point easily to Shylock as 'the outsider' if Antonio is, on some level, also an outsider in his own society.

And playing Antonio as someone who will not, in this society, find a partner whom he can openly love, has implications for the staging of the play's final scene. The final stage direction, '*Exeunt*', offers little information for how the seven major characters on stage (and perhaps attendants as well) are to leave, and with whom. But with three couples present, it's noticeable that Antonio is the only one without a partner, and productions have increasingly emphasized his alone-ness, or loneliness. The RSC productions of 1960 and 1971 left Antonio alone on stage, while in 1965, he walked off, but on his own. In 1971, the accompanying sound cue was the blowing of the *shofar*, the often discordant sound associated with the Jewish High Holy Days, and one had to think of 'the other lonely, isolated figure, the one who is mentioned only as "the rich Jew"' (Gilbert 2002: 153). Once again, the Olivier-Miller production at the National Theatre seems influential. There, Gratiano and Nerissa exit, with a whoop of laughter. Bassanio follows, although Portia stands on the stairs outside the house, as does Antonio. Lorenzo tries to get Jessica to enter the house, but she moves away from him, reading the document that had been handed to them, so Lorenzo leaves by himself. Portia seems concerned, looks towards Antonio but cannot reach out to Jessica and so she leaves. Thus we have Antonio and Jessica, each holding a document, each in some way troubled. Antonio stretches out his hand towards Jessica – is he inviting her to enter the house with him, or does the gesture imply a wish to comfort her? We can't be sure, but the off-stage chanting of the Kaddish, the prayer traditionally said in honor of the dead, makes clear where Jessica's thoughts are, and reminds us that the 'manna' (5.1.294) Lorenzo has delighted in comes at the price of Shylock's death.

This pairing of Antonio and Jessica in 1971 was deeply disturbing, but it was even more painful in 1987:

Portia and Bassanio left first, followed by Gratiano and Nerissa, so eager for bed that they were already touching each other's bodies. Lorenzo and Jessica also left, moving upstage, with Lorenzo going first. Then Jessica suddenly turned back, looking for the little cross that she had worn on her belt. She knelt to retrieve it, but Antonio, left alone on stage, got to it first. He picked it up and held it out to her – but also out of reach. The Jewish woman reached up for the symbol that had so oppressed her father, held by the Christian homosexual who would never be able to express that love again to Bassanio. Deliberately he withheld the little cross, as if to taunt her with her 'otherness' – both like and unlike his. (Gilbert 2002: 153–4)

The 'othering' of Jessica is not obligatory, of course, but it has become more and more frequent, often foreshadowed by the playing of her dialogue with Lorenzo, 'In such a night'

(5.1.1–23), at the beginning of the play's final scene so as to emphasize not the lyricism of the balanced phrases, but the potential separation and disquiet of the lovers, as they invoke famous – and unhappy – lovers from the past. Certainly, productions can play this section as a lovers' duet, with attractive young people, often dressed in white (reminding us that Jessica is a very recent bride) on a moonlit stage (Gilbert 2002: 147–8). But we might also see an incipient breakup, as in 1987, when Lorenzo and Jessica were on separate sides of the stage. Or, on Broadway in 2010, in an ironic reversal of the *Romeo and Juliet* balcony scene, Lorenzo stood above, on the set's structure of stairs, while Jessica sat below, her feet in a pool; the tone of their exchanges got sharper and sharper, so that Lorenzo finally descended and held out his hand to her, but she didn't take it. In 1999, at the National Theatre, the 'duet' seemed relatively happy (it is, however, cut in the video version), but as Jessica and Lorenzo lay stretched out on the floor, only their hands touching, Jessica suddenly broke into sobs on 'I am never merry when I hear sweet music' (5.1.69) and had to be comforted. And at the end of the play, Jessica looked questioningly at Portia, who directed her line 'And charge us there upon inter'gatories' (5.1.29) to her. Then Jessica began to sing lines that Shylock had sung to her earlier in the play; his singing was tender, hers was bitter and fierce. The tonal change is crucial, as are the words – which we hear only in Hebrew. The words are from Proverbs 31.10–12, beginning with '*Eshet Chayil*', a woman of worth, or valour, or a 'capable wife', and are traditionally sung by the husband to the wife at the Sabbath meal. In this production, Shylock sang them to Jessica, and she sang with him, showing how well she knew their meaning. But the line she sings at the play's end is the verse, 'She does him good, and not harm, all the days of her life', and clearly this Jessica was aware of the irony that such lines had ever been addressed to her.

Though isolating Jessica and/or Antonio has become almost traditional, a different approach, namely, isolating Portia, was the stunning interpretation of the RSC's 2011 production. Right from the beginning, the production showed Portia as a woman trapped in a game-world, where she was both the hostess and the prize of a TV show, 'Destiny'. Portia looks like – and there really is no other description – a 'blonde bimbo', with a Dolly Parton wig, a very short, pink, checked skirt, huge high heels (albeit with Mary Jane straps) and bobby socks (see Figure 3). Her Southern accent is exaggerated, and only at the end of the first scene (when she is no longer beamed up to huge television screens) are we sure that what we've seen is the performance that she has to give, rather than the reality. When Morocco is considering his choice in the first casket scene, her smile is patently fixed, as if she is forced not to show any feeling at all; only her fierce tone at the end of that scene, 'Draw the curtains, go' (2.7.78), is the giveaway that she hates what she is doing. Similarly, at the end of the scene with Aragon, she seems to stagger up the stairs, trapped in the charade. Thus, her appeal to Bassanio, to wait before he chooses, comes from her wish

FIGURE 3 *Susannah Fielding as Portia, with blonde wig, in 1.2, in the 2011 Royal Shakespeare Company production, directed by Rupert Goold. Photo by Ellie Kurttz © RSC.*

to escape, now that she sees a man she can love. And once he's chosen the right casket, and kissed her – briefly – Portia takes off her high heels, removes her blonde wig, revealing brown hair, held back with a headband, as she confesses, 'You see me, Lord Bassanio, where I stand' (3.2.149), and she does indeed sound like an 'unlessoned' and 'unpractised' girl (3.2.159), trying, haltingly, for honesty. What makes the moment memorable, and painful, is that Bassanio just gazes at her with no real emotion or surprise. In other words, he doesn't react to the change, perhaps because he can't see her when she's not the image from the TV show, perhaps because he doesn't want to.

Given this Portia, trapped in a costume and wig and role that she finds constricting, we're not surprised that she becomes increasingly strident, even vicious, in the trial scene, because now she has some control over the situation, once she's figured out how to stop Shylock. She pounces on the word 'Jew', almost relishing her power, although she comes to find that power temporary. Like most Portias, she is disappointed when Gratiano comes in with Bassanio's ring. But this Portia faces an even sharper disappointment in the final scene as she sits on a sofa, sandwiched between Antonio and Bassanio. When Antonio intercedes for Bassanio, saying, '… your lord / Will never more break faith advisedly' (5.1.252–3), Bassanio reaches across Portia and takes Antonio's hand – briefly – but long enough for Portia to look down and see the gesture. She chokes a bit but hands over the ring to Antonio, then crosses over to stage right and from her traveling bag retrieves her blonde wig, puts it on somewhat crookedly, revs up her Southern accent, and gets on one of her very high-heeled lucite shoes. And in the last moments of the production, she takes off her wig (see Figure 4), and as Launcelot Gobbo starts singing, 'Are You Lonesome Tonight?' she dances, one shoe on, one shoe off, in a little circle, holding up the wig; Bassanio is on the sofa, Antonio is standing slightly upstage of the sofa. The spoken part of the song seems especially relevant, with the Shakespeare allusion ('someone said that the world's a stage'), and the references to a play ('You read your line so cleverly and never missed a

FIGURE 4 *Susannah Fielding, a disappointed Portia, without her wig, in the final scene of the 2011 Royal Shakespeare Company production, directed by Rupert Goold. Photo by Ellie Kurttz © RSC.*

cue', 'Now the stage is bare') adding extra bite to the crucial line, 'But I'd rather go on hearing your lies / Than go on living without you'. In a spotlight, Portia is alone, dancing, having gotten what she thought she wanted. It is a very bleak ending.

Making the audience uncomfortable, both with the characters, and on behalf of the characters, has come to be the dominant mode of ending the play. While the 2011 production focused on Portia's isolation, a reading that seems congruent with readings that stress a homosexual Antonio – here finding himself in a *ménage à trois* – such a focus is not the norm. More usually, the audience will be reminded of Shylock, and in recent productions, that reminder grows out of a series of choices that emphasize Shylock's Jewishness, not simply his otherness. Just as Henry Goodman [at the National Theatre] in 1999 reminded the audience of Shylock's love for his daughter by singing the Hebrew words of praise, and at the play's end Jessica repeated those words with a bitter ironic tone, so productions, in the trial scene, or in the play's final moments, have stressed Shylock's loss of his Jewish identity. Almost every Shylock I've seen has either taken off a yarmulke, or had it ripped off him, although Olivier's Shylock kept his on while he was helped offstage by two attendants; the shock came a few seconds later as an awful wail, lasting at least fifteen seconds, was heard, and, in the TV version, the camera pans slowly from Portia to Bassanio to Antonio to the Duke, each one registering the appalling noise and pain. In the BBC version (1980), Gratiano removes the yarmulke, and Salerio presses a crucifix against Shylock's lips. In John Barton's two productions (1978, with Patrick Stewart as Shylock, and 1981, with David Suchet as Shylock), Shylock gets to take off the yarmulke himself: Stewart with a quick hand gesture that implies 'this doesn't matter'; Suchet with slowly dignified resignation. Antony Sher in 1987 was forced to make the sign of the cross. Henry Goodman in 1999 turned the moment into one of defiance; not only did he rip off his yarmulke, but he also removed the tallit under his jacket, then wadded both yarmulke and tallit into a small bundle and dropped it into the scales he had brought to measure the pound of flesh. Al Pacino, forced to his knees, crumpled even further as Antonio insisted that he 'become a Christian' (4.1.383) and dangled a crucifix (see Figure 5). Patrick Stewart, in 2011, took off his tallit and yarmulke, dropped them and left quietly, but couldn't avoid the large gob of spittle from Gratiano. What Shylock didn't see came a few moments later after all the characters had left the stage, as a Hispanic janitor with a large black garbage bag entered and put the tallit and yarmulke into the bag; the marks of the Holocaust survivor who could defy Salerio and Solanio were now simply rubbish, picked up by yet another outsider.

Even more disquieting is the choice in two recent productions (2010 in New York; 2015 at the Globe) to stage the conversion of Shylock, thus taking the BBC's gesture of forcing Shylock to kiss a crucifix even further. In 2010, the moment came after Portia had received Bassanio's ring. Bells chime, a priest leads in a small procession, with Shylock

FIGURE 5 *Lily Rabe (Portia), Al Pacino (Shylock) and Byron Jennings (Antonio) in the trial scene of the 2010 New York production, directed by Daniel Sullivan.* © *Joan Marcus.*

guarded; he's now completely vulnerable, wearing just his white shirt and dark trousers, and his yarmulke. A burly guard snatches off the yarmulke, forces him to kneel in a small pool, and while the priest chants a baptism ritual, the guard pushes Shylock's head into the water, the third time holding him there for so long that it seems he might drown him. The guards and priest leave as Tubal and another friend rush to help Shylock out of the pool. He staggers to an upright position and then picks up the yarmulke from the floor; looking at it, he defiantly puts it on, and then lurches offstage, not with Tubal but towards the departing Christians. All the while, the bells keep chiming, relentlessly; the entire sequence lasts for two minutes.

By placing the baptism ritual directly after the trial scene, the Sullivan production essentially 'ended' Shylock's story before the play was over, although since the 'baptism pool' then became the site of the Lorenzo–Jessica scene, we couldn't really forget him. In contrast, Munby's Globe production inserted an even longer and more elaborate conversion/baptism ritual at the play's end, once again surprising and shocking the audience, just as the beginning had done. We see three couples and Antonio on stage; Nerissa slaps Gratiano's face after he jokes about 'keeping safe Nerissa's ring' (5.1.307) but then kisses him; Portia and Bassanio embrace; Antonio is far stage left; and centre stage, Lorenzo and Jessica, with Jessica holding the document she has been given. She moves downstage, falls to her knees, chanting a Hebrew prayer, drawn from the Yom Kippur liturgy, asking for pardon and forgiveness, and ending with blessing God who graciously forgives. Lorenzo starts to go to her but Gratiano, amazingly sensitive for an instant, stops him. Jessica, kneeling, her low-cut dress emphasizing the gold cross she wears around her neck, is inconsolable (see Figure 6). Drums start to beat, and from the central doors a procession of white-clad monks enters, the first holding a large golden cross, and everyone, including the characters on stage, joining in a Latin hymn. Shylock is there, barefoot, bare-headed, wearing a long white robe. The priest intones ritual questions, all in Latin:

> *Credis in unum deum patrem omnipotentem creatorem celi et terram?*
> [Do you believe in one God, the Father almighty, Creator of heaven and earth?]
>
> *Credis in Iesum Christum filium eius unicum dominum nostrum natum et passum?*
> [Do you believe in Jesus Christ, his only Son, our Lord, who was born and suffered?]
>
> *Credis et in spiritum sanctum, sanctam ecclesiam catholicam, sanctorum communionem, remissionem peccatorum, carnis resurrectionem, vitam eternam?*
> [Do you believe in the Holy Spirit, the holy Catholic Church, the communion of saints, the forgiveness of sins, the resurrection of the flesh, and the life everlasting?]

And to each question, Shylock chokes out '*Credo*'. The priest pours water from a goblet over his face – '*Ego te baptizo in nomine patris, et filii, et spiritus sancti*' (I baptize you in the name of the Father and of the Son and of the Holy Spirit) – three times, as he names each part of the Trinity, and then Shylock forces himself to join in the final Amen. Shylock turns to look at Jessica, then turns away and slowly exits off the front of the stage, into the crowded audience. And everyone else on stage slowly exits through the central doors, with Jessica the last to leave. The whole sequence, from Jessica's prayer through her exit, takes four minutes. When it begins, Jessica's anguished voice and the Hebrew text express her need for forgiveness; when Shylock is being 'converted' and baptized, she is kneeling, head down; but when he leaves the stage, she stands and sings with everyone else, becoming a part of the Christian community that has forced her father into this agonizing spectacle. Indeed, so appalling were the final moments that the usual song and dance (the 'jig') that has concluded every other Globe performance that I've seen was omitted here.

What, one might well ask, is the source of the interpretative choice to stage the scene of Shylock's conversion and baptism?

FIGURE 6 *Phoebe Pryce as Jessica, in the 2015 Shakespeare's Globe production, directed by Jonathan Munby. Photographer Manuel Harlan.*

Not even the 2004 film, where 'illustration' seems frequent, offers such a spectacle, although at the very end of the film, we move from Belmont back to Venice; Jews enter the synagogue, but Shylock stands isolated outside, and our view of him disappears as the synagogue doors are closed. But both Daniel Sullivan (in New York) and Jonathan Munby (at the Globe) chose an extended and disturbing intervention. They are not the only directors to have made this choice to foreground the viciousness of Venice's treatment of Shylock. One thinks of George Tabori's production at the 1966 Berkshire Theater Festival in Stockbridge, Massachusetts, which set the play in a concentration camp, and which included Shylock's death, after he attacked a Nazi guard and was shot; or Tabori's 1978 plan, while working in Munich, to actually stage the play in Dachau, transporting his audience on buses and trains (as if they were prisoners) from Munich to Dachau (Schülting 2017: 232). Though this version was never realized, Tabori might have included a baptism scene, according to Anat Feinberg's description of Tabori's idea: 'The audience would be taken back to Munich by buses, leaving behind the dim site and the lonely Shylock, only just baptized' (Schülting 2017: 234). Tabori's *Improvisations on Shakespeare's Shylock* (his substitute for his planned Dachau production) in 1978 was deliberately meant to disturb and embarrass the audience. So, too, the production in Weimar in 1995 (directed by Israeli director Hanan Snir), staged just six kilometres away from Buchenwald, and set in the 'SS Officers' Club' as a play-within-a-play, aimed to make its German audience as uncomfortable as possible. It included a Shylock stripped naked, the rape of Jessica, and the death of Shylock, 'drowned in our production by the Venetian Nazis during his baptism rite' (Kaynar-Kissinger 2017: 271).

What strikes me as different about the 2010 and 2015 productions is that the audiences, whether in Central Park or on Broadway or at the Globe, probably would not have imagined that they would have to see Shylock's forcible conversion; both of these productions are, in many ways, 'conventional', not set in the clearly oppressive setting of a concentration camp, not presented as a play-within-a-play, not stylized. The Globe even gave its audience the comforting distance of Renaissance costumes. So forcing the audience to *watch*, not just to hear, the ramifications of Antonio's line, 'that for this favour / He presently become a Christian' (4.1.382–3), adds a level of emotional engagement with Shylock that might otherwise not be present. Indeed, many Shylocks have listened to that line without registering a great deal of emotion: Patrick Stewart in 1978 was vocally outraged and panicked when threatened with the loss of his money, but gave only a blank stare when told he must convert; David Suchet in 1981 maintained a dignified silence; in the film version with Olivier, the camera shows us a man beginning to crumble, physically, as he hears the line. Henry Goodman (National Theatre, 1999) seemed more upset when Antonio insists that half of Shylock's fortune will go to 'the gentleman / That lately stole his daughter' (4.1.380–1) – he beat his chest in pain, while the stipulation of conversion drew only an incredulous look. The most anguished response to Antonio's line came from Jonathan Pryce in 2015 at the Globe. For most of the production Pryce was a dignified and composed Shylock, wiping off spittle with a handkerchief during 'Hath not a Jew eyes?' (3.1.53) and building to a vow of revenge. But when Antonio demanded that he become a Christian, Pryce's Shylock cracked, screaming 'No', clutching Antonio in appeal, bowing to kiss Antonio's hands. Staging his conversion thus became particularly painful, because the audience had already seen how even the verbal threat had destroyed Shylock's outward calm; and in the conversion/baptism ritual, the outward calm became the defensive mask that covered, but did not hide, the pain.

Perhaps one can argue that staging the conversion/baptism takes us back to the portrayal of hatred so evident at the beginning of many productions. That is, the logical extension of hating 'the other' is to erase that otherness – in this case, through conversion. And thus the choice of actors and directors to make Shylock more obviously Jewish – by means of interpolated lines in Yiddish (Henry Goodman and Jonathan Pryce both scolded Jessica in Yiddish), interpolated

Hebrew blessings (Henry Goodman again, with '*Eshet Chayil*'; Patrick Stewart in 2011 blessing Jessica with the traditional prayer, 'May God make you like Sarah, Rebecca, Rachel and Leah'), and even the Hebrew prayer from the medieval Haggadah, 'Pour out thy wrath upon the nations that know thee not' (Antony Sher in 1987) – shows that the physical and verbal abuse is directed specifically towards the Jew. The other major interpretation, to make Shylock *less* Jewish and more assimilated, runs as counterpoint, so that these Shylocks come to recognize that they cannot ever escape being Jewish. In a sense, the experience of Patrick Stewart, who played Shylock at the RSC in 1978–9, and then in 2011, also at the RSC, is exemplary. Talking in 1984 about the 1978 production, and his concept of Shylock, heavily influenced by the director, John Barton, Stewart insisted that 'Shylock is an outsider who happens to be a Jew'; only to be countered by David Suchet, Barton's 1981 Shylock, arguing that 'as Shylock I'm not an outsider who *happens* to be a Jew, but *because* I'm a Jew' (Barton 1984: 169). But as Stewart prepared to play Shylock in 2011, he talked with Rabbi Lionel Blue (a major British rabbi) and travelled to Israel, this preparation reflecting the centrality of Judaism to an understanding of the role. Certainly, in a post-Holocaust world, productions have increasingly forced audiences to confront not only Shylock the Jew, but the society that cannot tolerate him, and may even try, unsuccessfully, to eradicate him.

2

Dangerous Border Crossings: Nicolas Stemann's *Merchant* in Munich

Benjamin Fowler

Der Kaufmann von Venedig, dir. Nicolas Stemann, premiered at the Munich Kammerspiele on 9 October 2015. I saw it on 21 December 2015. Any dialogue quoted in this essay comes from the German prompt script (in my own translations) rather than an edition of Shakespeare's play.[1]

This is a comedy. LAUGH!

Until the end of 2.2 (in which the Prince of Morocco opts for one of three caskets in an attempt to win Portia as his bride), Nicolas Stemann's 2015 production of *The Merchant of Venice* for the Munich Kammerspiele followed the established chronology of scenes. However, after Morocco chose incorrectly and withdrew from Belmont, the actor Niels Bormann interrupted the linear progression of Shakespeare's play (and the entrance of Launcelot Gobbo) with a crude summary of 1.3. Returning to a scene that had played some fifteen minutes earlier, the actor performed a madcap recap with a biting satirical edge. Bormann prefaced each line in his comic solo by announcing the speaker ('Antonio said: Give me 3,000 ducats now; Shylock said: Yes, but I want your heart …'), dancing between Christian and Jew in this negotiation of Antonio's bond (and eliciting titters from spectators). Then Bormann's sassy routine took a sour turn as he adorned himself with props fished out of his pockets: plastic vampire fangs and a golden elasticated hooked nose as he parodied a vampiric Jew drinking the blood of Christians, then a Nazi armband and officer's cap as he goose-stepped up and down the stage shrieking: 'The Jewish devil cites scripture for his own aims'. In this guise, Bormann pantomimed shooting Shylock dead before turning his imaginary gun on the now-silent audience. 'This is a comedy', he yelled. 'Laugh!' Bormann's monologue put the play into dialogue with the tenacious demons that shadow it still, engaging not only Shakespeare's text but also the fraught histories of representation and prejudice with which it intersects. It is emblematic of a production that raided the past to address tensions currently simmering, using Shakespeare to interrogate contemporary forms of social exclusion and the violence that they prompt.

Any recent production of *Merchant* would be hard-pressed to ignore the re-entrenchment of nationalist and xenophobic attitudes characterizing what is ostensibly an era of 'globalization'. US president Donald Trump's pledge to build a wall on the United States-Mexico border at Mexico's expense and his attempts to instigate a 'Muslim Ban' in early 2017 are perhaps the most flagrant examples of populist governments stirring negative sentiment towards 'outsiders' in their attempts to harness the support of citizens who feel dispossessed. Fifty-two per cent of those who voted in Britain's so-called 'Brexit' referendum expressed a desire to cut ties with the European Union, and the pressures of migration have led the EU itself to strive continuously to harden its borders, forcing refugees to pursue ever-more cataclysmic routes; over the last decade, the edges of the EU have become the site of over half of all deaths at borders, making it the most dangerous border crossing in the world (Jones 2016: 16). Mass migration poses one of the leading global challenges, which will only intensify as populations flee not only war but economic and environmental catastrophe. As of August 2017, according to the UN Refugee Agency's website, there are 65.6 million forcibly displaced people worldwide, the highest number in recorded history. In contrast, the number of refugees resettled in 2016 totalled a meagre 189,300. Reece Jones (2016: 68) seems justified in his claim that globalization isn't undermining the position of the state; instead, 'as the movement of people threatens their ability to control resources and populations, states around the world have responded by hardening borders [in a] rearticulation and expansion, not a retreat, of state power'.

Terror attacks involving Islamic State sleeper cells in the West have exacerbated anxieties over migration. In the month in which I sat down to write this essay (August 2017), two terror attacks claimed by the Islamic State group unfolded in Spain, where vehicles ploughed into crowds on Las Ramblas in Barcelona and in the coastal town of Cambrils, killing fourteen people instantly.[2] Across Europe, similar attacks have emboldened far-right groups such as Patriotic Europeans Against the Islamisation of the Occident (PEGIDA), founded in Dresden in October 2014 and anticipating, ten months later, Angela Merkel's announcement of the 'open-door policy' that saw over a million refugees enter Germany by the end of 2015. The perceived threat of outsiders to 'Western' cultural values intensified in January 2015 when two Islamist extremists linked to Al-Qaeda forced themselves into the offices of French magazine *Charlie Hebdo* and shot dead twelve editors, columnists and cartoonists, targeting the publication because of a series of satirical cartoons of the prophet Muhammad. These and similar attacks have helped right-wing movements consolidate into tribes whose members find amity in their self-regard as victims, scapegoating minority groups in the process. Political parties such as Alternative for Germany (AfD), formed in 2013, poise their definitions of nation and nationalism against the perceived dangers of multi-cultural society. The often-patriarchal attempts of such groups to protect their privileges frequently draw racism, misogyny and homophobia into their ideological constellations, and although apparently formed in response to local concerns, they signal the rise of what is becoming, paradoxically, a trans-national force. Five days before the attacks in Spain, a 'Unite the Right' white supremacist rally in Charlottesville, Virginia, was the scene at which a man rammed a car into anti-racist and anti-fascist protestors, killing one and injuring nineteen others. Driving vehicles into crowds at high speeds is not solely an instrument of Islamist terror, but a tactic used by followers of extreme alt-right ideologies permeating the fringes of Western liberal democracies and encroaching on their centres. Such contradictions signal frightening and intolerant times.

Against this wider context, Germany (and Munich, the early nucleus of the Nazi regime) provided an especially charged location for a production of *Merchant* intended to probe the political and ethical responsibilities of state theatres and the stories they animate. In late 2015, the city had these themes on its mind. Two nights before seeing Stemann's production, I sat in the same theatre to watch *Mein Kampf*, a work by Helgard Kim Haug and Daniel Wetzel (of Rimini Protokoll) responding to the imminent authorized reprint of Hitler's inflammatory autobiographical manifesto.[3] The state of Bavaria had made it illegal to distribute *Mein Kampf* following Hitler's death, inevitably burnishing its taboo status, but it was about to resurface following the expiration of copyright bestowed on the Bavarian ministry by the Allies after the Second World War. This situation triggered much debate, including in the Israeli Knesset, where one deputy refused to say the name of the book out loud and some asserted that it endangers the mental health of the people (Kasiske 2015). In addressing this predicament, Bavaria's state parliament decided to support the Munich-based Institute for Contemporary History (IfZ), part-financing the preparation of a 2,000-page critical edition of the text, including more than 3,500 scholarly annotations contextualizing Hitler's antisemitic rhetoric and elucidating his propaganda. Facing protests from Holocaust survivors, the state retracted its endorsement, ultimately allowing the project to proceed and retain its funds but removing the state's imprimatur. Now that this new edition is on the shelves, there is fresh debate about whether it should be taught in schools (Doerry and Wiegrefe 2016).

Both *Merchant* and *Mein Kampf* were produced in Munich at a time when debates about stereotype, difference and tolerance fanned out through German society. In the year Germany received over a million refugees (2015) – the majority of whom were fleeing conflict in countries including Syria, Afghanistan and Iraq – attendance at PEGIDA rallies spiked, revealing deep fractures. These productions responded by putting their respective texts on trial. They refused to make them serve polemical statements, insisting on the need to formulate proper questions: how to combat political ideologies (e.g. an anti-immigrant, radical-right populism) that, although founded on intolerance, offer simple answers to complex difficulties? How to deal with works that so easily twist to assert the claims of antagonistic groups? And, perhaps most pertinent in the case of *Merchant,* against the backdrop of the refugee crisis, how to reconcile the tension between a will to open borders and a tendency to ghettoize minorities (much like the cosmopolitan Venice of the sixteenth century)?

Why *Merchant* now?

I defer my discussion of Stemann's production a moment longer to establish the resonances of a play that often provokes the question: to what extent it is antisemitic and to what extent it is *about* antisemitism? That question was underscored in 2016 when *Merchant* was selected for performance at the Jewish ghetto in Venice as one of a series of events commemorating the site's 500th anniversary.[4] Hemmed in by tall buildings and a network of canals, today's picturesque Venetian campo doubles as the original ghetto (whose name stems from the site's previous usage as a copper foundry – a *geto* in Venetian, which the first settlers, German Jews, pronounced with a hard 'g'). From 1516 onwards, the Jewish population was required to live within the ghetto's bounds, with strict employment controls and a curfew policed by Christian guards at the Jews' expense (the gates were also locked during Christian festivals, probably to safeguard, as well as restrict, inhabitants). However, by 1525, Greek merchants settled their own Venetian district and invested in an Orthodox Church on the condition that they enjoy the same rights as the Jews. The complexities and ambiguities of this arrangement are hard to process given the intervening history, but the Venetian Republic's commitment to cosmopolitanism (driven by trade) is staggering for the times. In the context of the expulsions of Jews across the Continent, Venice pioneered ways for minorities to co-exist in urban centres, and ghettos would soon replicate across Europe. Facilitating trade and cultural exchange as well as segregation, the Venetian ghetto was, as Stephen Greenblatt (2017b) argues, 'a compromise formation, neither absorption nor expulsion. It was a topographical expression of extreme ambivalence'.

Although Shakespeare demonstrates no knowledge of the ghetto (Shylock lives on a public street), the play clearly absorbs the 'extreme ambivalence' characteristic of its real-world setting. A month-long conference held in Venice in the summer of 2015, titled The Shylock Project, drove this point home.[5] As a participant, I joined a group of scholars and students exploring the play and its production history as a precursor to its production the following summer in the Campo del Ghetto Nuovo. The forty-eight papers given during the conference repeatedly established that *Merchant*'s knotty ambiguities are central to its endurance. So, too, is the generic instability perceived by critics from this side of the intervening history between Shakespeare's then and our now; given the loaded ethnic and religious stereotypes that the play draws into its scheme, it is hard to identify much in this play that accords with its listing in the First Folio as a 'comedy'. What also transpired was that this play's very allusiveness, more so than perhaps any other of Shakespeare's works, exacerbates fault-lines dividing the contemporary societies in which it is staged.

This is most obviously so in the account Bill Alexander (2015) gave of the electric moment during the 23 April performance of his 1987 RSC production when, in the heat of the trial scene, the South African actor Tony Sher (playing Shylock) dragged Akim Mogaji (a black actor in the company playing an Officer) to the front of the stage as he admonished the Venetians for having among them 'many a purchased slave' (4.1.90). Sher's improvised move appropriated Shakespeare for anti-apartheid protest, prompted by his knowledge that the cultural attaché from South Africa was sitting in the stalls; as Sher (2002: 193) experienced it, 'the magical fourth wall suddenly shattered'. Avraham Oz (2015) also gave a fascinating overview of the play's treatment on the Hebrew stage, detailing Israeli director Omri Nitzan's divisive 1994 production in Tel Aviv, which countered tradition by presenting Shylock as a Jewish terrorist. In the wake of the massacre of twenty-nine Muslims praying at a mosque in Hebron by a fanatic settler doctor (Baruch Goldstein), Nitzan had Shylock mime firing a sub-machine gun at Salerio in 3.3, intolerance breeding religious extremism on both sides of an intractable divide: 'It is as much Baruch Goldstein as it is Hamas', argued Nitzan (in Hundley 1994), connecting the play's Christian-Jew conflict with socio-political antagonisms directly outside his theatre's walls.

Like a fluid, the play adapts to new moulds. It also seeps through the fissures in ideological systems, prompting labourious efforts to dam up its potentially subversive flows, such as in Nazi Germany, where its popularity necessitated monitoring by a regime under which, as Tobias Döring (2015) outlined, ambiguity proved problematic. Joseph Goebbels, the Reich Minister of Propaganda, licensed all productions from 1933 onwards, censoring Shylock's forced conversion (conversion was, of course, impossible under Nazism). Jessica's elopement with Lorenzo had to be recast to circumvent the suggestion of miscegenation, criminalized by Nazi legislation. This meant re-writing her as an adopted child rescued by the good Christian Lorenzo. How the play is handled speaks as loudly as the play itself, or, as James Shapiro (2015) argued in Venice, *Merchant* is 'a canary in a coal mine', liable to expose noxious and residual bigotry as much as the compassion that frequently attends portrayals of Shylock in a post-Holocaust context; more reason, for Shapiro, why the play must not be censored or suppressed.

Steven Greenblatt (2017b) made a similar case in *The New Yorker*, using *Merchant* to intervene in the complex culture wars embroiling American universities. Having observed acute anxiety among students 'asked to confront the crueller strains of our cultural legacy', Greenblatt insisted that such encounters are vital in order to enable critical opposition to alt-right aggressions: coming to terms with 'repellent' as well as 'beautiful' cultural legacies is, according to Greenblatt, a fundamental preparation for 'a world that you did not fashion but that will do its best to fashion you'. Cries of censorship dominate recent arguments around free speech in universities but in ways that signal perplexing times. Tom Slater's polemical edited collection, *Unsafe Space: The Crisis of Free Speech on Campus,* uses the language of 'crisis' to identify a 'distinct and dangerous' trend across North America and the UK, criticizing 'fragile' students for calling for 'course syllabi to be slapped with trigger warnings' (2016: 2). Slater makes unflattering comparisons with students mounting free speech crusades in the 1960s, whose demands he terms an 'assertion of their resilience and resolve' (1). However, such logic cleaves to old-school scripts without acknowledging the ways in which the context has shifted. Do all have an inalienable right to a platform in a culture where, as Angela Nagle (2017: 28) points out, the 'aesthetics of counterculture, transgression and nonconformity' have been appropriated by the 'new right-wing sensibility'? And is an educator's insistence that students should be more 'resilient' deaf to the ways in which today's students – to borrow Slater's description of activists in the 1960s – are seizing agency differently, 'rethinking and reshaping their world' (1)?

These disorientating debates mimic the play's oscillations, its propensity to slide between and elide the categories of victim and perpetrator. It has the potential to upset and offend, but also to magnify and inflame prejudice, raising major questions about the ethical responsibilities of pedagogy and art. Voices clamour to stress the need to grapple with *Merchant* now, in a world where such an undertaking seems more fraught than ever. Confronting these very difficulties, the German director Nicolas Stemann used his staging as a way of questioning how to react to a moment of intense European crisis through the lens of a text liable to fuel and fan hate.

Stemann's 2015 production

Stemann's strategy, in his production for the Munich Kammerspiele, involved turning the play quite literally into an echo chamber for contemporary moral and mental situations. His procedures forced critical distance between actors and text, creating an elaborate counterpoint between Shakespeare's words and their present-tense enunciation that foregrounded the play's *handling* to the same extent as its dramatic action. Flatscreen televisions suspended from the fly tower functioned throughout as textual surfaces on which Shakespeare's words appeared (in German), and the actors – as if confronting this dialogue for the first time – read and reacted to the lines in changing configurations. Although the displayed text always indicated which character was talking, the six performers slid between roles. The monitors showed Shakespeare's script, gliding upwards as if on a teleprompter, but they also blazed with full-screen words in bold, blood-red letters (such as 'bloodsucker' or 'dog'), emphasising keywords in Shylock's account of Christian abuse. These words provided an ironic gloss on his 'merry jest' in calling for Antonio's forfeit on a defaulted loan to be 'a pound of flesh': was Shylock playing (with) the roles his oppressors bestowed on him, was he deferring to (stereo)type or mocking it? Supplementary screens would register the act and scene divisions, evoking a rehearsal mood, and English subtitles were projected above the proscenium, a constant flow of German re-translated into English rather than Shakespeare's original lines (every performance being subtitled in this way). Juxtapositions of pixelated languages were the constant visual accompaniment to speech, as the ensemble of six read, reacted to and commented on Shakespeare's script.

This approach borrows from Stemann's work on a contemporary Austrian playwright, Elfriede Jelinek, whose 'postdramatic' plays jettison plot and character and favour floods of associative text: dense arrangements of what she calls 'Textfläche' (text surfaces), sometimes spoken simultaneously and always requiring the director's collaboration as Jelinek rarely allocates speakers (see Jürs-Munby 2013). Plot no longer impels the event. Instead, linguistic puns, repetitions and motifs provide footholds for disoriented listeners as they attempt to navigate Jelinek's textual surfaces. Commenting on Stemman's decision to treat Shakespeare like Jelinek, the critic Patrick Bahners (in Slagman 2015) found that the actors' artless reading of the text, as if for the first time, seemed to signify that the only means of bringing *Merchant* to the stage today is *as* text, with all of the critical distance that implies.

This certainly seemed to be the case for vast swathes of the production, where the de-linking of performer and character opened space for meta-commentary (as we saw in Bormann's summary of 1.3) and undercut the notion of bounded identities on which prejudice is grounded. It also offered an effective performative response to the play's slipperiness. A quotation that surfaced often in papers during The Shylock Project was Portia's line on entering the trial scene in Act 4: 'Which is the Merchant here, and which the Jew?' (4.1.174). As Döring (2015) noted of the play, 'everything slides towards its opposite', an instability that Jonathan Miller capitalized on in his 1970 production, in which Portia's question was a genuine one: Shylock and Antonio, indistinguishable in dress, speech and behaviour, could not be told apart.[6] Their identical attire complemented a text that repeatedly thwarts classifications of identity and (im)morality.

In Stemann's production, and at different times, everybody was the Merchant *and* the Jew. After reading 'Hath not a Jew eyes' in unison, five of Stemann's cast performed separate sections of the speech as individuals, beginning with Hassan Akkouch, born in Lebanon and raised in the Berlin district of Neukölln (known for its large Turkish, Arab and Kurdish communities). 'I am Muslim', Akkouch announced, claiming Shylock's words to rebuff anti-Muslim sentiment; Jelena Kuljić followed, a Serbian speaking as a representative of the Roma; casting himself as a spokesperson for Jewish homosexuals, Niels Bormann asked, 'If you prick us, do we not bleed?'; then Julia Riedler took up the speech as a woman addressing patriarchy, asking, 'if you inflict injustice on us, should we not revenge?' But in a subversive twist typical of the production, Thomas Schmauser broke in as the last speaker with: 'What can I say? I am a white male heterosexual! I am healthy. But I also have hands, organs, limbs, senses, affections, passions ...'. As he tried to complete Shylock's speech, battling the irritation of the ensemble, the audience laughed. The production undercut this monologue's traditional deployment as rousing humanism (by mocking the appropriated victim-status of the non-minority cast member), puncturing its pathos and dissipating its emotional power. In the hysteria, Bormann reminded the audience once more: 'This is a comedy'.

This moment illustrates Stemann's intention to stage an encounter with the play rather than the play itself. As if observing a workshop, audiences watched actors debate the play's contents, forward conflicting readings, and bring associations in and out of the frame. Niels Bormann's 'improvised' interjections – titled 'intermezzos' in the prompt-script – detoured from Shakespeare's text to offer the dramaturgical equivalent of Gobbo's comic banter, refracting the play's themes through the prism of historical and contemporary events. Shortly after Bormann parodied 1.3, 'Hath not a Jew eyes' returned, voiced simultaneously by three performers, one of whom (Akkouch) spoke in unsubtitled Arabic. This recitation was violently interrupted by the anarchic Bormann firing shots (two pointed fingers and a convincing sound effect). The other actors ducked as Bormann shouted through a megaphone, 'This is a comedy! This is funny!', borrowing Gratiano's rebuke to the sad Antonio in 1.1 ('Why should a man whose blood is warm within [...] creep into the jaundice by being peevish?') and telling his fellow performers: 'Look, this is how comedy functions'. He then began handing out copies of the *Charlie Hebdo* magazine. When Akkouch pointedly refused to take a copy, Bormann addressed the audience: 'Did you see that? He attacked me! Yes, the Jew who wants only the heart!', before shooting around a stage that, with its desks and open laptops, now resembled the offices of the magazine in Paris where assassins had opened fire twelve months earlier. Bormann then mimed shooting himself in the head before telling us, straight-faced, 'This is a comedy', and introducing 2.2: Launcelot Gobbo the clown.

The layers of meaning here are complex to negotiate, as Bormann's role-play collapsed the violent extremist with the offended liberal, overlaying the Jew (Shylock) with the Muslim (Akkouch) in the crosshairs of (offensive?) satire. The classic question about this play – is it antisemitic or about antisemitism? – was obliquely raised but provocatively unanswered, pulling questions of genre and its political implications into the production's web of meaning. Does the play (like a satirical cartoon) sketch 'the Jew' as a comic grotesque villain, a knife-whetting monster, playing into age-old anxieties surrounding Jewish bloodlust (Shylock as the vampiric predator of early modern morality tales, sustained by the blood of Christian children)? Is the comedy too hot to handle, and what is at stake in our laughter? Stephen Greenblatt (2017b), describing his first encounter with *Merchant* as an undergraduate, remembers asking himself, 'What, exactly, are you applauding and smiling at?'. He lists the plot points on which the 'comedy' depends, including Jessica's betrayal of her Jewish father in bestowing his savings on her Christian suitor; representations of Christian abuse; Shylock's own 'vindictive, malignant rage'; and the forced conversion that proves Shylock's only recourse once outmanoeuvred in the courtroom. There is a tension, Greenblatt notes, between the play's 'formal design' and our 'attempts to bring it into the Enlightenment'.

Rather than navigate a path through these difficulties, this production escalated them. Its goading doubled as an invitation to reflect on the nature of our own prejudices. However, satire and irony were not Stemann's only methods for interrogating the text and the reactions it provokes. The director also found ways of capitalizing on the gaps between speaking and reading caused by his mise-en-scène. During Shylock's first appearance (the initial version of 1.3 in this production), the three white men in the ensemble performed the dialogue between Antonio, Bassanio and Shylock. Halfway through, Akkouch entered for the first time and danced a fluid solo-choreography at the edges of the stage, disrupting speech-driven theatre with the language of abstract movement. A further instruction in the prompt-script reveals that he was also speaking the 'Shylock-Text in Arabic'. Haunting a scene of thinly veiled hostilities and misunderstandings, his literally 'marginal' presence opened a breach in the communicative flow of the stage. Akkouch's softly spoken words resisted incorporation into the trans-lingual flows linking actors and screens. Is he another Shylock? What is he saying? Disrupting the seemingly smooth translation between script and stage, and between English and German, Akkouch's Arabic aroused interest in a presence made notable by its exclusion from the production's semantic web. Making Arabic the only spoken language banished from the stage monitors insinuated into Stemann's staging (for this spectator at least, and presumably for the theatre's mainly white middle-class audience) contemporary debates around integration raging in German society.

Although at times he also voiced Shylock (in Arabic and German), Akkouch was most consistently affiliated with Jessica, whom he played in a sequined dress and a blonde wig. With his thick beard, Akkouch's Jessica resembled Conchita Wurst, singing Barbara Streisand's 'Papa Can You Hear Me?' in pastiche-Eurovision mode on Jessica's first appearance – another astute contemporary reference. Wurst's victory at Eurovision 2014 proved divisive. The head of Poland's public broadcaster (and former politician of the right-wing United Poland Party) Jacek Kurski described Wurst as a 'homo-unknown' whose victory marked an act of 'cultural aggression from the West' (qtd. L. Smith 2016). Jessica's status – a daughter to the Jew's blood, but not to his manners (2.3) – complicates the supposedly inviolable racial, religious and cultural categories used to establish difference and police division. As we have seen, the Nazis had to re-write her. By stabilizing Jessica in the body of Akkouch (he was the only performer who played her), the production's gendered and ethnic drag excluded her from the dominant heteronormative economy of Belmont (mirroring the fates of Antonio and Shylock). Additionally, having Akkouch play the Jewess who couples with the Christian, the production also touched on the frisson of miscegenation (an attendant fear of integration) between ethnic groups living in close proximity, like those bounded by invisible ghettos in Germany's urban centres today.

It was in the trial scene, however, that Stemann's academic strategies – reviewer Christine Dössel (in Slagman 2015) called the production a 'seminar' on the text – generated the most powerful theatrical results. The lead up to Portia's 'Tarry a little' was played as a fast-paced sequence of individual and choral speaking. Key terms like 'knife', 'blood' and 'justice' punctuated the scene on screens as they were spoken, and the number of speakers varied in response to unanticipated power reversals. For example, all six actors chanted Gratiano's accusation ('Thy desires are wolfish, bloody, starved and ravenous') as a pack mentality bore down on the maligned minority figure, Shylock. Similarly, when Shylock seized the moral high ground, his lines attracted more and more speakers, until finally Julia Riedler's Portia emerged as the individuated force, crying out four times to halt the confusion: 'Who is the Merchant here, and who the Jew?' Then the stage's aluminium flooring began to peel up like a plaster being teased off the skin, knocking the actors off their feet and rolling them downstage. Riedler, the last one standing, ended the sequence by proclaiming as Portia-Bellario: 'A pound of that same merchant's flesh is thine; The court awards it, and the law doth give it!' Then she, too, fell down on the floor and the theatre became, for the first time that evening, silent.

'Wait a moment!' flashed up on the centre-stage monitor. 'And another.'

After a long pause, Riedler stood up to read '... There is something else' from the same monitor. As other characters (Gratiano, Bassanio et al.) responded to Portia's revelation that Shylock mustn't draw blood when removing his pound of flesh from the merchant defaulter Antonio, Riedler called upon the ensemble by their real names to read lines from the screen. Whenever Shylock had a line, nobody stirred. His words for the rest of the scene remained unvoiced. During each of his textual responses, the (now upright) actors stared at the monitors and, together with the audience, read his words in silence. As Portia's questionable mercy stripped Shylock of his wealth and his religion, Stemann the director stripped the character of embodiment. As a result, Shylock's lines became focused by his absence.

In the last stages of the trial scene, the onstage monitors got stuck on Shylock's final line:

I ask you to allow me to leave. I do not feel well.

In a breathtakingly simple but surprising use of the technology, Shylock's final words stayed put, frozen above the stage for the entirety of the fifth act, transcending the character's bounded textual appearance in only five of Shakespeare's scenes. As Bormann, Riedler, Kuljić and Schmauser played the revelations around the rings in Belmont as a hyperactive boulevard comedy (while Akkouch's Jessica vomited into a champagne bucket, realizing her assimilation attempt was doomed), Shylock's line lingered above them all. The four lovers tangled limbs, exiting the stage as a single writhing unit producing a cacophony of chatter as if the play's comic mechanism had been horribly overwound. Bormann's assertions that this is a 'comedy' broke apart completely as they pressed too hard on the humour, and in their place Stemann left us with a final tragic image of the excluded. Under Shylock's shining line (white text on a black background), Akkouch's Jessica whirled, then collapsed in a heap. Then Walter Hess walked on stage and slumped against the proscenium, the actor who had most often voiced the lines of Shylock and Antonio due to his seniority within this otherwise young ensemble. But was he the Merchant now or was he the Jew? Or was he both – a stage presence conflating the two men barred from the 'ideal' community at the end of this play, two men whose tragedies are symbolized by a ring?[7] As the play elides the Merchant and the Jew – both excluded from this scene of hetero-normative unions – Stemann left us with the comedy's collateral damage, made visible in Shylock's last line, indelible above the stage, and the crumpled bodies of Akkouch's Jessica and Hess's Antonio/Shylock.

Stemann's closing tableau leant on the tragic, but the production's jocular and farcical tone had always only thinly veiled its menace. Despite (or perhaps because of) frequently undercutting the farce with disturbing contemporary associations, Stemann inflated the play's comic dimensions to frightening proportions. In this sense, the production exacerbated Greenblatt's (2017b) assertion that the play provokes an 'unsettling from within', but it also departed from Greenblatt's reading in significant ways. The unsettling he perceives is produced by one character, Shylock, who is given 'more urgent, compelling life, than anyone else in his world', thus coming 'perilously close to wrecking the comic structure of the play'. Such a reading relies on modes of humanist identification that Stemann's production, particularly in its treatment of 'Hath not a Jew eyes', sought to complicate. One major reason for this difference in emphasis is the particular context in which Stemann encountered the play. In Germany, the refugee crisis has put Enlightenment values (and Western Euro- and ethno-centrism) under intense pressure, causing state theatres to examine their defining feature since the eighteenth century as venues for bourgeois self-understanding and reflection. Although a discourse of 'human rights' has long shaped European culture and identity, the pressures of migration (alongside the growing prevalence of calls to address colonial history and decolonize) have exposed this self-image as naïve, if not hypocritical and specious, presenting huge challenges for those working in its cultural institutions. Unpacking those challenges helps us see what is at stake in Stemann's meta-theatrical interrogations, raising important questions about what it means to bring Shakespeare to the stage in a prominent German state theatre today.

The refugee crisis and German state theatres

In 2014, Stemann was among the first theatre directors to address what has become the most significant refugee crisis in Europe since the Second World War, staging a new play by the Austrian playwright Elfriede Jelinek (whose works he had premiered across German-speaking theatres since 2004). Jelinek wrote *Die Schutzbefohlenen* in reaction to two main events. The first occurred in 2012, on the International Day of Migrants (24 November), when forty asylum-seekers pitched a protest camp outside the Votive Church in Vienna, having marched from their refugee centre 20 kilometres outside the capital.[8] This began a five-week occupation of the church and a hunger strike protesting Austria's harsh asylum laws, mass deportations and the poor conditions in which asylum-seekers were maintained. The majority of those involved were extradited by the Austrian government the following summer. The second event, in October 2013, was the death of over 360 adults and children from Ghana, Somalia and Eritrea, whose 20-metre-long fishing boat sank off the coast of the Italian island of Lampedusa – a principal European entry point for migrants.

Loosely translated as *Protection Orders*, Jelinek's title invokes legal safeguards protecting society's most vulnerable, but also plays on a verbal association with its primary source-text, Aeschylus's *The Supplicants* (*Die Schutzflehenden* in German). She appropriates a play from ancient Athens, traditionally perceived as the cradle of European civilization, as the vehicle for an excoriating rebuke of the exclusion of those in peril from the systems of protection enjoyed by European citizens today. At moments her play gives voice to the experiences of refugees (as imagined by the European Jelinek), but it also interweaves citations from sources including Ovid, Heidegger and contemporary government handbooks.[9] It mentions key figures who have paid their way into Austrian society, thus evading the convoluted bureaucratic performances required from those seeking asylum, showing that all are not equal under law; the protections denied those fleeing crisis after lengthy adjudication processes can, it seems, be purchased by high bidders. When the production played in Amsterdam, the Holland Festival Programme (2014) advertised that it 'confronts us with a Europe which has never fulfilled its promise as a protector of human rights'. Questioning a central tenet of Europe's cultural identity, Jelinek paints Europe as a fortress bordered by fences and Frontex patrols.

The way Stemann handled *Die Schutzbefohlenen* sheds light on his production of *Merchant* the following year. He presented Jelinek's text in various iterations, each involving the participation of actual refugees. When staged at the Thalia Theatre in Hamburg, the production highlighted the unexamined whiteness of the theatre's ensemble as refugees from Ghana and Afghanistan entered the stage half-way through. As they began to perform Jelinek's words, their inclusion also raised hard questions about the dynamics of European cultural production and its capacity to give voice to others in an event written and controlled entirely by elite white artists. The production culminated in the sentence, spoken by the theatre's ensemble and addressed to the refugees, 'We cannot help you, we can only play you'. Pointing to the complications of artistic responses to humanitarian crisis, Stemann told Patrick Wildermann (2015) that he is conscious of the pitfalls of appropriating refugee narratives: 'Nobody is out of this problem, no matter how he deals with the subject. We are not part of the solution, we are part of the problem.' It would seem that many critics agreed with this assessment. Ralf Remshardt saw the production in Berlin where, following its Hamburg run, it opened the 2015 Theatretreffen (an annual showcase of ten German-language productions, as selected by a jury of critics). Seeing refugees onstage in the context of 'an elite social occasion studded with high-culture celebrity', Remshardt (2016) felt uneasy and concluded that 'the production was performing its own inefficacy'. The critic Christine Dössel (2015) argued that, 'authentic and touching as such projects often are, they never entirely escape the basic suspicion of artistically exploiting human suffering'. *Die Schutzbefohlenen* initiated a slew of productions across Germany that presented 'real' refugees onstage, a trend that can be viewed as evidence of state-subsidized cultural institutions swerving their own histories of complicity in structural inequality by falling back on the sort of sham humanitarianism that such productions nominally seek to critique and expose.[10]

Germany's state-funded city theatres have certainly sought an active and politicized role in the crisis, chiefly by providing material support. During its run at the Thalia Theatre, *Die Schutzbefohlenen* collected over €100,000 in donations, which it funnelled towards local charities working with refugees; in September 2015, the Deutsches Schauspielhaus offered shelter for refugees arriving at Hamburg's main station, accommodating them in the foyer of the Malersaal (its studio stage); the director of the Gorky Theatre in Berlin, Shermin Langhoff, devoted the theatre's resources to helping refugees fill out forms and obtain work permits. All over the country, theatres transformed into emergency accommodation camps, provided food and clothing, offered language lessons and programmed panel discussions. The German news website nachtkritik.de collated a list of these actions under the hashtag #refugeeswelcome that ran to seventy-eight examples at its last update in January 2016. Does this turn to practical support on the part of Germany's theatre institutions signal artistic paralysis? What role, if any, might staging *The Merchant of Venice* play in the face of these critical events?

Conclusion: Artistic renewal at the Munich Kammerspiele

To conclude, I want to view the politics of Stemann's 2015 *Merchant* through the lens of his engagement with bourgeois canonicity in the wake of *Die Schutzbefohlenen*'s problematic success. This also involves considering the particular choice of *Merchant* as the first production at the Munich Kammerspiele under its new artistic director, Matthias Lilienthal. Lilienthal had helped to shape the radical era of the Berlin Volksbühne as its chief dramaturg in the 1990s, after which he ran the Berlin HAU (Hebbel am Ufer) for nine years, cultivating an independent scene of experimental work defined in opposition to the state-subsidized, middle-class repertoire dominant in

Germany's city theatres – which Lilienthal had derided as 'art shit' ('Kunstkacke': see Kümmel 2015). Many worried about Lilienthal's arrival in the conservative city of Munich at the helm of a theatre (the Kammerspiele) famed for its sensitive interpretations of literary classics. Since his controversial appointment in 2015, theatre commentators in Germany have made his directorship the locus of passionate arguments concerning 'the role of the performing arts in today's radically shifting world' (Lilienthal 2017). Given concerns about his potentially agonistic relationship with the bourgeois institution, we can read Lilienthal's choice of *Merchant* to open his first season as a conciliatory gesture; rather than mark a contrast between his and a previous regime, Lilienthal used Shakespeare as the border at which old and new audiences (and different traditions of thinking about theatre and performance) might meet.

This context conditions the questions Stemann used the play to address. As Jelinek had done with Aeschylus, Stemann complicated an audience's easy identification with a staple of the bourgeois canon. His staging techniques rejected humanist readings of Shylock to focus instead on questions of representation itself. In Shylock's post-trial absence, the production put its habitual strategies up for negotiation to ask how suffering might be represented on stage and on whose behalf. As the German critic Esther Boldt (2015) argued at the time, 'Theatre is political above all when it reconsiders its own structures, which, after all, arose from that cultural history whose validity is today being so urgently questioned'. Stemann's production questioned that cultural history by making explicit the ethnic and religious identifications and sexual orientations of his cast, highlighting the lack of inclusivity in traditional German ensemble systems and signalling Lilienthal's broader intentions for politically reshaping the state theatre as an institution. *Merchant* thus became the vehicle for an examination of the institutional frameworks within which work is made, under an artistic director who sought to 'form new alliances and new audiences from different social classes and interest groups'

(Lilienthal 2017). It formed part of a season that questioned assumptions about what constitutes state theatre repertoire, featuring work by the independent group Rimini Protokoll alongside gigs by artists like Peaches. Since then, Lilienthal has opened the theatre to more international influences and hybrid artistic genres. The 2016/17 season saw directors Amir Reza Koohestani (Iran) and Toshiki Okada (Japan) invited to work with Lilienthal's ensemble, establishing relationships that have developed over subsequent seasons. As Ralf Ramshardt (2016) argues, the theatre itself – especially in its iteration as a highly subsidized German state theatre – is a 'border […] centred chiefly in cosmopolitan cities and concerned with the movement of information and people'. Lilienthal, like other artistic directors across Germany, has attempted to enable new border crossings, tackling themes of diversity, mobility and migration not only in the artistic repertoire but also in the theatre's personnel. At one of the Kammerspiele's 'Open Border Congress' panel discussions, Lilienthal committed to reflecting the migrant share of the population of Munich (37.2 per cent) in his workforce, raising it from 20 per cent (Dössel 2015). A second initiative aimed to deliver on this promise. In 2015, Lilienthal set up the 'Munich Welcome Theatre', funded by the German Federal Cultural Foundation, transforming the Kammerspiele into a place where refugees are invited to participate in projects that give them a working perspective on theatre. Two years later, the Kammerspiele announced that it was integrating four performers from their Open Border Ensemble into the main house ensemble for the 2017/18 season (Lilienthal 2017).

These moves build on gestures in Stemann's production of *Merchant*. Rather than interpret the production's use of satire and irony as a cynical commentary on the impotence of art, I am inclined to view it within its larger context as a vision of vital renewal that mingles art with institutional critique and practical transformation. One must not idealize the Lilienthal regime. A number of prominent performers have decided to leave the ensemble based on perceived neglect, and at the beginning of the 2016/17 season, audiences fell to 60 per cent capacity and 18 per cent of the theatre's annual subscribers cancelled their memberships (Lutz 2016). The sustainability of Lilienthal's regime is far from assured, but in beginning with *Merchant*, his programming showed that socially conscious artistic renewal isn't necessarily predicated on a break with old texts. In 2015 in Munich, Shakespeare didn't serve conservative agendas that buttress canonicity or bourgeois Enlightenment values. Instead, it became the vehicle enabling a new artistic team to enact its own border crossings, ones that are cognizant of the limitations of the culture industry (especially within elite mainstream institutions) but don't give up on art's ability to move people and ideas in ways that respond to, but also help to shape, rapidly shifting realities.

A brief coda

This essay was written from the vantage point of August 2017, but as this volume enters production (September 2019) I have been offered space for a brief coda. In confronting this two-year gap, it seems like we have been living through a perplexing era of tumult and stasis. Despite a diet of daily news that in previous years might have ended political careers, Trump remains in the White House, Brexit remains unresolved, and Lilienthal remains in post at the Kammerspiele. Hate crimes periodically spike as intolerance continues to penetrate mainstream politics. In May 2019, the Muslim Council of Britain formally requested that the UK's Equality and Human Rights Commission (EHRC) investigate Islamophobia in the Tory Party; in the same month, the EHRC launched a probe (still ongoing) into antisemitism in the Labour Party. The United States has seen the deadliest attack yet on its Jewish community in the Pittsburgh synagogue shooting of 27 October 2018. Killing eleven and injuring six others, the terrorist expressed his motive in advance on the far-right social media site Gab, attacking HIAS (Hebrew Immigrant Aid Society) and its support for 'invaders' – his term for those entering the United States in migrant caravans from

Central America. The times remain frighteningly intolerant and frighteningly difficult to interpret. Are we witnessing the violent lashings out of a white supremacy on its last legs, or a neo-fascism that is becoming mainstream?

In Munich, although Lilienthal remains in post, the fate of the Kammerspiele is also an uncertain one. In March 2018, local members of the Christian Social Union (CSU) – the conservative Bavarian party that works in coalition with Angela Merkel's Christian Democrat Union (CDU) – made it clear that they would not support an extension to Lilienthal's contract when voted on by the city council. These CDU representatives have come to oppose Lilienthal's tenure at the Kammerspiele, citing low subscriptions, an artistic programme that undermines the illustrious German tradition of spoken-word theatre, and their dissatisfaction with the political orientation of the public institution under his management. Lilienthal responded by announcing that he would step down when his current term ends in the summer of 2020, even though Munich's cultural adviser Hans George Küppers expressed regret at this decision. These events suggest that Lilienthal's attempt to artistically and politically reboot the Kammerspiele has failed, and yet the theatre's 2018/19 season led to it being voted 'Theatre of the Year' by *Theater Heute* – a German-language journal that bestows awards annually, in this instance based on the rankings of forty-four critics (the winner of 'Best Production' also hailed from the Kammerspiele – Christopher Rüping's ten-hour production, *Dionysos Stadt*). This national critical recognition might be connected to the resistance Lilienthal has met at the level of Munich's local city politics. It also signals that Lilienthal's project at the Kammerspiele is being aborted prematurely. Nevertheless, a final season awaits, which will complete five years of vibrant artistic programming that has broadened cultural discourse and opened up new collaborations – locally and internationally – to fashion the theatre as an inclusive space for expressing stories and perspectives hitherto shunned by the mainstream. The Open Border Ensemble goes from strength to strength, having invited three Syrian performers to join the 2018/19 ensemble as well as hosting a number of other guest artists. By the time Lilienthal steps down he will have presided over a very full five years of artistic and political programming at the Munich Kammerpspiele: five years of holding open borders separating communities, constituents and artistic practices to facilitate multiple crossings, which are sure to have consequences as we move into a future that remains decidedly undecided.

Notes

1 I am grateful to Manon Haase at the Munich Kammerspiele for providing access to the prompt script and archive recording of this production.

2 Thirteen people died on the scene in Barcelona, and one person in Cambrils. More than 130 pedestrians were injured in the Barcelona attack, one of whom later died in hospital. The Barcelona van driver also killed the owner of a hijacked car to make his escape, bringing the death toll to sixteen (not including the six terrorists shot dead by police).

3 For more information on this production, see: https://www.rimini-protokoll.de/website/en/project/adolf-hitler-mein-kampf-band-1-2

4 Directed by Karin Coonrod of Compagnia de' Colombari, this open-air production played from 26 to 31 July 2016, marking both the 500th anniversary of the Ghetto and the 400th anniversary of Shakespeare's death. For more information, see: http://www.themerchantinvenice.org

5 This event was organized by Shaul Bassi, Carol Rutter and Maria Ida Biggi. For more information, see: http://www.cini.it/en/events/shakespeare-in-venice-summer-school-the-shylock-project-2

6 *The Merchant of Venice*, dir. Jonathan Miller, The National Theatre, London, 1970.

7 I'm thinking here of Shylock's agony over Leah's ring – which Jessica steals, and which he would not have parted with for a

'wilderness of monkeys' (3.1.122) – and the ring that Antonio, at Portia's behest, uses to bind Bassanio and Portia in Act 5. In standing once more as his 'surety', Antonio is forced to renounce his claim on the man for whom he hazarded all.

8 I use the term 'asylum-seekers' to describe those leading the protest, but as Monika Mokre (2018: 205) clarifies: 'The protest movement called itself "Refugee Protest Camp Vienna" and involved asylum seekers, rejected asylum seekers, and other *sans-papiers* (*refugees* in the protest camp's terminology), as well as EU citizens, third-country citizens with valid documents for residence in Austria and (a few) recognized refugees (*supporters* in the protest camp's terminology). At their first press conference, the refugee activists emphasized that they would speak for themselves and that they understood the term *refugee* to include all asylum seekers, recognized refugees, migrants, and *sans-papiers* in Austria.'

9 One of Jelinek's source texts is the brochure of the Austrian Ministry of the Interior titled 'Living Together in Austria: Values That Connect Us'. It prioritizes 'fair play', conveyed through the analogy of competing swimmers who acknowledge mutual respect, no matter who wins, because they have struggled against the same conditions. Jelinek's coruscating irony exposes the insensitivity of such platitudes for refugees who have risked drowning to arrive on European shores.

10 The enterprise has also attracted hostility. In response to the Stemann/Jelinek production at the Thalia, the Latvian director Alvin Hermanis pulled his work from the theatre's repertoire because of its support for refugees, criticizing Merkel's open-door policy as misguided because of the risk that terrorists would enter the country (see Höbel 2015). During a performance of *Die Schutzbefohlenen* in Vienna in 2016, a right-wing group bearing the symbols of the Identitarian Movement stormed the stage and distributed leaflets saying 'multi-culturalism kills', whilst splashing artificial blood.

3

Thomas Jordan's 'The Forfeiture': A Mercantilist Rewriting of Shakespeare

Katherine Romack

As early as the first decade of the eighteenth century, critics have been perplexed by Shakespeare's depiction of Shylock in *The Merchant of Venice*. In 1709, Nicholas Rowe indicated that Shakespeare's original was better characterized as a tragedy. Rowe writes of the 'incomparable Character of *Shylock* the *Jew*': 'tho' we have seen that Play Revived & Acted as a Comedy, and the Part of the *Jew*, perform'd by an excellent comedian, yet I cannot but think it was designed tragically by the author' (1709: xix–xx). He was referring to George Granville, Viscount Lansdowne's return of *The Merchant of Venice* to the stage in an immensely popular reworking titled the *Jew of Venice. A Comedy* (1701) – an adaptation that reduced Shylock to a racist caricature that would carry the stage for the half-century to come.[1] A year later, Charles

Gildon conversely lauded the superiority of Granville's comic adaptation, characterizing Shakespeare's representation of Shylock as 'so vastly out of Nature, that our Reason, our Understanding is everywhere shocked' (1710: 321). What both of these early critical appraisals of the play suggest is that Shakespeare's representation of Shylock did not conform neatly to dominant early modern portrayals of Jews. Critics would debate the ideological import of Shakespeare's depiction of Shylock for the next 300 years.

Instead of engaging with the ongoing question of Shakespeare's implicit attitude toward Jews, I will look at the anchoring of *The Merchant of Venice* to an agenda that is unquestionably anti-Jewish in Thomas Jordan's seventeenth-century ballad adaptation of the play entitled 'The Forfeiture: A Romance' (1663: 36–40). Jordan's ballad contributed to a flood of literature about Jews that attended the mid-seventeenth-century debate about formal Jewish readmission.[2] In the context of an outpouring of writings about Jews that included everything from theological treatises and political petitions to plays, poems and polemics, a renewed interest in Shakespeare's *Merchant of Venice* in this period isn't surprising. In 1652, William Leake hastily reissued the third quarto of Shakespeare's play, appending a fresh title page to the remnants of 1637 editions (Erne 2013: 130). Jordan's ballad adaptation of the play was first printed in his *A Royal Arbor of Loyal Poesy* (1663). Like so much of Jordan's literary output during the Interregnum, the book is a miscellany of works assigned dates of composition and performance that range from the outbreak of civil war to the early years of the Restoration. The internal evidence supplied by 'The Forfeiture' indicates that the ballad may have been composed (and disseminated in manuscript form) sometime between 1653 and 1656, but the volume also speaks to Jordan's early Restoration audience, when the adjudication of the question of readmission was redirected from Cromwell to Charles II, prompting a renewed flood of antisemitic literature about Jews, both foreign and domestic.

Conflicting approaches to the question of Jewish readmission converged in December 1655, when a number of lawyers, ministers and merchant representatives convened at Whitehall, at Cromwell's behest, to consider the future of Jews in England (Green 1875: 15). The Whitehall Conference was the culmination of a gradual increase in 'philo-Semitic' ideas promulgated by a diverse spectrum of political, religious, literary and intellectual writers. There was a longstanding scholarly interest in biblical Hebraism that intensified with the religious conflict of the period (Osterman 1941: 302–5; Matar 1990). Between 1645 and 1655, the theological arguments for the readmission of the Jews increased in volume and intensity. Millenarian Protestants, who regarded the conversion of Jews to Christianity as requisite for the return of Christ, were especially passionate in their justifications for readmission (Williams 1643; Peters 1647; Nicholas 1649). In 1648, Johanna and Ebenezer Cartwright issued a petition requesting a repeal of the 1290 Edict of Expulsion (published in 1649). The 1650 repeal of the Act Against Recusants (1593), which had enforced participation in Anglican services, promised a new liberty of conscience and toleration in England. In 1653, the Instrument of Government went further to maintain that 'none shall be compelled by penalties or otherwise' to profess the Christian religion upheld by the State.[3] By the mid-1650s, radical Protestantism had become attached to Jews in the popular imagination. For closet Royalists, support for readmission was synonymous with republicanism and dissent. The Whitehall Conference only confirmed their association of Jews with Cromwell.[4] Protestants too, contra their millenarian contemporaries, issued violent condemnations of Jews in this period (Matar 1985: 121–3). Appointed by Cromwell, the assembly that gathered at the Whitehall Conference responded to a series of requests presented by Menasseh Ben Israel to the Protector that included naturalization and military protection, freedom of worship (including the establishment of synagogues and a cemetery), the election of an agent 'to receive our passports, and oblige us to swear fidelity, in order that those who come in may live without prejudice or scandal', the extension of judicial authority to the 'chief of the synagogue' in matters pertaining to Mosaic Law and the abolition of 'all laws against the Jewish Nation', including those restricting trade (Green 1875: 15).[5]

Jordan's ballad adaptation of Shakespeare responded to this mid-seventeenth-century debate about formal readmission and was, I contend, the first manifestly antisemitic adaptation of Shakespeare's play. Significantly, Jordon's adaptation was not driven by the inchoate residual medieval antisemitism that provides the backdrop of much of the literature about Jews in this period, nor was his adaptation motivated by the more targeted religious disputes between millenarians and their opponents that dominated the mid-century debate. Instead, Jordan's adaptation spoke to a more mercenary agenda. His rewriting of Shakespeare worked to buttress attempts to neutralize a perceived commercial threat by drawing a much clearer line of demarcation between the merchant and the Jew than is indicated by Portia's courtroom query: 'Which is the merchant here, and which the Jew?' (4.1.170).

***

One of the great ironies of the Whitehall Conference was that an assembly skewed by Cromwell's disproportionate appointment of millenarians and philo-Semites failed to endorse Jewish readmission. Henry Jessey, who issued the only detailed first-hand account of the proceedings, had kept up a correspondence with Menasseh and lobbied for admission as well as poor relief for Jews residing in Jerusalem.[6] He remarks that the 'Protector shewed a favorable inclination toward our harbouring the afflicted Jews ... in several speeches that he made. So did some of the council' (1656: 10). Justices Glynn and Steele had quickly dispatched any legal objections. Both Henry Lawrence and John Lambert, of the Council of State, endorsed readmission in the proceedings (Jessey 1656: 8; Crouch 1695: 168). Christopher Nye, along with Thomas Goodwin, held the opinion that 'due cautions warranted by Holy Scripture being observed, it was a duty to yield to their request' (Crouch 1695: 170–1; Jessey 1656: 3). Joseph Caryll, too, laid out the moral advantages of readmission and stated, 'we should the more pity and harbour distressed strangers, especially persecuted Jews' (Jessey 1656: 7; Crouch 1695: 171). While there is no direct evidence to confirm the positions adopted by other attendees, we do know that John Owen and Thomas Manton had expressed philo-semitic views in their sermons and that Hugh Peters had published at least one pamphlet encouraging readmission (Crome 2015: 295; Peters 1647). Professor of Hebrew Ralph Cudworth visited Menasseh while he was in England and his attitude toward Jewish readmission was likely positive (Lewis 2013). His fellow Hebraist, Benjamin Whichcote, was probably open to readmission in as much as it might contribute to Jewish conversion by facilitating a 'reasonable dialogue with liberal Christians' (51). While there are traces of less affirmative religious perspectives contained in the two seventeenth-century accounts of the proceedings, both Jessey and Crouch represent these viewpoints as exceptional. The first three sessions of the Whitehall Conference, which met on 4, 8 and 12 December, appear to have concluded, if not decisively, 'without any heat' (Thurloe 1742: 321).

What is certain is that the tone of the conference became more acrimonious on 18 December, as the deliberations were opened to the public and a crowd of spectators filled the 'long gallery at Whitehall' (Spence 1890: 108; Patinkin 1946: 167).[7] The final session appears to have been dedicated primarily to the question of the potential impact of readmission on trade. As Lucien Wolf reconstructs it:

> On this occasion the doors of the Council Chamber were, for some sinister reason, thrown open to the public, and an excited crowd, armed with copies of Prynne's newly published tract on the Jewish question, collected to hear the debate. The proceedings were tempestuous from the beginning, and gradually they took the form of a vehement demonstration against the Jews. Merchant after merchant rose and violently protested against any concessions,

declaring that the Hebrews were a mean and vicious people, and that their admission would enrich foreigners and impoverish the natives. (1901: li)

Although Wolf's account is speculative, it is clear that William Prynne began circulating advance pages of his *A Short Demurrer to the Jewes Long Discontinued Barred Remitter into England* (1656) on the eve of the final session of the Whitehall Conference to whip up public ire with a vitriolic rhetoric that invoked the traditional antisemitic image of the Jews as bloodthirsty crucifiers of Christ (and English children), representing them as a people of 'implacable transcendent malice' and more subtly invoking the longstanding popular association between Jewish money and aristocratic corruption as a way to cultivate suspicion about the parliamentary leadership (1656: A4v–r).[8] It is also plain that some merchant opponents worked hard to derail the proceedings. Jessey, a minister with ties to the Fifth Monarchists and a friend of Menasseh, is a biased reporter, but his eyewitness account indicates that he regarded some members of the merchant faction as the primary obstacle to Jewish readmission (1656: 8).

Cromwell dissolved the committee when it became clear that any decision that was arrived at would evoke a dangerous response from a public stirred up by Christian Zionist supporters, closeted Royalist sympathizers, disaffected Puritans and more mercenary city interests. The question of Jewish resettlement had, by 18 December, become a political lightning rod. Henceforth, readmission would remain an informal issue. This may have worked to the advantage of the Jewish community already residing in London – in as much as it deflected attention away from the Jewish question (deflating the fear-mongering surrounding the Whitehall Conference) and prevented the introduction of 'special' regulations for residents identified as Jewish. With the breakdown of the Whitehall Conference, English Jews were denied the rights and protections of naturalization. The failure of the conference was, not least, a result of the juridical quagmire introduced by the corporate merchant interest in the form of a slew of crippling regulatory stipulations restricting Jewish trade (Wolf 1901: liii). In the end, monopoly interests trumped free trade even as the fictions bolstering the idea of a godly cosmopolitan market proliferated. It is this fiction that Thomas Jordan's rewriting of the *Merchant of Venice* was designed to uphold.

Jordan has been characterized as a city poet whose 'constant values are moderation and peace, coupled with Protestantism, patriotism, the promotion of trade and a socially inclusive vision in which the city and its government have an important role in the nation' (Owen 1996: 299). Jordan had been raised as a boy actor in the King's Revels Company, where he performed at Salisbury Court. He would maintain his theatre connections for the rest of his career. During the Interregnum, he engaged in numerous theatrical experiments, was involved in the authorship of the lyrical 'Player's Petition to the Long Parliament' and was arrested for an illicit performance at the Red Bull in 1655. In the Restoration he would translate this experience into civic pageants and other municipal entertainments.

As an out-of-work actor, Jordan turned to the pen for a living. He circulated a large volume of manuscript material and issued more than twenty publications between 1642 and 1660 (many of these in multiple print runs). He styled himself a 'promiscuous poet' and produced a diverse range of materials, catering to a Royalist readership, publishing dramatic entertainments, poetic miscellanies and issuing mock diurnals, broadside ballads, speeches, military and political panegyric and other ephemera (Jordan 1665).[9] Jordan's appropriation of previously published material, often replacing the title page and inserting his own name as author, has caused more than one modern critic to dismiss him as a plagiarist. This is better read, I think, as a mark of Jordon's playfulness with the conventions of an emergent entrepreneurial esthetic. The dominant themes that unify Jordan's disparate publications are a passionate hatred of the Roundheads, a deep respect for the London tradesmen and merchants and love of the king. His works regularly criticized both hot Protestants and the administration that encouraged them even as they celebrated the nobility of the civic magnates who had remained true to their monarch. The entrepreneurial persona Jordan cultivated and the Royalist position he espoused so ardently during the Interregnum would elevate him to the role of poet of the corporation of London, a post that consisted primarily of the production of The Lord Mayor's Pageant each year.[10] On the eve of the Restoration, Jordan began generating civic entertainments for the London livery companies and city officials. He would go on to produce more than a dozen civic pageants in his position as London poet laureate (Hulse 2008).

The heterogeneity of the volume that contains Jordan's adaptation of the *Merchant of Venice* and strategic dating of the entries present the portrait of a Royalist writer-adventurer navigating the perilous waters of the Interregnum print market. *The Royal Arbor of Loyal Poetry* contains numerous references to the theatre and touches Shakespeare's *Othello* and *Henry IV, Part 1* in addition to *The Merchant of Venice*. The dedication – 'To the most liberal Lover of Sciential Industry and Native Ingenuity, the truly Noble, Mr. John Bence Merchant' – that prefaced the initial publication of the collection underscores the entrepreneurial spirit of the volume (1663: A2r).[11] As might be expected of a writer who so frequently praised loyalist city officials and London merchants, Jordan's ballad adaptation of the *Merchant of Venice* reflects their antisemitic, anti-admission attitudes in its strikingly mercantilist rewriting of Shakespeare. Set to the tune of 'Dear let me now this evening dye', 'The Forfeiture' reproduces Shakespeare's bond plot in its entirety, with two major alterations. First, the ballad's representation of the Shylock figure as a comic buffoon is unambiguous. The 'vilde' [*sic*], 'deformed' Jew is represented with the standard red hair and physiognomy of the usurer (36–7). Jordan's second innovation is to give Portia's courtroom performance to the Jewish daughter and marry her off to the merchant. If Jordan's alliance with loyalist London merchants and city officials accounts for the crude representation of Shylock in his ballad adaptation, his decision to sideline Shakespeare's crafty heroine, re-allocate her role to the Jewish daughter and have this 'Doctor' marry the merchant is more complicated.

***

When placed in the context of the mid-1590s – a period of severe economic crisis that saw bad harvests, war, famine, a sharp increase in unemployment, poverty, debt and food riots that threatened a repetition of the 1517 Ill May Day – the explicit economic language of *The Merchant of Venice* was hardly conducive to comedy (Burnett 1991: 35–7). For Shakespeare's audience, the central issue of the play was not usury but an interrogation of the ground of credit (Cohen 1982: 769; Korda 2009). The disastrous harvests of the mid-1590s, a growing population, the ongoing shortage of coin and expanding credit networks drove up inflation, borrowing and consequent default as debts were recalled by lenders who themselves found their credit frozen. Debt litigation exploded, and many people found themselves incarcerated for forfeiture. Most day-to-day transactions in the early modern period were conducted through credit agreements that were often informal and largely supported by Christian principles of neighbourly obligation (Muldrew 1993: 179; 2001: 84). During the economic crisis of the 1590s, trust and, therefore, credit evaporated along with the ethic of Christian benevolence that provided the market with liquidity.

Although Shakespeare set his play in the distant Venetian Republic, not London, the play nonetheless spoke to an audience dealing with the problem of community estrangement. Set in a cosmopolitan market economy requiring exchange with religious and ethnic strangers possessing inscrutable social rules and dubious motives, what, the play seems to ask, guarantees the 'trust' required of the contracts and promises that drive commerce? First off, Shylock is hardly a stereotypical representative of Jewish venery. He does not engage in usury anywhere in the play, nor does he seem to be especially interested in the acquisition of ducats, though he is certainly guilty of hoarding. As Amanda Bailey and Lauren Garrett rightly point out, Shylock adopts what is, in effect, a Christian lending practice, offering a 'kind', no-interest, debt bond to Antonio – knowing that Antonio is likely to default (Bailey 2011; Garrett 2014: 33). The play reminds us just how easily people possessing less-than-benevolent intentions can 'play' the Christian debt bond.

Shakespeare's ethical critique is not limited to his representation of Shylock. The ostensibly universal Christian values that ground love and honest trade are repeatedly contradicted – Shylock delights in pointing out – by the Venetians' ethical relativism and hypocrisy. The unresolved commercial and amatory explanations of Antonio's sadness that open the play set an ominous tone for the subsequent economic and amatory venturing of Bassanio. Representations of paternity and friendship, too, are conditioned by the language of debt and calculation, from Shylock's conflation of daughter and ducats to Antonio's characterization of his obligation to Bassanio as impressment (1.1.153–60). The language of amatory accounting in the play is patently excessive, and the prodigality of both Bassanio and Antonio, when set against the poverty of the 1590s, dissipated. The domestic retreat of Belmont is similarly infected by the commercialism of the city as Portia is figured as the object of international competition between Naples, Poland, France, England, Scotland, Germany, North Africa and Spain.

Contradicting Antonio's insistence that it is the universality of Venetian law that greases the wheels of commerce are the machinations of Portia, who exploits her family connection to the central representative of the traditional moral arbitration of economic law, the Schoolman Doctor Bellario, to fraudulently adjudicate Shylock's suit. Her theatrical wrangling reveals that Venetian law is incapable of addressing the pervasive conflict and unfairness at the heart of commerce between strangers. In the casket scene, for example, Bassanio's position as an insider gives him a distinct advantage in the casket trial. He does not need to bother reading the inscriptions on the caskets;

his choice is guided by Portia, whose song opens with two lines that rhyme with 'lead' (3.2.63–4). The consequences are devastating for his rivals, the prohibition of marriage, which grants Venice an obvious edge over its foreign competition.[12] In the end, as much as Portia has been lauded as clever and autonomous, and her marriage to Bassanio portrayed as representative of a liberal cosmopolitanism, Shakespeare represents Portia as deeply xenophobic and her marriage to Bassanio as both insular and endogamous.

The nepotism and endogamy of the play's Christian protagonists indirectly touch a final 1590s context for the play that is particularly salient to the concerns of this essay: the growing popular recognition of and protest against the deleterious effects of newly minted monopolies that culminated in a series of feisty debates in the Commons between 1597 and 1601, a period directly coincident with the probable composition of *Merchant*.[13] The primary complaint was that Elizabeth had exceeded her prerogative by issuing a number of patents on staple domestic products. One MP asserted that monopoly brought the 'General Profit' into a 'Private Hand' that could only result in 'Beggary and Bondage' to the monopolist (Townshend 1680: 237). Of Elizabeth he maintained, 'There is no Act of Hers that hath been, or is, more Derogatory to Her own Majesty, or more Odious to the Subject, or more Dangerous to the Common Wealth, than the Granting of these Monopolies' (237). The popular attribution of steep increases in the cost of staple goods to the monopolists spurred numerous civic actions in the decade that preceded the parliamentary debate. In June 1595, apprentices in Billingsgate seized butter and fish in order to sell them at a fair price. Eighteen-hundred apprentices, galvanized by the fish and butter initiative, tore down pillories, threatening to kill the Lord Mayor, 'rob wealthy inhabitants', and 'take the sword of authority from the governors' (Burnett 1991: 36). Undeterred by the 24 July execution of the ringleaders of this tumult, apprentices in Cheapside stole a cart of starch from one of the Queen's patentees in October. These events surely influenced the Elizabethan reception of the prodigality of the protagonists, the conspicuous wealth of Belmont and Antonio's suicidal decision to throw himself into a life-or-death, 3,000-ducat debt bond with an avowed enemy. By the mid-seventeenth century, these early debates over monopoly and private interest would congeal into a polarized rift between mercantilist monopolists, who argued that monopoly was to the benefit of the nation, and those who opposed them (Barth 2016: 273–7).

Although it is impossible to say for sure how the merchants who worked to derail the Whitehall Conference might have received William Leake's 1652 reissuing of Shakespeare's play, we can make some conjectures. Shakespeare's exposure of the morally relativist and nepotistic motives of the Venetians would certainly have made Sir Christopher Pack, the most influential merchant representative to the Whitehall Conference, uncomfortable. Pack, a Presbyterian Parliamentary sympathizer, was one of the few Merchant Adventurers that had not been purged from city government by 1655. As such, Pack had a greater stake than most of his commonwealth merchant contemporaries in the preservation of an ideology supporting a state-chartered marketplace. Again and again, Pack defended the ostensibly immemorial rights of the nation's oldest external monopoly. In his description of a January 1657 conflict between the 'Free Merchants' and Merchant Adventurers, Thomas Burton says that Pack 'did cleave like a clegg', in defence of the Adventurers' monopoly over wool against new merchant interlopers, 'and was very angry he could not be heard *ad infinitum*' (Burton 1828: 308–9).[14] He goes on to observe, 'The man will speak well, and I heard that when the consultation was at Whitehall, about the admission of the Jews, of all the head pieces that were there, he was thought to give the strongest reasons against them coming in, of any man' (309). The seamless transition from commercial to Jewish trespassers in Burton's account is indicative of Pack's protectionist desire to shore up a hierarchal commercial and ethnic pecking order. His presentation, a month later, of the *Humble Address and*

Remonstrance, which petitioned Cromwell to assume the title of King, underscores his absolutist tendencies.[15]

Conversely, conference delegate, independent wool merchant, and Baptist William Kiffin epitomized the progressive vanguard of the Commonwealth merchant oligarchy. The new wave of traders Kiffin represented – influenced, if not uniformly won over, by the revolutionary and millenarian spirit of the transatlantic economy – saw their fortunes rise dramatically during the Interregnum and were also more open to Jewish readmission (see Donoghue 2013). It is easy to picture former Mayor Pack going toe-to-toe with Kiffin at Whitehall on 18 December 1655. Pack had long campaigned against this new class of trespassers and viewed Kiffin and the Jews with equal disdain. The documents surrounding the Whitehall debate attest, in short, to a strong tension between economic monopolists and other protectionists and those who believed that the introduction of Jewish merchants into the English economy would greatly improve the overall fiscal health of the nation.[16] As Jessey reports,

> Some judged, seeing the Jews deal chiefly in way of Merchandize and not in husbandry, nor buying houses, nor in Manufactures; that the Jews coming and so trading might tend to the bringing lower the prizes of all sorts of commodities imported; and to the furtherance of all that have commodities vendable to be exported; and to the benefit of most of our Manufactares (where they shall live) by their buying of them. And thus, though the Merchant's gains were somewhat abated, it might tend to the benefit of very many in our Nation even in outward things, besides the hopes of their conversion; which time (it's hoped) is now at hand, even at the door. [This last was spoken of at a more private meeting.] (Jessey 1656: 9)

It is probable that Jessey's 'more private meeting' about the commercial benefits of Jewish readmission included Kiffin, who had become a Baptist under Jessey's ministry. Five months before the Whitehall Conference began, Kiffin had been dragged before the then Lord Mayor Pack for preaching against infant baptism (Gordon 1909: 99). In 1663, Kiffin would go on to testify, before a House of Commons subcommittee, 'against granting to the "Hamburg Company" a monopoly of the woolen trade with Holland and Germany' (99). Jessey's elision of the spiritual and economic benefits of Jewish readmission was much in line with the progressive 'free merchant' spirit Kiffin appears to have embraced.[17]

Crucially, Kiffin's commercial success was conditioned by an attitude toward strangers that extended the Christian benevolence that characterized the communitarian markets of Shakespeare's England to an international community. Had Kiffin picked up a copy of Leake's 1652 reprinting of *The Merchant of Venice*, Shylock's 'deadly spirit of revenge' might well have struck him as the logical outcome of an economic environment structured by religious hypocrisy, enmity and self-interest (Rowe 1709: xx). Kiffin's ethical understanding of Christian trade was shared by groups like the Quakers – whose early history of persecution and economic resistance (in the form of refusing to tithe), as well as their philanthropic traditions, placed them in an exterior relationship to the state. Central to the Quaker's spectacular eighteenth-century commercial success was a reputation for Christian 'truth' and 'honesty' with regard to craftsmanship, the exchange of goods and financial arrangements – dealing with a Quaker ensured a fair investment. Their principled religious attitude towards commerce, conjoined with a vast international missionary network, gave them a distinct edge in international trade and finance. Quakers were especially friendly to religious and ethnic strangers, including Jews, and were the first to compose polemics calling for the abolition of African slavery. Reading the writing on the wall perhaps, Pack's violent loathing of Quakers was rivaled only by his hatred of Jews.[18]

Weighing in heavily on the side of commercial monopolists and nativists like Pack, Jordan's 'The Forfeiture: A Romance' converts Shakespeare's economic realism into romance, eliminating any traces of questionable Christian business ethics. Jordan figures deceptiveness as an essential attribute of the Jewish 'race' and distinguishes carefully between the 'deformed' Jew who accumulated his wealth through usury and the 'gallant Christian Merchant' '[w]hose love unto a friend' is characterized as 'knit, / As strong as the bonds of nature' (Jordan 1663: 37). Just so there is no confusion about the nature of the bond between Bassanio and Antonio, Jordan also provides Antonio with a wife. This marriage serves a number of functions. For one, by eliminating Portia, Jordan is able to deflect the nepotistic manipulation of the law onto a Jew. Replacing Portia with the Jewish daughter, Jordan, in effect, reallocates courtroom theatrics to an alien, eliminating the questions Shakespeare had raised about the fairness of Christian courts (and commercial adjudication more generally) – a stranger is technically performing the manipulation of the law.

Once Jordan has displaced Portia's performative wrangling onto the Jewish daughter, he can marry her off to the merchant. The ill-gotten gains of the usurer are now transferred into Christian hands by ethnic coverture. Reversing the flow of capital, Jordan offers to the likes of Thomas Violet a remedy to the perceived problem of the Jewish extraction of bullion from England. Violet's *Petition against Jews* (1661) had blamed Jews for the shortage of coin.[19] He suggested that the 'many score pounds of our Gold and Silver' drained from England by Jews could be repaid by taking all Jews discovered in England hostage, reckoning 'the Jews of the world will ransom these Jews Bodies at a great rate' (5, 7). Cromwell's toleration, Violet explains, had allowed Jews to 'keep public worship in the city of London to the great damage of the Kingdome, especially our merchants, whose trade they engross and eat the children's bread' (2). Nonsequiturs such as these abound in the anti-Jewish literature of this period as Christian values are attached to an amorphous idea of honesty and trustworthiness in commercial dealings, and avarice is assigned to Jews. Although the attempt to extricate 'honest' Christian trade from corrupt commercial practices was at least as old as Aquinas, the desire to distinguish wholesome Christian trade from greed and self-interest is asserted with an increased urgency and tenacity – if decreased critical acumen – in this period. The diminished perspicacity and logical inconsistencies of monopolist discourse in this period were a product of the moral bankruptcy and ethical vacuity of the men who espoused it.

Jordan refigures Shakespeare's Jewish daughter in order to model an essential Christian credit. Even as she takes on the role of the 'Doctor' and performs the court scene, the Jewish daughter exhibits an idealized brand of trustworthiness and sincerity that distinguishes her from Portia's more ambiguous 'credit'. Jordan's Jewish daughter, after all, has only engaged in a 'subtle slight' that is excused by her 'true heart' and desire for marriage. '[F]or the love she long time bore' the merchant, the Jew's daughter is rewarded with marriage and her father's estate and 'baptized in Christendome' (Jordan 1663: 40).

> The Jew inrag'd doth tear the Bond,
> And darest not do the slaughter,
> He quits the Court, and then 'twas found
> The Doctor proves his Daughter;
> Who for the love she long time bore,
> From a true heart derived
> To be his wife, and save his life,
> This subtle slight contrived.
>
> (39–40)

Jordan converts the Jew's daughter into an emblem of Christian sincerity that supersedes the performative vagaries of juridical and ethnic custom.

> So sweet a Virgin never Lad
> Did ever set his eyes on;
> He that could call this Lady foul
> Must be a purblinde Noddy,
> But yet she had a Christian soul
> Lodg'd in a Jewish body.
>
> (37)

Jordan here depicts Christian 'credit' as a quality inhering in the Jewish daughter's 'soul', a soul housed in a Jewish body. Such a formulation is inconsistent with the opening interpellation of Jordan's ballad, which announces Jordan's belief that Christian credit is an essential, internal, but also somatic, attribute: 'You that do look with Christian *hue* attend unto my sonnet' (36; emphasis added). Jordan's characterization of Christian credit as a 'hue', a moral quality as indelible as skin colour, is peculiar given his depiction of the Jew's daughter as a Christian trapped in Jewish flesh.

The reason the Jewish daughter's flesh does not constitute an obstacle to her conversion into an emblem of domestic Christian credit is, I suspect, the product of Jordan's investment in an extremely retrograde and absolutist model of coverture. The Jewish daughter's forfeiture of identity in marriage is, in a word, total. Such a model of coverture, of course, flies in the face of the customary early modern maxim that the rights of a human being, even a wife, could not be curtailed to the point that their personhood was given up entirely to the dominion of a master. The motivations behind Jordan's adaptation are brought into sharper focus when we consider the career of the first merchant dedicatee of Jordan's *Royal Arbor,* John Bence. Bence was born to a family with a high commercial and municipal standing in Aldeburgh dating back to Elizabeth I, and was a powerful shareholder in the Royal Africa Company established in 1660, a company that would hold a monopoly over the trade in flesh until 1688 (see Watson 1983). Shylock's defence of his entitlement to a pound of flesh through a reference to Christian slaveholding and the silent figure of Lancelot's impregnated Moor in Shakespeare's play had taken on new meaning by the time Jordan penned his ballad adaptation. Addressing a commercial class increasingly at pains to provide ideological cover for its activities in an ever more ruthless economic environment, Jordan's antisemitic adaptation worked to obscure the bad faith at the heart of his mercantilist romance.

Notes

1 The adaptation is characterized by George C. D. Odell as 'dreadful', 'a gross vulgarization', 'the worst in the whole realm of Shakespearean alterations' and 'a rouged corpse – a thing too ghastly to conceive of' ([1920] 1966: 78–9).

2 Conducted under the auspices of a consideration of Jewish 'admission', the readmission controversy was equally concerned with the status of the crypto-Jews who already resided in London. Ariel Hessayon has identified, for example, at least one diurnal circulating an overblown report of public Jewish prayer meetings in Hackney in the months leading up to the Whitehall debates that is suggestive of increased anxieties about resident Jews in this period (2011: 1). For an excellent discussion of attitudes toward London Jews, see James Shapiro, *Shakespeare and the Jews*, especially Chapter six.

3 See The Instrument of Government (16 December 1653), articles XXXV and XXXVI (Gardiner 1906: 416).

4 For a discussion of the Royalist frustration with the Jews' perceived collusion with Cromwell, see Nabil Matar 1990: 84–8.

5 Book-length studies of the readmission debate include: Lucien Wolf, *Menasseh Ben Israel's Mission to Oliver Cromwell* (1901), H.S.Q. Henriques, *The Return of Jews to England: Being a Chapter in the History of Law* (1905), David Katz, *Philo-Semitism and the Readmission of the Jews to England, 1603–1655* (1982) and Eliane Glaser, *Judaism Without Jews: Philosemitism and Christian Polemic in Early Modern England* (2007).

6 Brief mentions of the conference appear in the diurnals of the period, but the only published eyewitness account is Henry Jessey's *A Narrative of the Late Proceeds at White-Hall Concerning the Jews* (1656). A second seventeenth-century description of the conference, 'The Proceedings about the Jews in England in the year 1655', is contained in Nathaniel Crouch's *Two Journeys to Jerusalem* (1695).

7 Joseph Spence reports that 'Sir Paul Rycaut, who was then a young man, pressed in among the crowd, and said he never heard a man speak so well in his life as Cromwell did on this occasion' (1890: 108).

8 Prynne's letter to the reader is dated 14 December 1655 (four days after the last session of the conference).

9 Jordan frequently offered up the same work to multiple dedicatees. 'His plan seems to have been to print a book with the dedication in blank, and to fill in the name afterwards by means of a small press worked by himself' (Seccombe 1892: 198). The individuals populating Jordan's many dedications were primarily prominent civic figures, merchants and tradesmen.

10 He was city laureate from 1671 to 1685 (Nichols 1824; Knight 1844: 145–160).

11 Other merchants targeted by Jordan include Merchant Adventurers William Christmas and Nathaniel Lownes as well as William Barkeley and Thomas Bridges.

12 '[E]ffectively sterilizing some of the more influential members of a generation of foreign bachelors, disrupting local dynasties across the Mediterranean and Europe' (Darcy 2003: 190).

13 I lack the space to capture the complexity of this debate here. Generally speaking, monopoly was regarded as beneficial to the economy as long as it served public, not private, interest. Monopoly became a problem when it came to constitute an 'abrogation of the right of all subjects to engage in a trade and as a harm to the public in the form of reduced employment and higher prices' (Nachbar 2005: 1327).

14 'Before the civil war ... the Merchant Adventurers and newer Eastland, the East India, and Levant Companies, monopolized foreign trade. As a new class of unincorporated merchants specializing in trade in North America and the West Indies, who "interloped in the East Indies", became more affluent and powerful, merchants with more established pedigrees worked to restrict their trade and keep these intruders out of city government' (Samuel 1988–90: 157). See also Brenner 1993: 633.

15 Barth notes that mercantilist monopolists would find a home in the Tory Party (2016: 274).

16 For similar opinions see the 12 December letter of Major General Whalley to Thurloe (Thurloe 1742: 308) and Collier (1656: 13).

17 For the economic interests of the other Merchant representatives see Brenner 1993: 118, 134, 155–6, 402–7, 544; Helms and

Ferris 1983; and Smythe 1808: 236–7. Some of these men may have had a hand in the strategic dissemination of Prynne's *Demurrer* (Samuel 1988–90: 164).

18 He was, for example, an enthusiastic participant in the persecution of James Naylor (Lindley 2008).

19 Violet's xenophobic hysteria was characteristic of the restored city oligarchy. A petition issued by the Mayor and Aldermen of the City of London just months after the Restoration requested that Charles II pass a formal expulsion edict. The petition is reproduced in Wolf (1901: 186–8). The previous year, Richard Baker had published a pamphlet requesting that Richard Cromwell expel the Jews (1659).

4

Jessica, Women's Activism and Maurice Schwartz's 1947 *Shayloks Tochter*

Sara Coodin

In 1947, the famed Yiddish actor-producer Maurice Schwartz staged an adaptation of Shakespeare's *Merchant of Venice* at the Public Theatre in Manhattan. *Shayloks tochter* (Shylock's Daughter) was a reworking of the Hebrew novel *Shailok ha-yehudi mi-venetsiya* (Shylock the Jew of Venice), by Ari ibn-Zahav, that was first published in 1943 and then reprinted in a second edition in 1947, appearing in Yiddish translation alongside Schwartz's play that same year.[1] *Shayloks tochter* opened to great success in September of 1947, receiving popular and critical acclaim with Yiddish- and English-language audiences and critics alike and touring across several major North American cities in 1947 and 1948. Schwartz's adaptation is not a faithful transcription of Shakespeare's text; instead, it substantially revises *Merchant* in ways that reimagine the play entirely from a Jewish perspective. Set on the eve of

Passover in the year 1559 in the Jewish Ghetto in Venice, the play focuses much of its action on Shylock's daughter Jessica, played in Schwartz's production by the celebrated Yiddish actress Charlotte Goldstein, dramatizing the struggle of a young Jewish woman caught between worlds. Jessica's character longs to escape her cloistered Jewish life, a move enabled through marriage and conversion, as it is in Shakespeare's comedy. However, over the course of Schwartz's play, Jessica shifts directions and pledges a newfound commitment to the Jewish community, one that prompts her to perform rescue work for Inquisition prisoners in Rome. Jessica's self-reinvention over the course of the play sees her evolve from love-struck object of romance to young activist determined to redress the suffering of her fellow Jews, to tragic victim who fails to attain belonging in either Christian or Jewish worlds. In the play's most radical departure from Shakespeare's text, Jessica is discovered drowned in the canal at the play's conclusion after abandoning her Christian marriage and suffering permanent exclusion from the Jewish community.

Schwartz's most innovative departures from *The Merchant of Venice* also reflect a series of definitive shifts taking place in the lives of Jewish women during the first half of the twentieth century, shifts aligned with women's long history of participation in labour activism in North America that prompted new modes of social organization both inside and outside the Jewish community. Jessica's identification with her Jewish heritage through activist work in the play has thus far evaded the attention of scholars, who have focused more intently on this play as an example of post-Holocaust literature.[2] *Shayloks tochter*'s deep relevance to its 1947 North American Jewish audience, though clearly linked to the play's close historical proximity to the Holocaust, is also markedly implicated in questions about social justice and, particularly, young women's roles in advancing it. In this essay, I consider Jessica as a figure whose turn towards activism speaks in significant ways to the lived experiences of Schwartz's Jewish-American audience and their own history of participation in both factory labour and labour activism. The ways in which *Shayloks tochter* appeals to that history, I argue, queries the bonds of Jewish social solidarity, exploring new sources of Jewish community that move away from esoteric scholarly study and instead emphasize active modes of advancing social reform.

***

What sorts of strategies represent the best, most productive responses to Jewish suffering and persecution? Are messianic passivism and retreat into Torah study preferable to active and worldly intervention? During the late 1940s, such questions took on a unique urgency and relevance among Jews. Yiddish theatre scholars have drawn lines of connection between Schwartz's play, which foregrounds these concerns, and the Holocaust, its most proximate and momentous historical precedent, arguing for the Holocaust's priority as the principal inter-text against which the play ought to be read.[3] Positioned at the juncture of a series of key upheavals implicating American Jews, Schwartz's play engages with the Holocaust, the creation of the Israeli state one year later in 1948 and the twin poles of communism and fascism that consumed global and American politics throughout the 1930s, 1940s and beyond. *Shayloks tochter* is no simple translation; it stands as a complex literary work in its own right, invoking the horrors of the Holocaust as well as the idealistic zeal of contemporary Zionism, while exploring forms of Jewish collective organization that bear on communism and socialism's formidable presence within twentieth-century Jewish American life. Its opening stage directions, 'Two Jews, bearing bundles of old clothes, approach' (Schwartz 1947: 12), evoke this complexity, recalling the infamous piles of Jewish clothing left at the entryways of Nazi death camp gas chambers, refugees arriving at Ellis Island with little aside from bundles of garments, and the North American garment industry that would employ Jewish immigrants in such prodigious numbers. Despite its Inquisition-era setting, *Shayloks tochter* reflects the distinctly contemporary and layered set of lived experiences of its twentieth-century

Jewish American audience, which includes a long history of participation in factory work as well as activism for workplace reform.

For many of Schwartz's Yiddish-speaking audience members, low-wage, toilsome factory work and the labour activism fuelled by its abject working conditions formed part of a shared backdrop of Jewish immigrant history. Industrial sweat-shop labour and the protests and reforms that emerged from it were in fact formative experiences for large numbers of North American Jews, even in contexts where the exploitative employers were also Jews.[4] Twentieth-century union organizers' recruitment materials reflected the prevalence of Jewish workers in industrial settings, and were often printed in Yiddish and tailored to speak to large numbers of young Jewish immigrants, and women workers particularly.[5] The needle trade – sewing – constituted an important source of employment for young Jewish women (some younger than fourteen years of age), who typically worked in factory settings until they married and began having children. During the early decades of the twentieth century, women often found themselves employed in the trade's least remunerative and secure jobs as seasonal and temporary workers.[6] It was during this same period that the garment industry's labour force grew, in step with industry demand. Garment factories that employed 39,000 workers in 1889 had, by 1905, expanded to over 150,000 employees (Waldinger 1988: 89).

Shayloks tochter offers a view into workplace conditions and their attendant tensions, rendering its Jewish ghetto a complex site of encounter not only between Christians and Jews, but also workers and employers. Through its exploration of the relationship between Shylock and his Christian servants, the play directs attention to characters who represent the play's working poor, and positions Shylock as an ambivalent figure who proves indifferent to the effects of his exploitative demands on his workers, some of whom have served him for twenty years. Launcelot calls attention to the importance of the work he performs in Shylock's household that helps Shylock uphold Jewish ritual.[7] In one instance, Shylock maligns and harasses his employees, denigrating their work ethic and productivity: 'Lorenzo, Launcelot, Stephano! Stone-dead are they all! Where are they, the lazybones, the useless wage-takers?' (Schwartz 1947: 22). This kind of harsh treatment provides a rationale for his employees' willingness to conspire against him, as it does with Shylock's servant Launcelot in Shakespeare's *Merchant*. However, for this Jewish adaptation staged for a Yiddish-speaking audience, the proximate history of factory work and workplace exploitation experienced by American Jews contributes additional significance. Shylock's oppositional posture towards his employees frustrates any possibility of solidarity between them, even in the face of shared concerns such as a common dissatisfaction with Pope Paolo the Fourth. According to Salanio, 'the common people hate [Paolo] more than they do the Jews' (Schwartz 1947: 13).[8] Despite sharing a common enemy who institutes oppressive conditions for Venetians (and based on the historical Paul IV), Shylock's indifference to material life corresponds with his equally indifferent attitude towards the exploitation of his servants. Their plight punctuates the play, and their schemes to stage an exit from their present poverty and low-wage labour is framed, at times, quite sympathetically, as in the following exchange between Launcelot, Stephano and Shylock.

SHYLOCK
You are leaving my house?
LAUNCELOT
For twenty years I have served you, honoured Signor. A faithful dog I have been to you.
STEPHANO
And I have served you thirteen years ... like a faithful dog.
LAUNCELOT
We wish to provide for our old age.
STEPHANO
To marry at least once in our lives
(Schwartz 1947: 108)

Whereas in Shakespeare's text it is the plight of the Jewish moneylender that provokes Shylock's 'if you prick us do we not bleed' speech, in *Shayloks tochter* it is the men who comprise the play's downtrodden workers who pine for basic material amenities such as a rye field, a modest house and the financial security to marry and start families of their own.[9] It is worth remarking that at the outset of this Yiddish-language adaptation staged for a Jewish audience, it is Shylock's Christian employees who evoke a sense of humanitarian pathos, while Shylock himself is positioned more ambivalently as both the play's acknowledged centre (with Schwartz as its undisputed star) and its exploitative employer.

As the centre of a play whose title emphasizes Jessica but names only Shylock, Shylock also embodies a traditionalism that is both prominent and problematic. Shylock exemplifies this through his insistence on Talmudic study, his contempt for Christian life and his resistance to the claims of urban assimilation represented by the city of Venice. Unlike his employees, who continuously narrate their desire to improve their material lives, Shylock sees little value in working to improve the conditions of ghetto existence; instead, he imagines spiritual fulfilment and happiness through the retreat of Torah studies. Where contemporary twentieth-century Jewish writers, including Sholem Aleichem, tended to portray ageing Jewish patriarchs as sympathetic figures positioned against the encroaching claims of a secularizing modernity, *Shayloks tochter* lays its ageing patriarch open to more substantive critique, particularly as he becomes increasingly consumed by an obsessive vendetta for his pound of flesh.[10]

As a counterpoint, the play foregrounds Jessica, who offers a contrasting perspective to her father's messianic passivism and rigid traditionalism. From the outset, Shylock's acceptance of status quo living conditions clashes with his daughter's profound dissatisfaction with them. Jessica associates ghetto life with poverty, restriction and unhappiness, declaring that '[i]n the Ghetto, people should mourn, not imitate the gay Venetians. In the Ghetto, Jewish daughters should sit by the window and pine away with longing for the magic City' (Schwartz 1947: 54). For Shylock, the Venetian ghetto is a permanent home, one that he insists his daughter must regard as an immutable reality, and to whose features she must learn to acquiesce. He asserts that 'Shylock's daughter must find her happiness between the narrow walls of the Ghetto, even as her mother, peace unto her memory, has found hers' (Schwartz 1947: 24). This early allusion to his dead wife Leah, who perished within the ghetto walls, proscribes a grim future for Jessica, generating one of the play's key dramatic tensions surrounding her choice of suitor. The Christian Lorenzo holds out the possibility of escape for Jessica to a life defined by art, beauty and material luxury. Conversely, Samuel Morro, the Jewish refugee and Torah scholar taken in by Shylock, counsels a retreat from the impoverished conditions of ghetto life in favour of a highly developed inner spiritual sensibility fulfilled through the study of Torah. Shylock intends Jessica to marry Morro, a suitor whose stoic approach to ghetto life parallels Shylock's, and who arrives at Shylock's doorstep with only 'the books of his teacher, the *gaon*, Rabbi Samuel Aqualti' (Schwartz 1947: 25).

The play is set on the eve of Passover, using the biblical story of Exodus as an inter-text to suggest that something more than inward retreat and acceptance of the status-quo is necessary to advance the fortunes of Jews under the oppressive Inquisition. The Passover story, itself a narrative of liberation featuring Moses leading the Hebrews out of slavery, forecasts the play's concern with strategies of active resistance in the face of oppression. In a debate about how to organize aid efforts to help Jews imprisoned in Rome under the Inquisition, Tubal declares that funds have been amassed to help Jewish prisoners. 'But who will be the messenger to go to Rome?' he asks (Schwartz 1947: 36). A rabbi describes this mission in terms that explicitly recall the Exodus narrative: 'the great *mitzvah* of "Redeeming the Imprisoned." ... *Avadim Hayinu* – slaves we were unto Pharaoh in Egypt, and even now we are slaves unto Paolo the Fourth' (Schwartz 1947: 37). However, the rabbi lacks a prescriptive plan, instead emphasizing the importance of keeping faith in God and a commitment to Torah study. 'God will aid us in our need, and will send us his messenger in due time', he pronounces (Schwartz 1947: 65). Shylock reiterates the rabbi's perspective by emphasizing that the current situation for Jews under the Inquisition will only be resolved by patiently waiting for the messiah. 'Only Messiah, the son of David, can save us from the Inquisition flames and the ghettos' (Schwartz 1947: 39). Samuel Morro echoes this same line of reasoning, locating salvation in the end times after the arrival of the messiah. 'Then shall we sing "*Az Yashir*" – the song of Moses and the Israelites – in the streets of Jerusalem. We shall live to see the Third Temple rebuilt in glory. And the nations of the world will rejoice in the spiritual light that will reach them from Jerusalem' (Schwartz 1947: 39).

Morro's comments reflect a Zionist hope that was actualized in 1948, only one year after the play was first staged at the Yiddish Art Theatre. And yet, while both Shylock and Samuel Morro express a spiritual longing for a better future that parallels some of the more idealistic aspects of Zionism, their comments also indicate a conspicuous lack of active strategizing to rehabilitate the material conditions of their present-day lives. As a piece of post-Holocaust writing, *Shayloks tochter* reflects on the horrific actuality of Jewish persecution and the lack of practical options for Jews living in Nazi-occupied Europe in the face of encroaching genocide. The question of Jewish suffering raised insistently in the play does, however, also query the type of spiritual patience advocated by Shylock and Samuel Morro by positioning it in stark contrast to the approach taken by Shylock's daughter.

The crux of *Shayloks tochter* rests on Jessica's deliberation between two options that she attempts but fails to reconcile – conversion to Christianity through marriage to Lorenzo; and a traditional life in the Jewish community via an arranged marriage to Samuel Morro. Her development remains rooted in her materialism, initially figured as pining for material luxuries and a deepening relationship with the pleasure-seeking

Lorenzo. That luxury-focused materialism is subsequently redirected, reframed as a concern for the physical suffering of Jews imprisoned under the Inquisition, which ultimately determines Jessica's course of action in the play. In the end, she chooses a path that cannot be reconciled with either of her available options: she marries Lorenzo and converts to Christianity, and commits to subversive activism on behalf of her Jewish community. In effect, she chooses an option that is not yet an option, since it undertakes to improve the lot of the most vulnerable members of her community while rejecting the prescribed role of Jewish wife to a man cut from the same cloth as her father, while using the limited freedoms her marriage to a Christian affords to attempt to undertake her activist work. What emerges clearly is that Jessica's shift from diversion-seeker to committed social activist crucially hinges on her character's acute sensitivity to the material dimensions of everyday living, an attunement closely associated with activism and workplace reform in the twentieth century. As I discuss in the remainder of this essay, it is through her that *Shayloks tochter* puts pressure on passive religious messianism by questioning its viability as the basis for strong community-building. As an alternative to esoteric spiritualism, Jessica's character instead builds on a deeply felt commitment to practical social justice. By examining the play's intersections with contemporary North American labour history, I discuss how it interrogates the usefulness and limitations of an activist approach as a foundation for Jewish identity and new source of community for diasporic Jews.

***

If Jessica's central choice in the play hinges on two religiously distinctive suitors, Christian and Jewish, hers is also a choice between what initially manifests as a diverting if glamorous materialism in the Christian Lorenzo, opposed to the otherworldly Jewish spiritualism of Samuel Morro. For the first half of the play, Jessica's desire for Venetian commodities and freedoms drives her relationship with Lorenzo closer to marriage and transports her away from Morro, the man who embodies the traditional Jewish values and committed spiritualism of her father. Lorenzo prefaces his courtship with Jessica upon her predilection for luxuries unattainable in her ghetto poverty. In one instance, he warns her that if she eschews him and returns to her Jewish life she will lose access to those luxuries and their attendant freedoms: 'No more shall you float on the canals, no more hear the songs of lovers in the gondolas' (Schwartz 1947: 103).

Jessica's pursuit of worldly pleasures has been cited as evidence of her character's flightiness;[11] and indeed, her initial desire for material pleasures corresponds with a desire to depart from aspects of traditional Jewish life, including the pursuit of learning through devotion to Torah study. However, assessments of Jessica as merely a shallow girl also miss the larger point of her attunement to material pleasures, which signals an acute investment in material culture that ultimately transforms her into a socially conscious young woman. Although her father identifies her longings as part of a misguided desire to become a 'daughter of Venice' and assimilate to the dominant Christian culture, Jessica's material longings also point towards a desire for liberation from her father's way of life. In this sense, she reflects a broader tendency among early twentieth-century working-class women, who often succeeded in fashioning their political subjectivity through the idiom of commercial goods, using consumer choices to escape the traditional worldviews and practices of patriarchal households.[12] Jessica's material longing is itself a complex text, allowing the play to designate her difference from her father and serving as a means for her to eventually resist him in less 'flighty' ways, as the issues that underwrite her materialism are explored and developed over the course of the play.

The life that Lorenzo exposes to view – pleasure-driven, focused on physical beauty (he repeatedly calls Jessica a 'Madonna') and reinforced by his friends' Portia and Antonio's splendid displays of wealth – charts a clear, materially focused path of escape for Jessica from the ghetto's constraints. Portia and Antonio reside in a marble palace surrounded by objects of beauty; their life is made up of lively celebrations, beautiful clothing and dancing. 'Our home is a temple for those who love life', Portia pronounces (Schwartz 1947: 43). For Jessica, such scenes point up her own dissatisfactions with the dreary conditions in the Jewish ghetto while also suggesting a clear and existentially transformative course of action in the present to remedy those sufferings. However, the life showcased by Lorenzo is rooted in Christian Venice, and the cost of entry for Jessica is a very public rejection of her Jewish identity. Moreover, the play makes clear that the prevailing attitude of Christian Venetians towards Jews is avidly antisemitic. Antonio has a pointed hatred of Jews – in *Shayloks tochter* he speaks the line, 'my hatred for them [the Jews] is in my blood, a heritage of many generations' (Schwartz 1947: 41) – which plays on Shylock's line in the original play: 'I hate him for he is a Christian' (1.3.38).

In setting out conversion as an avenue of escape from the Jewish ghetto, Portia and Antonio supply Jessica with a way – a terribly compromising one – for her to create an identity for herself as a woman of action rather than remaining a passive spectator to her own and others' suffering. However, that same course of action also fails to address the root cause of Jewish suffering. Antisemitic persecution during the Inquisition underwrites Jewish existential misery in the play; for Jessica, the kind of escape bound up with conversion would effectively align her with her Christian oppressors. Her desire to improve her lot and, eventually, that of her community, positions her between two uncomfortable options: convert and hope to secretly help Jewish Inquisition prisoners (an option that would place her in permanent exile from the Jewish community), or remain within the confines of ghetto life and accede to the passive approach advocated by her father and Jewish fiancé. The moments leading up to Jessica's marriage to Lorenzo and conversion highlight the acute anguish she experiences when faced with this choice.

PORTIA
> After the ceremony, we shall all fare to the Ghetto. Let the Jewish virgins of the narrow Ghetto-lanes see how Venice exalts a Christian daughter.
>
> JESSICA
> No! No! *(Attempts to go. Portia prevents her. Bells toll. Enter Lorenzo in wedding costume, a bouquet of flowers in his hand; with him, Antonio and Cardinal Roberto.)* ... *(Quietly, like a faraway echo.)* The flames of the Inquisition are flaring up. Rabbi Benjamin Nehemiah prepares to leap into the fire, in sanctification of the almighty.
>
> (Schwartz 1947: 117)

Jessica's description of Benjamin Nehemiah, the teacher and mentor of Samuel Morro, whom she visits in a Roman Inquisition prison, highlights Jessica's strong self-identification with Jewish resistance figures at this juncture of the play, even as she prepares to marry Lorenzo and convert to Christianity. Her movement towards marriage and conversion is here aligned with a form of self-sacrifice born of religious persecution in which she understands her imminent marriage via the imprisoned rabbi who refuses Christian conversion.[13] Jessica's identification with Jewish martyrdom marks a significant turn in her character's development that stems from her ability to identify other Jews' suffering and persecution as her own. Her 'awakening' initially takes place prior to the prison mission in the form of a fevered dream in which she experiences visions of the Talmud being burned by Catholic bishops and cardinals. Reflecting on the dream, she comments, 'I have just seen how the Talmud was burned at San Marco Plaza, and the mob laughed and laughed' (Schwartz 1947: 61). In an exchange with her father, she proclaims a newfound sympathy with his sorrows and those of other Jewish ghetto-dwellers and the Jewish people more broadly. 'I understand you [Shylock] now more than I did before my illness. How your face is lined with wrinkles, Ghetto-wrinkles ... mother's death ... the sorrows of the Jews ... the pain I cause you ...' (Schwartz 1947: 63).

Jessica's commitment to 'faring forth on a sacred mission to save refugees from prison' (Schwartz 1947: 83), born of fevered images of infernal religious persecution and martyrdom, reinterprets the religious content – Talmudism and rabbinic heroism – that had previously been identified with Shylock and Samuel Morro and their brand of messianic passivism. Jessica's path to reclaiming her Jewish identity refashions those conventional Jewish symbols into important catalysts to activist work, which she undertakes by volunteering for the rescue mission.

The fire and flame imagery in these scenes also evoke a tragic chapter from local twentieth-century workers' history in New York City that signalled both the horrific actuality of factory work as well as the desperate need for reformed working conditions. The Triangle Shirtwaist fire, whose horrors remained etched in the minds of Jewish New Yorkers for generations, resulted from a deadly mix of unsafe working conditions and a cutter's wastepaper basket fire, and took the lives of 145 employees, a majority of whom were young Russian-Jewish immigrant women working twelve-hour days for less than $15 a week.[14] In the aftermath of the Shirtwaist tragedy, the workers' union set up a strike that was attended by 80,000 people, and the union's subsequent efforts led to the adoption of improved workplace fire safety laws in the city of New York.[15] By alluding to a historic local tragedy that had become emblematic of the horrors of factory work and the possibility of reform, Schwartz's play reimagines the bonds of Jewish solidarity as ones forged in suffering but subsequently reinforced through collective effort, mobilization and solidarity around social justice issues.

In *Shayloks tochter*, Jessica's activism is brief and confined to her single trip to a Roman prison undertaken with aid from Lorenzo, Portia and Antonio, who hope to incite her to repudiate her Jewish faith. Jessica's story ends in tragedy when she absconds from her marriage and is discovered drowned in the canal after her conversion to Christianity, which she is told is irrevocable. Jessica's tragedy in *Shayloks tochter* is also the absence of any viable alternative to Jewish ghetto life that doesn't entail a fatally self-sacrificial form of martyrdom. Bound up with her search for alternatives to that martyrdom in the play is a set of concerns about the fate of Jewish women and their roles as domestic caregivers and child-bearers, which the play aligns specifically with Jewish life. When Lorenzo pressures Jessica to marry him, he is emphatic about saving her from a life of relentless marital duties and the rigors of frequent childbearing. He describes the condition of married Jewish life for women as a form of enslavement and submission to patriarchal authority, insisting that '[y]our father will never again permit you to leave the Ghetto. This is your last visit to Venice. He is waiting impatiently for your return to Rome, and for your marriage with Morro. Then you will be imprisoned in the bed-chamber, that you may enrich the Ghetto with a little Jew yearly' (Schwartz 1947: 103). Although he does not specifically prescribe a childless life for their own future, Lorenzo's comments disparage toilsome Jewish reproduction, and imply that their own future life of luxury and ease would entail considerably more freedom for Jessica than Jewish ghetto life. *Shayloks tochter* revises Shakespeare's characterization of Portia and Antonio by presenting the two as a married couple who are conspicuously childless, in contrast to the image of ceaseless childbearing that Lorenzo recalls when he describes the ghetto.[16]

Jessica's fate as an exile scripts a tragic outcome to her search for renewed direction, meaning and belonging. The impetus that motivates her turn from frustrated daughter to brief activist would have been entirely comprehensible to this play's original audience, for whom committed struggle to improve the material conditions of working life often helped forge identities that diverged from traditional religious and domestic roles. In the decades leading up to the Second World War, public perceptions of Jewish workers were strongly influenced by fears of communism's global spread. In the period between the two World Wars, mounting concerns about communism's reach and the ongoing association of Jews with its proliferation meant that Jews often found themselves at the centre of pointedly anti-communist propaganda, some of which succeeded in bolstering local American support for Hitler and the Third Reich in the 1930s.[17] Under communist direction, workers' unions during the first half of the 1930s had overseen a series of combative, highly confrontational workers' strikes that prominently featured Jewish women, who were depicted in mainstream media outlets as wild, disruptive, and inassimilable to normative values and 'proper' womanly conduct.[18] These women and the perceived threat they posed remained closely aligned with a perceived communist threat to the democratic social order. After 1935, when labour unions moved away from communist leadership, less combative strategies for resolving workplace disputes were implemented that resulted in fewer employee strikes, fewer confrontational episodes between striking workers and 'scab' employees, and more positive perceptions of women factory workers. In response to the purging of communist strains from the labour unions, as well as the normalization of women's presence in factory work during the wartime years, social attitudes towards Jewish industrial workers and Jewish women workers became more sympathetic.[19]

Although the wartime period saw a de-escalation of workplace protest in North America, and industrial work itself came to be valued as an important national contribution to the global fight against fascism, the decades following the war also featured renewed debates about women's presence in the workforce and their public voice and mobility outside the domestic sphere. In discussing the roots of modern feminism, some scholars have argued that figures such as Betty Friedan, whose *Feminine Mystique* shaped much of the discourse of first-wave feminism in the 1960s, owed a great deal of their momentum as well as their key insights to earlier years spent working as labour activists.[20] If the social activism of Jewish women in the 1940s and 1950s served as an important engine of 1960s and 1970s feminist thought, that same history also provided a significant re-entry point back into Judaism for progressive, socially conscious women during later decades of the twentieth century. Judith Antler introduces her study of highly influential twentieth-century activist Jewish women, *The Journey Home: Jewish Women and the American Century*, by narrating her own experience of early disenfranchisement with Judaism. Where Antler initially experienced her Jewish heritage as alienating, she identifies her ability to subsequently reconcile with Judaism as heavily indebted to Jewish feminism. Antler cites the women's activism in her own family as her key point of access, relayed in stories about the exploits of her great-aunts and grandmothers who worked, protested, marched and resisted (Antler 1997: xi–xviii).

Antler also cites the often-rocky relationships that Jewish activists of the 1970s and 1980s forged with mainstream American feminism and its antisemitic undercurrents; tensions that she maintains exemplify the challenges that modern Jewish women have faced while integrating the various strands of their identities into a cohesive, ideologically consistent whole.[21] In a twenty-first-century context, those challenges have become even more acute under third-wave feminism, a movement defined by intersectionality's key claim that all forms of social and political injustice are interconnected, which has created unique tensions for Jewish women.[22]

Jessica's shift from passive romantic subject to determined social justice actor to tragic outcast without a community in *Shayloks tochter* reflects, on the one hand, some of the key driving factors that mobilized Jewish women's activism in the first half of the twentieth century; while on the other, it forecasts some of the problems that have faced Jewish women activists in the decades since Schwartz's play was first produced. In working with people outside her ethnographic community, Jessica shows a willingness to move between worlds and set aside fixed, insular notions of identity in the interests of advancing the cause of justice in solidarity with the disenfranchised. There is little question that for her, movement outside the confines of the Jewish world is experienced as a profoundly disturbing crisis, one that resides at the centre of the play's story of turmoil and loss. Jessica is no overt beacon of feminism; on the contrary, many of her actions and choices in the play reflect a helpless fragility in the face of difficult choices. However, her character does model the very resistance activities that have remained a vital part of Jewish women's histories in the twentieth century, and upon which subsequent generations of Jewish activists and feminists built their commitments to social and political progressivism. In the year of its debut, Schwartz's play was already making concessions to the decline of the rich cultural life associated with Yiddish theatre. Its playbills, written in English rather than Yiddish, reflect Schwartz's awareness at this late stage of his career, that Yiddish theatre was already becoming a spectre of a fast-receding Jewish immigrant past. And yet, in framing Jewish identity as a two-fold struggle for both an improved world and a sense of belonging in that world, Schwartz's play was also determinedly forward-looking, and remains a distinctly timely adaptation of Shakespeare's Jewish play.

Notes

1 The Yiddish translation of ibn-Zahav's novel by Menachem Glen, titled *Shaylok und zayn tochter: a roman fun amol und itst* (*Shylock and his daughter: a novel of past and present*) was published in serial format in the Yiddish newspaper *Morgen-Zhurnal* in the autumn and winter of 1947.

2 For recent examples, see Nahshon 2017 and Chaver 2011.

3 Nahshon has called attention to a series of contextual events surrounding Schwartz's production that emphasize its relevancy as a piece of post-Holocaust writing, including Schwartz's own adoption

of two Holocaust-survivor children the same year the play opened, and his playbill's introduction, which draws a number of explicit parallels between Renaissance Italy and twentieth-century Germany. In the essay 'New York City, 1947: A Season for Shylocks', Nahshon quotes Schwartz's playbill: 'All this occurred in Italy during the famed Renaissance period, when art and science prospered as much as in latter-day Germany; although of course without the same German thoroughness and technique of the Twentieth Century. ... Paul IV's period was a small-scale precursor of Hitler's time, and the Nuremberg laws were practically a copy of Paul's Roman edicts against the Jews. A description of the time is almost a replica of the anti-Jewish practices in our own day' (2017: 164).

4 Tensions between Jewish workers and owners sometimes meant that protests would be staged between immigrants and the individuals who had sponsored their immigration to North America. See Giesbrecht 2010: 6 for a discussion of this issue in the city of Winnipeg.

5 Women workers were often the objects of intense recruitment efforts on the part of union groups, including such organizations as the Women's Trade Union League (WTUL), the primary collective organization for the garment industry in the early twentieth century. Throughout the first three decades of the twentieth century, WTUL organizers actively engaged with immigrant women factory workers in the housing settlements where they lived, and made deliberate efforts to approach women in their vernacular languages. Among the WTUL's most effective activities was its educational outreach, which included programming efforts to 'promote self-organization and to train women workers as leaders' while imparting English-language skills to newly arrived immigrant workers who lacked proficiency in English (Hyman 1988: 29). The New York WTUL created a textbook, *New World Lessons for Old World Peoples*, which taught English vocabulary to women alongside the virtues of unionism. The primer was published in Lithuanian, Italian, Yiddish, Bohemian and English, complete with illustrations that established clear and visible contrasts between union- and non-union working conditions. The featured characters were very like the women these texts aimed to reach: mostly women, and often single immigrants (Hyman 1988: 36).

6   The seasonality of factory work led to hiring workers, particularly young, less-skilled female workers, on an intermittent or contingent basis. Women factory workers therefore often found themselves in less secure working arrangements, with poorer remuneration, than men. According to Waldinger, it was not unusual for the average length of unemployment each year to span eight to twelve weeks for women in this industry (Waldinger 1988: 93). On the whole, female garment factory workers tended to be young unmarried women, making this type of work the province of less-skilled female labourers than it was for men, some of whom performed specialized and highly paid functions as cutters and finishers. As late as 1920, 52 per cent of the female workers in manufacturing were under twenty-five years old, and the industry widely employed girls from as young as fourteen and, in the years between 1900 and 1920, girls even younger than fourteen, according to Waldinger's study.

7   Launcelot emphasizes his essential but unacknowledged contribution to Shylock's household early on, when he remarks: 'Who salts the meat according to ritual? Who cooks – who bakes the *challah* for the Sabbath? Jews are not permitted to employ Christian maids in their homes. Who, then, will run a *kosher* kitchen for Signor Shylock, since his wife is departed? It's twenty years that I am servant to Signor Shylock. All by myself, I can go through the *Passover seder* ...' (Schwartz 1947: 15).

8   In a modern context, Jewish men and women often found their ethno-religious identities reshaped or realigned through activism. Giesbrecht comments that the first half of the twentieth century constituted a new era of Jewish identity in which cultural bonds were forged around labour activism in ways that bypassed traditionally observant religious practices. She writes of this period in Winnipeg, a Canadian city renowned for its Jewish female labour protesters: 'During garment industry strikes, for instance, workers often gathered at the Jewish Peretz Hall, a socialist free school, or the Talmud Torah, a religious school dedicated to the Hebrew language, where union members spoke in Yiddish. Traditional cultural spaces thus took on new meanings when used in the context of labour protest. Leftist thought and Jewish culture were intertwined; strikes

and protests provided spaces within which ethnic identities were strengthened through resistance to bourgeois capitalism' (12). Narrow ethnographic loyalties were often broadened through participation in social activism and transformed into working-class solidarity that crossed ethnographic lines, either complicating or erasing tribal loyalties. As noted Canadian labour activist Joshua Gershman recalls, for many who had become involved in North American labour activism in the early decades of the twentieth century, labour activism provided a 'new home – and perhaps even more, a new spiritual temple … indeed, for most urban Jews, it constituted their first real introduction to [American and] Canadian life. It served not only as an agent for economic benefits, but also as a cultural shelter' (Abella 1977: 186).

9 Upon preparing to leave, Stephano exclaims: 'To be rid of the Ghetto; no more to hear Shylock yelling, "Launcelot! Stephano!"; no longer to have the Synagogue before our eyes night and day. To have a cottage of our own in the country, with a patch for wheat and rye' (Schwartz 1947: 80).

10 See, for example, Sholem Aleichem's celebrated short story 'Chava' as an example of an elegiac recounting of paternal loss when Tevye's daughter absconds from his home with a Christian man. I discuss this episode and its significance within Jewish-American writing as an engagement with the Shylock/Merchant trope in chapter 4 of *Is Shylock Jewish? Citing Scripture and the Moral Agency of Shakespeare's Jews* (2017: 197–244).

11 Nahshon views Jessica this way and writes that 'when she [Jessica] succumbs to Lorenzo's seductiveness and to the blandishments of Venice, she falls into the trope of a weak, confused female' (Nahshon 2017: 165).

12 This represents the central argument of Nan Enstad's *Ladies of Labor, Girls of Adventure* (1999). Enstad discusses how consumer culture and purchasing power were all associated with the ability to critique patriarchal culture, and consumer products therefore acquired important symbolic status as tokens of liberation from strict male-dominated families where fathers traditionally called the shots (11).

13 This figure is based on the historical sixteenth-century Rabbi Benjamin Nehemiah ben Elnathan, who chronicled

the persecution and imprisonment of Jews, including his own, under Pope Paul IV.

14 On 25 March 1911 the Lower Manhattan Triangle Shirtwaist factory burst into flames after a fire in a cutter's wastebasket on the eighth floor quickly spread to other parts of the overcrowded, unventilated workspace. Lacking even the basic safety provisions that would have allowed workers to escape a factory fire – there was no functional sprinkler system, and only one operational elevator that workers had to file down a long corridor to reach – the fire rapidly consumed the interior of the eighth, ninth and tenth floors of the building whose facade was, ironically, fireproof, and still stands today. What remained after thirty minutes of consuming flames were the charred remnants of bodies from a fire escape that had collapsed under the weight of desperately fleeing victims, the broken corpses of those who had chosen to jump to their deaths rather than be engulfed by the flames, and dozens of twisted carcasses burned beyond recognition on the factory floor. The escape door to the street had remained locked to those attempting to flee as the fire completely consumed the workspace and all those trapped within it. A 2011 *New York Times* article profiles the way in which families of the victims have contended with the memorial legacy of the fire. See Berger (2011).

15 Other forms of collective action among garment workers also began to stir in earnest during the first decade of the 1900s, and remained a potent force through the 1910s, 1920s and 1930s across major cities in North America. Between 1906 and 1909, women workers engaged in several short-lived walkouts to protest working conditions in New York City. These labour uprisings were occasional and limited to a select few factories. However, when wages dropped in 1909, grievances over fines, disciplines and new requirements that forced workers to pay for their own needles and thread led to a series of spontaneous strikes among shirtwaist workers that became the famous 'uprising of the 20,000' that had thousands of workers on the picket lines for an extended period that lasted months, to the surprise of industry owners and newspapers who covered the story (Waldinger 1988: 96). During the Great Shirtwaist Strike of 1909, it was Jewish women activists such as Clara Lemlich, Pauline Newman, Rose Schneiderman and Fania Cohn who

played instrumental and highly visible roles in organizing and implementing the walkout.

16 Portia, who assumes a dominant role advising and pressuring Jessica to convert, also models an alternative of wilful femininity firmly embedded in a world of material luxuries, while enjoying substantial freedom from the kinds of domestic responsibilities that determine Jewish women's lives.

17 Bradley W. Hart discusses the American religious leader and radio host Father Charles E. Coughlin, who insisted that a communist-Jewish alliance constituted a pernicious threat to American security, and disseminated his message to a wide audience of American listeners throughout the 1930s (Hart 2018: 69).

18 During the first half of the 1930s, communist-led unions such as the Industrial Union of Needle Trades Workers (IUNTW), which dominated North American garment industry activism, directed increasingly fractious, even violent, encounters between striking workers, often Jewish women, and members of anglo-Protestant society. During one of the largest IUNTW-led strikes in Canada in 1934, perceptions of Jewish workers as foreign agitators intensified, valourizing 'good' female factory workers who were not agitators, while demonizing 'radical' communist-led ones. Tactics included spreading stories of violent threats and warning of the evils of falling under the sway of communist pro-labour propaganda (Giesbrecht 2010: 12).

19 In 1935, after the Communist International urged union organizations to join forces with mainstream labour organizations to help combat the rise of global fascism, the more moderate International Ladies' Garment Workers' Union (ILGWU) took over union leadership. In many North American cities, this meant an increasingly top-down leadership style in which male union leaders quieted worker complaints while generating smoother relations with owners, resulting in fewer overall disputes that escalated to strikes (Giesbrecht 2010: 14–15).

20 Friedan worked as a labour journalist and radical activist in the 1940s and early 1950s before receding into the kind of suburban domesticity that informed her feminist critique in *The Feminine Mystique*. Daniel Horowitz has convincingly argued that in fact it was Friedan's radical labour activist past, which she deliberately muted as she promoted her book, and not her suburban

experience, that represented the more vital foundation for *The Feminine Mystique*'s key feminist insights (Horowitz 1998).

21 Antler 1997.

22 Under the aegis of that imperative, activist events such as the 2017 Chicago dyke march, intended to celebrate queer pride, also called for the exclusion of Jewish symbols, including the Star of David, which organizers associated with the oppression of the Palestinian people. During that march, several Jewish women carrying rainbow-coloured Star of David flags were asked to leave the event. Such occasions showcased tensions between activism and progressive politics on the one hand, and Jewishness on the other, rendering them mutually exclusive and fundamentally incompatible with a core tenet of contemporary progressive feminism. For a particularly vocal editorial response to the exclusion of Jewish women from the dyke march – one that proved to be very inflammatory in the face of an already inflammatory issue – see Weiss (2017).

5

'Woolly Breeders': Animal Generation and Economies of Knowledge in *The Merchant of Venice*

James Kearney

In their first scene together in *The Merchant of Venice*, Shylock and Antonio exchange heated words that establish their antagonistic personal history and the position each character occupies both within the community of Venice and in relation to Judeo-Christian traditions. Mostly though, they talk about sheep. This essay looks at this give-and-take concerning Laban's sheep to ask why so much weight is placed on the generative capacities and accomplishments of these 'woolly breeders' (1.3.79). Animal generation was of significant interest to early modern economic thought, particularly with regard to questions of economic risk and its management. And early modern conceptions of risk were often defined in relation to epistemological certainty and uncertainty. Risk was a function of the contingent or accidental, which were considered the province of the divine and thus located beyond human knowledge and economic calculation. In late medieval and early modern controversies regarding usury in particular, one key area of dispute concerned proper domains of influence and action: where must one acknowledge the limits of human knowledge and industry? In this essay, I address the ways in which Shakespeare's *The Merchant of Venice* thinks with sheep as it addresses notions of property and risk at the heart of its economic and theological investments. Tending to Shakespeare's sheep not merely as property but as creatures that figure property helps shed new light on some of the play's fundamental concerns: debt and ownership, economic production and reproduction, inheritance and generational transfer.[1] More specifically, by reflecting on the skirmish regarding Laban's sheep and on Antonio's identification as a 'tainted wether' in the trial scene, I hope to show how the play's staging of the opacity or unknowability of creature or beast speaks to a larger conversation about risk and calculation in early modern culture, a conversation that revolves around a recognition of the limits of human knowledge.

'Innocent profitable beasts'

In his classic essay 'Of Gentlemen and Shepherds', Louis Montrose asks that we pause for a moment and take seriously the fact that in the early modern period the literary form of pastoral was fundamentally a 'poem about shepherds' and that both sheep and shepherds were essential to the economy of early modern England:

> Nine out of ten people in Elizabethan England were rural dwellers, and sheep outnumbered people, perhaps by as many as three to one. This was a society dependent upon unreliable sources of agrarian production for its physical

survival, and dependent upon sheep for food and fertilizer as well as for wool, the raw material of England's basic industry. Foreign visitors were repeatedly struck by the abundantly pastoral quality of the English landscape, its inhabitation by 'countless numbers of sheep' (Montrose 1983: 421)[2]

Thinking about the genre of pastoral in relation to history and ideology, Montrose asks us to attend to the ways in which the invocation of the shepherd and his world touches on the material realities of early modern life. Taking Montrose's cue, I want to dwell for a moment on the fact that the material realities of sheep were shaped by the fact that sheep were, first and foremost, property; that is, a material investment that needed to be safeguarded, managed and induced to propagate. This was particularly evident in early modern England, where sheep enjoyed a privileged status. Montrose cites William Harrison's observation in *Description of England* that 'this kind of cattle is more cherished in England than standeth well with the commodity of the commons or prosperity of divers towns, whereof some are wholly converted to their feeding' (Montrose 1983: 421). In discussing sheep as 'this kind of cattle', Harrison makes reference to the practices of enclosing and engrossing property that eliminated areas of common pasturage in sixteenth-century England; practices designed to exploit the profitable wool industry on a grander scale.[3] 'Cattle' is etymologically related both to 'chattel' and to 'capital', and the success of sheep as capital investment in early modern England gave rise to practices that famously threatened social institutions and arrangements. With the material realities of this situation in mind, it is no wonder that sheep in early modern England seem at times to *figure* property. To be sure, the long history of domestication necessarily transforms the relation of domesticated animals to the world in ways that have everything to do with their status as property. But sheep in the early modern imagination often take on the symbolic burden of this domestication; this is necessarily consequential both for the way they are thought about (and with) and for how they are cared for and managed.[4]

In *The Historie of Foure-Footed Beastes* (1607), Edward Topsell devotes over forty folio pages to the discussion of sheep. Although Topsell begins with an overview of what he calls 'the generall nature of sheepe' as well as the 'diuers and strange kinds' of sheep 'in other nations', what follows is only intermittently interested in addressing sheep in terms of either natural philosophy or early ethno-zoology (1607: 601). What Topsell is most concerned with is the maintenance and reproduction of sheep.[5] While the focus on the care and upkeep of sheep certainly points to their status as valuable property, Topsell also wants to convince his readers of the manifold *virtues* of sheep. Describing the honour and 'dignitie' sheep were accorded in antiquity, Topsell hopes to inspire his readers (or perhaps just 'one noble spirited learned man ... furnished with witte, meanes, and opportunitie'):

> to diue and pierce into the secrets of English sheepe, and Shepheards, and to manifest vnto the world the best, and most approoued meanes and medicines, for the propulsing and driuing away of all manner of diseases from those innocent profitable beasts, and for their conseruation in all manner of health and welfare. (1607: 621)

Piercing the secrets of 'English Sheep' will help conserve the health and welfare of these 'innocent profitable beasts', a striking formulation that gets at the strange mixture of creature, ethical figure, and economic good that sheep become in Topsell's account. Indeed, as the phrase 'innocent profitable beasts' suggests, the notion of sheep as property is delivered in terms of the rich metaphorics of sheep we find in the early modern period. Below, I suggest that the proverbial innocence – specifically, as Bruce Boehrer writes, the 'endangered innocence' – of sheep is in part a function of the ways in which they figure property or capital (2010: 164, 170). Here, I simply want to note the ways in which the sheep's evocation of innocence and predation, property and theft plays into many of *The Merchant's* narrative arcs and thematic motifs.

Property and theft are at the heart of the scriptural contention between Shylock and Antonio. Turning to Genesis, Shylock instructs his interlocutors to 'mark what Jacob did'. Although Shylock never gets to complete the lesson, it seems that he will attempt to defend his economic practices, practices repudiated by the merchant Antonio, by way of scriptural text:

> When Jacob grazed his uncle Laban's sheep,
> This Jacob from our holy Abram was,
> As his wise mother wrought in his behalf,
> The third possessor; ay, he was the third.

Here Shylock is interrupted by Antonio: 'And what of him? Did he take interest?'

> No, not take 'interest', not, as you would say
> Directly 'interest'. Mark what Jacob did:
> When Laban and himself were compromised
> That all the eanlings which were streaked and pied
> Should fall as Jacob's hire, the ewes, being rank,
> In the end of autumn turned to the rams;
> And when the work of generation was
> Between these woolly breeders in the act,
> The skillful shepherd peeled me certain wands,
> And, in the doing of the deed of kind,
> He stuck them up before the fulsome ewes,
> Who, then conceiving, did in eaning time
> Fall parti-coloured lambs, and those were Jacob's.
> This was a way to thrive, and he was blest:
> And thrift is blessing, if men steal it not.

(1.3.67–86)

Shakespearean scholars have long puzzled over Shylock's use of the Jacob and Laban story to justify usury, since it seems not to have been so used in the period.[6] Moreover, invoking Jacob's inheritance and blessing – as Shylock does in referencing Jacob's mother's efforts on his behalf – is, as Lars Engle points out, very dangerous for Shylock 'in an exegetical argument with a Christian' (1986: 29). By referencing what 'his wise mother wrought', Shylock alludes to Jacob's theft of his brother Esau's blessing. And in the Christian tradition, the transfer of the blessing was thought to signify the transfer of blessing from Judaism to Christianity; Jacob emerges here as a figure of Christian supersession.

Against this tradition, Shylock is attempting to assert ownership over the text ('Mark what Jacob did'), the patriarchs ('our holy Abram') and this birthright ('The third possessor; ay, he was the third'). But Antonio interrupts Shylock at precisely the point when he mentions Jacob's possession of the birthright, enacting a kind of Christian supersession writ small.[7] As many readers have observed, the entire exchange calls forth competing exegetical traditions and announces the typological themes of new covenant superseding old and mercy sublating justice that we find in the trial scene. The evocation of the Jacob and Esau story within the Jacob and Laban story thus gives us a wrestling over patrimony and inheritance within a contestation over cattle, property and use of property. The plot of *The Merchant of Venice* is driven by property and the conditions of inheritance. More specifically, the play seems concerned with the interruption of the social and economic norms of generational transfer. The bond plot is a function of the casket plot, which is a function of Portia's father's rewriting of inheritance. Likewise, the fate of the failed suitors, the romantic subplot between Lorenzo and Jessica, the apportioning of Shylock's capital in the trial scene, all suggest the disruption of the normal mechanisms of the transfer of wealth and property. In this matrix, Jacob's appropriation of Esau's inheritance might be considered not simply an allusion within the play but an origin story or primal scene for the play. And here we get that primal scene not only referenced but *repeated* in a different key in the Jacob and Laban episode where sheep-as-property are entangled in disputes over possession and use.[8]

For his part, Antonio denies Shylock's application of the passage to his practice of taking interest: 'Was this inserted to make interest good? / Or is your gold and silver ewes and rams?' For Antonio, the crucial distinction between the profits of the usurer and the profits of the merchant is risk: 'This was a venture, sir, that Jacob served for, / A thing not in his power to bring to pass'. Antonio's response that this episode was 'swayed and fashioned by the hand of heaven' is perfectly orthodox in the period (1.3.87–91).[9] The key to Antonio's response, however, is the term 'venture', which had become the preferred term of merchants to describe their profit-making endeavours. Risk is a key distinction between the usurer and the merchant, and the emergent ideology of risk has often been aligned with modernity and capitalism.[10] Here, I want to hold off modernity for a moment and return to a theology of risk, which is part of the scholastic inheritance addressing usury.[11]

Animal generation and the limits of knowledge

Risk is at the heart of the critique of usury in the theological tradition, and this is because risk is deployed to clarify the complexities of ownership in certain financial arrangements. To use or profit from a possession one must establish ownership, which is demonstrated through risk or exposure to loss. If you cannot lose something, the logic goes, then you do not own it. Note that in this theological context risk is, first and foremost, a juridical category that demonstrates possession rather than some virtue that warrants reward. An important aspect of theological notions of risk is that the sphere of the *contingent* is the domain of the divine.[12] As mentioned earlier, in early modern discourse concerning usury, acknowledging the limits of human knowledge and influence proves crucial. Whether referring to the manipulation of time or the mitigation of loss through increasingly sophisticated financial arrangements and instruments, early modern economic discourse often laments the hubris of assuming mastery in areas where only God can hold sway. In this context, early modern merchants seize on risk not only as that which distinguishes their economic activity from usury in technical terms but also as that which establishes the piety of their endeavours. The image of the heroic merchant adventurer is laid over the image of the pious man of faith who puts all his trust in providence as he exposes himself to loss.[13] In this paradigm the risk of the merchant venture is authorized in theological terms as an act of faith. And the emphasis on a passive acceptance of God's will and giving oneself over to divine will through risk and exposure to loss has new force in a post-Lutheran moment.

When Martin Luther himself turns his attention to economics in *The Long Sermon on Usury*, his object of analysis is less usury per se than economic calculation and risk.[14] In fact, in *The Long Sermon*, Luther does not spend much time railing against usury narrowly defined, since it is obvious to him that usury would and should be condemned. Instead, he attacks predatory financial arrangements and instruments that *amount to usury*. This is something we see in early modern economic discourse generally: usury is both a significant technical term for a particular practice and a term deployed to critique predatory economic behaviour generally. If Luther is attacking usury writ large, then he defines that category via risk, which becomes the key criterion for determining whether a financial arrangement is predatory. In other words, risk is how one recognizes 'usury' even if we are not talking about an interest-bearing loan. For Luther it is not simply that risk entails exposure to loss and is therefore a sign of proper ownership; it is that risk marks the realm of the *incalculable*. The relation of risk to calculation that someone like Luther takes as natural is a relation in which human calculation reaches its limit in things unknowable, at which point human agents must put themselves in divine hands.[15]

For the purposes of this essay, the crucial point is that in discussions of risk in early modern economic discourse, the two standard arenas invoked are maritime trade with its obvious hazards, and agriculture, in particular the uncertainty surrounding the generation of crops and livestock. Because natural reproduction is something outside of human hands, it can serve as a figure for the risk one takes in investing in certain forms of human industry. For instance, when looking for an example of the kinds of risk he is talking about in his *Long Sermon on Usury*, Luther invokes the uncertainties of agricultural production.[16] By turning to the manipulation of natural reproduction in the Jacob and Laban story, then, Shylock addresses directly one of the places that early modern criticism of usury staked out for itself. In terms of early modern economic discourse and a theology of risk, the question here has to do with knowledge and its limits: does Jacob embrace the unknown and put himself in God's hands, in which case he can figure his profit as blessing? Or does he have certain knowledge that allows him to manipulate capital in such a way that he profits at Laban's expense? Again, Shylock gets to the heart of the matter by offering blessing and theft as the two ways to read Jacob's action: 'thrift is blessing, if men steal it not' (1.3.86). Are Jacob's efforts to manipulate the woolly breeders to his advantage hard practices that amount to fraud because there is no real risk of loss, or are they legitimate (and risky) enterprises that have the blessing of God?

Early modern husbandry manuals certainly support the viability of this mode of reproductive intervention. Topsell rehearses various accounts in which sheep that drink from particular rivers produce offspring of certain colours. Topsell authorizes these accounts as natural and not miraculous by referencing the story of Jacob and Laban itself:

which things do not come to passe by miracle ... [but] by the power of nature, as may appeare by the History of *Iacob*, when he serued his father in law *Laban*. ... For after that he had couenanted with *Laban* to receaue for his stipend all the spotted sheepe, the Scripture saith [here, Topsell recounts the biblical story] ... Vpon this action of the Patriarke *Iacob* it

> is cleare by testimony of holy Scripture, that diuers colours layed before sheepe at the time of their carnall copulation, doe cause them to bring forth such colours, as they see with their eyes: for such is the force of a naturall impression. (1607: 605–6)

Likewise, as Arnold Williams notes, the biblical commentaries in the period do not dispute the viability of Jacob's reproductive intervention, the sympathetic magic whereby he influences the reproduction of sheep; on the contrary, like Topsell, they tend to offer corroborating evidence of similar acts that demonstrate the same reproductive principles (Williams 1948: 170–1). In his *Lectures on Genesis*, Luther helpfully catalogues many of the examples that other commentators use before adding his own anecdote about a woman who gives birth to a dormouse (Luther 1955–86: 5.380–3). Like Topsell, the commentaries not only see this as a viable form of intervention, they tend to view the success of the breeding programme as a *natural* rather than miraculous occurrence. That Jacob thrives to the extent that he does, that he profits so greatly, they ascribe to God's grace or blessing. Like Antonio, they view the entire enterprise as divinely guided. But that Jacob manipulates events to his advantage and deceives Laban is undisputed. And this brings the ethics of the action to the fore. It is amusing to watch early modern commentators twist themselves into knots to defend Jacob's stratagem.[17] In his *Commentary on Genesis*, Calvin formulates the problem clearly: at 'first blush', this episode 'may seeme very absurde' as the 'purpose' seems to be 'either to condemne holy Iacob of deceit, or else to praise his industrie' (1578: 634). And it is the very confusion at the heart of the problem that tempts an enterprising exegete like Shylock. To be sure, both husbandry manuals and biblical commentaries agree that this is a natural rather than a miraculous occurrence, but in early modern thought it does not follow that what is natural is entirely knowable or calculable. There is certainly no sense that what is natural is devoid of either mystery or the shaping hand of divinity. The reproduction of sheep and other animals (human and non-human) falls into the rather large category of things in early modern thought that are simultaneously familiar and mysterious, manipulable and unknowable.

The Laban's sheep episode is richly overdetermined. The struggle over inheritance exemplified by Jacob and Laban (and Jacob and Esau) and played out in terms of sheep-as-property is central to the play's dramatic structure. The language of *both* animal generation and breeding barren metal calls forth theological discussions concerning risk and usury that shape the play's interest in the economic world of Venice. And it is not simply that the figure of the sheep evokes property and theft, but that the proverbial innocence of the sheep is a function of its status as 'endangered property', its vulnerability to loss. Finally, the play seems to dramatize an antagonism between an emergent way of knowing in which calculation subsumes risk, an epistemology that we now associate with modernity, and an older one in which epistemological humility reflects a fundamental unknowability at the heart of the natural world. In the famous trial scene in Act 4 of *The Merchant of Venice*, many of these same elements are marshalled into the kind of agonistic, binary structure that the courtroom setting solicits and affords. And at the centre of the scene, the figure of the sheep re-emerges in merchant's clothing as Antonio dramatically announces that he is a 'tainted wether of the flock, / Meetest for death' (4.1.113–14).

Tainted unprofitable beast

In the final scene of the casket plot as Bassanio turns to make his choice, Portia laments her lot in this game of love and chance. Comparing herself to Hesione before the sea-monster, she adopts a suitably melodramatic pose: 'I stand for sacrifice' (3.2.57). Portia here invokes the genre of romance as she claims the role of 'virgin tribute' that will be given to the creature unless redeemed by the hero (3.2.56). Like Bassanio's earlier comparison of himself with Jason in search of the golden fleece, this deployment of romance fits with the play's aligning of risk – commercial, nautical, amatory – with adventure. And this dovetails with the casket test's association of risk with sacrificial gift: 'to give and hazard all' (2.7.9). Indeed, the curious conjunction of *to give* and *to hazard* performs the ideological work of aligning risk with the sacrificial virtue of giving or expending all. Portia's affirmation – 'I stand for sacrifice' – resonates broadly in a play invested in pitting the logic of excess and extravagance and loss against the logic of scarcity and paucity and thrift. As readers have noted, Portia's stance anticipates the famous declarations of Shylock's in the trial scene: 'I stand for judgment' (4.1.102); 'I stand here for law' (4.1.141).[18] Judgment and sacrifice are a version of the possible poles around which the play organizes itself: usurious contract and merchant venture, justice and mercy, Old and New Testament. And if we hear 'I stand for sacrifice' echoed in Shylock's 'I stand for judgment', we might pull Portia's averred stance into the trial scene where she ultimately deploys the law to stand for Antonio, who explicitly characterizes himself as sacrificial victim awaiting the knife

Readings of the trial scene tend to locate Antonio's declaration that he is the 'tainted wether of the flock, / Meetest for death' in a binary scheme that would place (Christian) risk and exposure to loss on one side of the ledger and (Jewish) prudence and predatory calculation on the other (4.1.113–14). And in these readings, Antonio tends to emerge as a figure of ultimate sacrifice: Isaac on Mount Moriah or Christ on the cross.[19] As some scholars have observed, however, a '*tainted* wether' is *not* what you would sacrifice in Christian or Jewish religious observance since a 'tainted' creature is neither appropriate gift nor consequential expenditure or loss.[20] 'The weakest kind of fruit' that '[d]rops earliest to the ground' is obviously a meager offering (4.1.114–15). In fact, once 'tainted' creatures are invoked, the 'sacrifice' here makes more sense in relation to animal husbandry and economic calculation. In its treatment of sheep, Topsell's *Foure-Footed*

Beastes is fundamentally concerned with the prevention of maladies that might afflict the 'innocent profitable beasts'; and crucial to this prevention is culling the flock. As Topsell notes, it is the shepherd's duty 'to picke and cull out the aged and sicke Sheepe ... least they ... infect their fellowes, or least that the whole flocke do go to decay'; that culling more often than not means killing in these instances is clear within the context of the rest of the passage (1607: 611). The 'tainted wether' is 'meetest for death' not because it is an ideal offering to the divine but because it is a potential source of infection or contagion. In other words, one culls the 'tainted wether' from the 'flock' precisely to manage risk and decrease exposure. In economic terms, this is a simple calculation designed to protect one's investment, one's capital. The rhetoric of Christian excess and expenditure versus Jewish calculation that key Christian characters within the play articulate and that has been taken up by so many readers of the play would then seem to be undone – or at least complicated – by the figure of the 'tainted wether'. This is not to say that Antonio does not proffer himself as a sacrificial victim. On the contrary, as the trial scene proceeds, Antonio's language suggests that he would prefer to cast himself in the role of martyr for love (4.1.260–77) who meets his fate with heroic endurance (4.1.5–12). My point is that he chooses to cast that sacrifice in terms of managing risk and reducing exposure; in marking himself for death through the figure of the 'tainted wether', he is not simply playing the role of both priest and sacrificial lamb, but of proprietor and economic hazard. And this sacrifice is ostensibly performed in the name of securing collective good – flock or herd or tribe – and economic well-being.

A significant share of the emblematic force of Antonio's identification of himself as 'wether' facing imminent death is derived from the figure of Shylock as wolf. In his speech immediately prior to this assertion, Antonio implores Bassanio to forgo debating with 'the Jew': 'You may as well use question with the wolf / Why he hath made the ewe bleat for the lamb' (4.1.72–3). Within twenty-five lines of the 'tainted wether' declaration, Gratiano suggests that Shylock's 'currish spirt' was 'infused' into him while he still 'layest in' his 'unhallowed dam'. In Gratiano's fanciful Pythagorean theorem, the soul so infused into Shylock's form or 'trunk' was fleeing not simply from a dying wolf but from a wolf on the gallows, having been 'hanged for human slaughter'. Gratiano deduces this because, as he says, Shylock's 'desires / Are wolvish, bloody, starved and ravenous' (4.1.127–37). Antonio and Shylock thus emerge in the trial scene as predator and prey, vulnerable sheep and murderous wolf. Of course, as Carla Freccero reminds us, the rich and generative cluster of ideas and images that we tend to associate with the wolf-sheep relation or dynamic is precisely a function of the long history of sheep as property:

> the economic system of private property (and primitive accumulation) require an enemy. And 'enemy' is most often what wolf is, especially in the economic arena. The archive of wolves and humans in intimate naturecultures is a record of economic competition, top-of-the-food-chain predators finding themselves side by side, the one in the *polis* (the city), the other on its borders (2015: 114).[21]

The creaturely innocence of the sheep is a function of its status as capital to be protected and emerges in contradistinction to the anthropomorphic vilification of the wolf, figured not simply as predator but as thief, raider, plunderer. Moreover, this language and this imagery are charged with affect and significance in *The Merchant of Venice* precisely because they are invoked in a play concerned with staging the ethical, social and interpersonal complexities and consequences of property relations.

Moreover, it may be that Antonio's 'taint' does not simply speak to infection or to contagion but to being touched, marked, tainted or attainted. In a virtuosic reading, Jonathan Gil Harris associates Antonio as 'tainted wether' with 'Jacob's "pied and streaked" sheep' at the centre of the scriptural dispute earlier in the play. Noting that 'taint' was 'a hybrid term', Harris traces 'taint' in relation to both disease and 'tinct' or colour:

> The interplay between 'taint' as ... animal disease and 'taint' as color produced a variety of hybrid senses in Shakespeare's England, all of them with pathological connotations of varying degrees. First, 'taint' possessed the still familiar sense of stain, blemish, or spot; this was used almost invariably in a metaphorical sense. ... Second, 'taint' assumed the pathological sense of contamination or infection ... And finally, 'taint' became a more specialized medical term referring to a trace of disease in a latent state.

While noting that 'this last meaning seems implicit in Antonio's description of himself as tainted', Harris argues that we should keep the range of meanings of 'taint' open as we approach the play's deployment of the term. With that array of meanings in mind, he argues that 'the tainted Antonio is physically *stained* as much as he is pathologically *infected*, and in a way that harks back to Shylock's justification of usury. If the usurer's skill lies in the production and expropriation of hybrid goods, the 'tainted wether' Antonio has here become Shylock's 'parti-coloured' sheep' (Harris 2004: 77–8). Antonio has become hybrid – 'parti-coloured', 'pied and streaked' – marked or polluted or tainted in relation to his own flock or tribe. While I find Harris's reading of Antonio as tainted hybrid convincing and instructive with regard to the 'tribal' dynamics of the trial scene, for the purposes of this essay, I want to seize on the idea that Antonio, touched or marked by Shylock, has become 'property alienated to Shylock, legally comparable to the lambs that Jacob usuriously expropriated from Laban' (2004: 78). In this reading, the trope of sheep-as-property is crucial to the image of Antonio as wether; attainted by the hold Shylock has on him, Antonio self-identifies as 'wether' not – or not simply – because he becomes prey in relation to Shylock's wolfish predator but because he has become property.

A 'wether', of course, is a castrated ram. That Antonio identifies himself as a figure associated with castration or sterility has received significant attention. And sterility and castration haunt the play: the casket test threatens marriage and thus traditional modes of reproduction and inheritance; Antonio is presented from the outset of the play as neither father nor husband nor like to be; Shylock's threat to Antonio's flesh can be and has been read as the threat of castration; the list could go on. This haunting can also be read as part of the play's overall concern with animal (including human animal) reproduction and generational transfer. Looked at through a certain lens, Antonio's status as 'meetest for death' is overdetermined in economic terms: he is tainted and, therefore, seems to expose the flock or tribe to some threat of disease or contagion; he fails to contribute to the flock or tribe's reproductive mission; and by the trial scene, he is no longer an economically viable figure in the world of Venice. To paraphrase Topsell, he has become a tainted, unprofitable beast. Topsell suggests that if you are to select a sheep for household consumption, you should choose one that is fruitless and unproductive. He writes (pun intended, I presume) that the 'the counsell of Antiphanes is profitable to bee followed ... to kil those sheepe from whom you can neuer expect any more profit by their Lambs, milke, Cheese, or fleeces' (1607: 611). The curious thing about Shylock's threat to 'cut the forfeiture from that bankrupt there' as the threat of castration is that if Antonio is the tainted wether, he is already castrated (4.1.121). And this seems to fit with Antonio's fatalism and resignation; the sense that, for Antonio, Shylock's excision is simply the formal occasion that will publicize to the world at large his existential condition. That Antonio is *economically* castrated as we arrive at the trial scene seems clear. And as Shylock says later in the same scene, 'You take my house when you do take the prop / That doth sustain my house. You take my life / When you do take the means whereby I live' (4.1.371–3). The means whereby Antonio lives have certainly been taken away; reduced to an abjection always framed within an economic logic, Antonio is unable to give or offer anything in the trial scene other than his life, which he seizes as sacrificial expenditure through the image of the 'tainted wether'. This seizure is purely discursive, however, as his life is not his to give. If there is to be sacrifice, it will have meant that his life remains Shylock's possession.

Many scholars read Antonio's identification with the tainted wether in relation to his melancholy affective life and what it might portend.[22] If Antonio is already castrated even before the approach of Shylock's knife, is this state of affairs a function of his status, announced at the play's outset, as someone who is sad because he is not merry (1.1.1–50)? Antonio's melancholy, of course, is notoriously illegible or impenetrable. Framed from the first lines of the play as an indefinable affective *something* that both solicits and rebuffs interpretation, it is central to what Drew Daniel identifies as 'the play's concern with the epistemology and poetics of opacity' (2013: 97). And this unknowable affect follows Antonio to the courtroom where his raw emotion and extravagant rhetoric seem to reveal both everything and nothing. If, as I have been suggesting, Antonio's self-identification as 'tainted wether' resists any easy claims to heroic martyrdom or ethical self-sacrifice – given that its overdetermined relation to sheep-as-property muddies distinctions between economic calculation and some 'pure' Christian expenditure – the point is not to affirm or decide what 'tainted wether' means either for Antonio or for the play. On the contrary, Antonio-as-wether proves as resistant to interpretation as other avatars of the melancholy merchant; moreover, and like other such avatars, the 'tainted wether' explicitly performs that resistance. The play's 'poetics of opacity' here takes up not only sheep as slippery, protean trope, but also the unreadable 'creature', which both animates the trope and acts as its limit. Antonio's evocation of the tainted wether give us the image of a beast marked for death, but if this mark or taint remains mysterious and seems of a piece with Antonio's performance of unknowability or illegibility, so too does the wether, which resists knowledge in its creatureliness, remaining both familiar and alien.

Stone binding and familiar alterity

Given the significance and ubiquity of sheep in sixteenth-century England, most in Shakespeare's audience could be expected to enjoy a certain familiarity with matters ovine. And Shakespeare himself, with his Stratford background and a father whose various occupations included dealing in wool, would be familiar with the material realities of sheep, including, presumably, a conventional understanding of their reproductive ventures. When discussing sheep and generation, Topsell offers an extensive account of different strategies for manipulating reproductive activities and results; these include the use of 'salt Water'; the binding of the left or right 'stone of a Ram'; preferring water from a particular side of a river; attending to the direction of the winds, etc. (1607: 606–7). On the one hand, Topsell's description of various ways to maximize the generative capacity of sheep points to long-standing technologies of livestock reproduction. On the other hand, the sheer variety of techniques proposed suggests a certain mystery at the heart of the process. Topsell's text does not read like a modern 'scientific' account designed to engender knowledge and certainty; instead, it reads like a sheepish list of things people have tried or thought with regard to processes that remain in some sense unknowable.

This 'unknowability' or creaturely opacity is at the heart of Topsell's 'innocent profitable beast', which is in turn at the heart of *The Merchant of Venice*, where creaturely tropes breed and figure many things, including a certain epistemological humility in relation to the familiar alterity of the natural world. The struggle over Laban's sheep, a form of property simultaneously manipulable and unknowable, echoes throughout *The Merchant of Venice*. In Shakespeare's play, these 'profitable beasts' figure both the vulnerable 'innocence' of property – its exposure to loss rendered in moralizing terms – and the limits of human calculation. *The Merchant of Venice* thus employs homely sheep and familiar ovine discourse as a means of working through the theological preoccupations of property and risk at the core of its dramatic action. Shakespeare's 'woolly breeder' is simultaneously a dynamic and fluid figure on the move in a symbolic landscape, a commodity entangled in human economies, and an early modern beast – that is, something both familiar and beyond understanding.

Notes

1 On the complex interplay of economic and sexual generation in *Merchant*, see Shell 1982.
2 On things ovine in the early modern world, see Yates 2017.
3 This passage calls to mind Raphael Hythloday's famous account of English sheep in Thomas More's *Utopia*. For excellent recent analyses, see Raber 2013: 151–78 and Yates 2017: 35–89.
4 For scholarship that attends to the complexities of non-human animals as property in the early modern world, see the work of Erica Fudge and Karen Raber. On the complexities of debt and property in *The Merchant of Venice*, see Bailey 2013: 51–74.
5 A rehearsal of some of the sub-headings dramatizes Topsell's emphasis on the diseases and maladies of sheep and how to prevent or cure them: 'Of the diseases of Sheepe, and their causes in general'; 'Of the colds of Sheepe'; 'Of the Scabs of Sheepe, the first remedy'; 'Of the holy fire which the Sheapheards call the Pox'; 'Of the falling sicknesse'; 'Of phlegme in Sheepe'; 'Of the fluxes of sheepe'; 'Of the Feauers of Sheepe'; etc.
6 Joan Ozark Holmer notes that the usury tract, *The Arraignment and Conviction of Usurie,* makes use of the Laban story to critique rather than to defend usury. In fact, Laban is figured here and elsewhere in the period as a usurer in his economic predation. See Holmer 1985.
7 For an influential version of this argument, see Lewalski 1962.
8 Most readings see Shylock as playing the role of Esau in this scriptural exchange, as the loser in this wrestling over inheritance. As Engle writes, Shylock 'loses control of the Jacob story as soon as he introduces it' (1986: 32).

9 The standard move in the commentaries of the period is to defend Jacob from the imputation of wrongdoing by referring Genesis 30.37–43 to another passage in Genesis where Jacob retroactively explains that he was guided in all he did by divine will: Genesis 31.10–13. As the marginal note in the Geneva Bible argues: 'Iaakob herein vsed no deceit: for it was Gods commandement as he declareth in the next chapter' (1560).

10 See Nerlich 1987. On economic risk in *The Merchant of Venice*, see MacInnes 2008.

11 The two foundations of the critique of usury from Aquinas forward are *sterility*, or the alleged unnaturalness of breeding money; and hazard, or risk. The notion that barren metal should not breed, to borrow Antonio's phrase, goes back to Aristotle's well-known discussion of proper economic activity in book 1 of his *Politics*. See Aristotle 1984: 1.10, 49–50.

12 On contingency in relation to divine providence in the period, see Witmore 2001.

13 See Nerlich 1987.

14 First published in 1519 and then in expanded form in 1520, Luther's sermon tackles a number of dubious financial practices of the time. It was reprinted as part of *Trade and Usury* in 1524. See Luther 1955–86: 45.273–310.

15 This theological relation of risk to calculation will ultimately be overtaken by economic history as contingency and the unknown become calculable entities, things to be bought and sold.

16 At the end of his treatise, when Luther turns from critique to advocacy, he urges a return to the Old Testament tithe and jubilee. His advocacy of the tithe is explicitly connected to risk. With regard to the tithe, Luther writes that the 'creditor would … have to bear both risk and good fortune as well as the debtor, and both of them would have to look to God. In this way … it would always remain uncertain how much the title would yield, and yet the tithe itself would be certain … [and] all would depend on the grace and blessing of God' (Luther 1955–86: 45.308–9).

17 In his *Lectures on Genesis*, Luther measured Jacob and other Old Testament figures by ethical standards not relevant to ordinary mortals and contemporary life. See Luther 1955–86: 5.380–3.

18 See Lewalski 1962: 337–8. Julia Reinhard Lupton observes that in standing for law, Shylock also announces his 'symbolic function' in the play's 'archetypal confrontation between Law and Mercy' (2000: 123).

19 For instance, see John Drakakis's annotation in the Arden edition: 4.1.113–14.

20 To give a recent example, see Astington 2015.

21 Tracing the phrase/concept that 'man is a wolf to / for other men' to Plautus, Freccero also notes that the 'originating context' is 'economic' (2015: 115–16).

22 For a superb reading, see Daniel 2013: 92–119.

6

'The means whereby I live': Deep Play in *The Merchant of Venice*

Jeanette Nguyen Tran

Why do men engage in deep play, both passionately and often, and even in the face of law's revenge? Clifford Geertz poses this question in his classic essay, 'Deep Play: Notes on a Balinese Cockfight'. In the essay, Geertz explains why the Balinese engage so passionately in cockfighting, a particularly risky activity that is illegal and involves heavy gambling. Geertz's method, borrowed from literary studies, and his central question, adapted from nineteenth-century utilitarian philosopher Jeremy Bentham, travel far beyond the specific cultural contexts of Geertz's study. Bentham coined the term 'deep play' in a brief rumination on why certain individuals choose to participate in situations where the marginal utility of what they stand to gain is less than the marginal disutility of what they stand to lose (1882: 106). In other words, why do people appear to act against their best economic interests, and what role should the law play in protecting people from the consequences of deep play?

Geertz cites *Macbeth* to argue that the Balinese read and reread the cockfight, in the same way we might read and reread *Macbeth*, to gain insight into their own subjectivity. In this essay, I explore why we go to see *The Merchant of Venice*, and suggest that the reason is similar to why Geertz goes to see the Balinese cockfight. The lessons of *The Merchant of Venice* best appear on the stage precisely because it is a play about deep play. Both the Balinese cockfight and *The Merchant of Venice* offer audiences an opportunity to witness and investigate the logic of deep play, or the human willingness to court self-destruction or mischief. Bentham himself drew connections between gaming and the arts of amusement, claiming that both satisfy the urge for mischief. Bentham was not a fan of poetry because he believed there was a natural opposition between poetry and truth, but he was willing to praise poetry as 'excellent substitutes for drunkenness, slander, and the love of gaming' (1839: 254).

As a play about deep play, *The Merchant of Venice* satisfies the urge for mischief in a number of ways. Applying Bentham's standards to *The Merchant of Venice*, it becomes clear that Shakespeare presents audiences with two situations that qualify as deep play. The first is the sealing of the bond between Shylock and Antonio, and the second is the casket game. Both Antonio and Bassanio risk self-destruction by wilfully participating in deep play, and it is, of course, the law that ultimately intervenes to protect them from fully suffering the consequences of their actions. There is no other Shakespearean play that deals with risk in such an overt way, and the play, through the vehicle of the lead casket, seems to champion the idea that success depends upon one's ability to 'give' and 'hazard' all. Is Shakespeare's play promoting 'false morals' in order to stimulate our 'passions' and excite our 'prejudices', as Bentham might suggest, or does the play, like the Balinese cockfight, present a kind of metasocial commentary on the culture's attitude as it relates to risk that goes beyond the lead casket's celebration of hazard (1839: 253)? Centuries removed from the age of mercantilism, this play continues to resonate with business leaders and actuaries because of the way in which it represents risk.[1] *The Merchant of Venice* is less about a specific economic system than it is about the evolving attitudes towards risk that this new economic system demands. I argue that the play's representation of deep play illustrates how an attitude – a fitness or adaptation that responds to a change in the environment, stimulus or stress – can be understood as a kind of instrument, like insurance, to manage risk. In only allowing Bassanio and Antonio to participate in deep play, it also reveals how access to the ownership of risk is gendered and racialized in ways that foreshadow the findings of present-day studies on the relationship between social identity and people's perception that they have mastery over personal outcomes.[2]

I explain how the sealing of the bond and the casket game constitute deep play, but the primary focus of my analysis is how Antonio's and Bassanio's attitudes toward risk evolve such that they are both able to convince themselves to court self-destruction. While *homo economicus* is ideally rational and self-interested, Antonio's and Bassanio's reasoning is at once irrational and self-interested. Unhae Langis describes Bassanio's 'unrestrained optimism in spending' as indicative, in any other circumstance, of a gambler's addiction (2011: 23). This is a very apt description of what the economic actors, with the exception of Shylock, look like in the play. While Walter Cohen (1982) identifies Shylock as an irrational economic actor for his insistence on revenge over financial profit, it is clear that this specific transaction with Antonio is the exception, and not the norm, for Shylock. Shylock's ability to seek, and nearly exact, revenge on Antonio is a fruit of his prudence.

Shakespeare's Venetian heroes reject the Calvinistic, or Shylockian, solution to life, an incremental approach to long-range goals that eventually results in, for example, the accumulation of wealth vast enough that one may lend freely to one's enemies for the sake of sport or revenge. Like gamblers, as theorized by Erving Goffman in his article on the sociology of risk-taking, 'Where the Action Is', Bassanio and Antonio are 'action' seekers (1967). Goffman's theory of action is premised upon the idea that the human condition is such that it is impossible to avoid 'fateful' activities that expose the individual to risk (1967: 164).[3] The one thing humans can control is their orientation to fatefulness. One may choose to await passively the outcome of a fateful activity, or define oneself as having freely chosen the uncertainty at hand. When a fateful activity is undertaken for what is felt to be its own sake, it becomes what Goffman calls 'action' (1967: 185). Gambling is the prototype of action for Goffman, and Geertz similarly focuses more of his attention in 'Deep Play' on the gambling surrounding the cockfight, rather than the cockfight itself. If action involves a wilful undertaking of serious chances that are perceived as avoidable, then deep play is action par excellence. Shakespeare confronts Antonio and Bassanio with fateful activities, which they reimagine as action or deep play. Both men go to absurd lengths to recast their exposure to uncertainty as wilfully taking a practical gamble, danger into taken risk, and unfavourable possibilities into grasped opportunity.

Antonio's and Bassanio's mental gymnastics highlight the power and necessity of the illusion of self-determinacy in an emerging mercantile economy where individual profit and security are prioritized, but are also progressively riskier and more difficult to obtain. In the economic system that Shakespeare imagines, life and livelihood appear to be one and the same. Portia says, 'Live thou, I live', as Bassanio approaches the caskets in search of her portrait, the finding of which will give him access to her person and her inheritance (3.2.61). While there is no penalty for choosing the incorrect casket, Portia implies that choosing the correct profit-bearing casket is akin to life, whereas choosing the wrong casket is akin to death. Even more strikingly, Shakespeare has both Shylock and Antonio utter nearly identical lines regarding the relationship between their lives and their livelihood. Shylock tells the Duke, 'You take my life / when you do take the means whereby I live'

(4.1.372–3), and Antonio tells Portia, 'Sweet lady, you have given me life and living' (5.1.286). The contexts are clearly different as Shylock faces punishment while Antonio meets his reward, but the sentiment remains the same. Attempting to marry Portia, lending money and borrowing money appear to be equally hazardous to one's physical and financial health. As Ian MacInnes explains, the rapidly changing economic system required rapidly changing attitudes towards risk, as well as new means for raising and protecting invested capital by managing and describing risk (2008). Such means include the rise of insurance, which MacInnes suggests was still a fairly new concept in the 1590s, and the development of what Craig Muldrew calls a 'culture of credit' (1998). My essay explores the shifting attitudes towards risk that Shakespeare represents in his play, attitudes which are shaped by the same forces that propelled this larger cultural demand for new instruments to comprehend and contain risk.

Antonio

By beginning with the merchant Antonio's sadness, *The Merchant of Venice* invites audiences to attend to the ways in which individual bodies, which were always vulnerable, become increasingly so in this new economy. The fact that Antonio will eventually use his body as collateral, and that there are no laws or customs that prevent him from doing so, constitutes the fullest expression of this reality in Shakespeare's Venice.[4] While the source of Antonio's sadness has been heavily debated, Antonio's friends, Salerio and Solanio, logically assume that Antonio's 'mind is tossing on the ocean' with his ships (1.1.7).[5] Salerio's vivid description of how distracted he is by the thought of his ship *Andrew* just 'touching' some dangerous rocks and scattering 'all her spices on the stream', communicates the considerable financial and emotional risk that early modern merchants had to assume as part of their trade (1.1.31, 32). And yet, as Lars Engle writes, to admit to fearing risk puts the merchant at even greater risk. Antonio's credit, which he needs to do business, is 'threatened by his inability to look happy when his livelihood is at risk' (1993: 80). David Hawkes explains that within the context of an emerging global capitalism, the merchant's word is tied not to his personal integrity as an individual, but instead to the state of his finances and/or the chances of his ventures succeeding (2004: 128). The culture of credit depends on this kind of objectification, where the adjective 'good' no longer refers to Antonio's moral character, but to his creditworthiness, and yet the consequences of default remain highly subjective or individualized. Shakespeare's merchant's body suffers alongside his reputation. Antonio's statement, 'I have much ado to know myself', is devastating in the context of a world where life and livelihood are one and the same (1.1.6). Antonio's anxiety over his possessions abroad leads directly to a loss of self-possession. Save Portia's courtroom manoeuvres, the purported miscarriage of Antonio's ships would have led directly to the loss of his life. Thus, Gratiano's comments, 'You look not well, Signor Antonio', and 'Believe me, you are marvelously changed', reveal early on how vulnerable the merchant's body is to physical harm, and to the scrutiny of other members of the commercial community (1.1.73, 76).

If Antonio's sadness is caused by his exposure to risk, why doesn't Antonio simply purchase insurance? In this discussion of risk and insurance, it is worth noting that Shakespeare never uses the word 'risk' in his plays or poems. His preferred word is 'hazard', which makes sense given that 'risk' was a term that was most commonly used in the seventeenth century in the context of long-distance maritime trade. Risk was not synonymous with hazard in the sense that risk did not necessarily refer to the immaterial fear of an unfavourable incident, but most often to a financial instrument that prepared one to cope with unfavourable incidents. As MacInnes explains, insurance – the buying and selling of risk – turns chance from a manifestation of divine providence into a marketable, possessable commodity.

Because there is 'no good business reason' for Antonio not to insure his ventures, MacInnes argues that Antonio desires to own the risk of his ventures to increase his potential for profit (2008: 50). Luke Wilson, citing how routine the practice of insuring ships was among sixteenth-century London and Venetian merchants, argues that Antonio's refusal to insure exposes an ethic of risk that is masochistic and antisocial (2003: 33). While both MacInnes and Wilson present possible readings for Antonio's poor business decision, Antonio's status as an insolvent debtor whose credit in Venice is worthless suggests that he simply may be an inept businessman (Caldwell 2014: 363).[6] Given his reputation, it seems just as possible to imagine that he was unable to find someone to insure his venture. After all, this is a man who, as Amanda Bailey notes, must enter into this arrangement with Shylock because his body is his only remaining desirable asset to the one person in Venice who will lend him money (2011: 15). Bailey conjectures, however, that Antonio's situation would probably 'not be surprising to those audience members who understood that the impressive amount of capital needed to fund cross-oceanic expeditions made merchants notorious debtors' (2011: 14). Given the prevalence of debt bondage, she argues that Antonio's and Shylock's behaviours are not deviations from debt bondage practices and jurisprudence, but an amplification of their proprietary logic. Whether Antonio represents an exceptionally inept merchant or a prototypical one, Antonio's lack of insurance, like his lack of credit, puts him in a position where he must take, or appear to take, complete ownership of risk. In his claim that 'my merchandise makes me not sad', Antonio does just that (1.1.44).

In agreeing to stand surety for Bassanio, Antonio again exposes himself to a disadvantageous degree of risk. Antonio should not agree to the bond with Shylock for a number of reasons, the first being their enmity. Antonio casually refers to Shylock as 'the devil' in their first encounter on stage, even though he needs Shylock's help (1.3.94). Shylock recalls how Antonio spit upon his Jewish gabardine just last Wednesday, as well as a slew of other insults. Shylock keeps track of Antonio's offenses as meticulously as he keeps track of his money. Unable to deny his hatred of Shylock, or Shylock's claim that he has no reason to trust Antonio with his money, Antonio attempts to recast his enmity as goodwill. He argues that their enmity actually benefits Shylock, as exacting a penalty on an enemy can be done with a 'better face' than on a friend (1.3.131). Though the argument is clever, it does not change the fact that Antonio does not trust Shylock either, and that a functioning credit system depends on trust. In tempting Shylock with the possibility that he may profit off his enemy, Antonio also acknowledges that he may fail to repay Shylock. Antonio knows that Shylock, whether driven by a desire for revenge or profit, will only agree to a loan if there is a reasonable chance that Antonio might default. While one can interpret Antonio's willingness to stand surety for Bassanio, nevertheless, as noble and Christ-like, one can also interpret his actions as an attempt to transform fatefulness into action.[7]

Shylock agrees to offer the loan interest-free, demanding instead a pound of Antonio's flesh if he forfeits the bond. As Bassanio realizes that Antonio stands to lose far more than either of them stands to gain, he urges Antonio to reject the bond, claiming he would 'rather dwell in my necessity' (1.3.151). While Antonio speaks confidently about how he will not forfeit the bond, there are limits to how confident he can actually be, given the risky nature of his profession. Antonio can calculate the odds of success with respect to the number of his ships, the value of his merchandise and the calendar, but he can never be certain if his ships will succeed, and he is hardly alone in his uncertainty. And yet, Antonio attempts to rationalize his decision to seal the bond by insisting that there is a quantifiable relationship between time and profit: 'Within these two months – that's a month before / the bond expires – I do expect return / of thrice three times the value of this bond' (1.3.153–5). However, Solanio and Salerio have taught us that at the core of the merchant's emotional turmoil is the unpredictable relationship between time and profit. There is a clear tension between the time – typically months – it takes for a venture to produce profits, and the time it takes – a breath, a word – for a venture to fail and to produce loss. As Salerio muses, 'And, in a word, but even now worth this, / And now worth nothing?' (1.1.34–5). Antonio's use of the word 'expect' suggests that he still knows that his profit is not guaranteed, but once he gives Shylock his word – 'Yes, Shylock, I will seal unto this bond' – all doubt must be eliminated from his speech (1.3.167). Grasping even more firmly to the illusion of self-determination, Antonio closes the scene with a tidy rhyming couplet, assuring Bassanio that 'In this there can be no dismay; / My ships come home a month before the day' (1.3.176–7).

Because Antonio's sadness sets the tone of the play, his rejection of 'dismay', another affective term that conveys what the *OED* defines as an 'utter loss of moral courage or resolution in prospect of danger or difficulty; faintness of heart from terror or from feeling of inability to cope with peril or calamity' constitutes a turning point. In Goffman's terms, Antonio's attempt to manage his affective response to fatefulness is a 'defense' (1967: 177). Calculating, scapegoating, superstition and even a belief in pure, blind luck are defenses one can harness to combat the anxiety, remorse or disappointment that encounters with fatefulness inspire. Defenses are coping mechanisms that allow the individual to engage fully in deep play while deferring or denying responsibility for any possible negative consequences. By rejecting dismay, Antonio assumes a position of moral courage, resolve and bodily strength that the text's characterization of him hardly supports. His sadness, the debt bond he agrees to, his guilt-laden and masochistic demand to see Bassanio at his death and his near-demise at Shylock's hands only highlight the fragility of his resolve and body.

Bassanio

Though Antonio and Bassanio differ in class and age, they share an attraction to action that bonds them together. The word 'dismay' is used in just one other scene in the play, and that is when Bassanio takes his turn at the casket game. As

Bassanio approaches the caskets, Portia laments, 'Live thou, I live. With much, much more dismay / I view the fight than thou that mak'st the fray' (3.2.61–2). The casket game, which presents the suitors with a one-in-three chance of succeeding, similarly puts the participants in a situation where they stand to lose more than they stand to gain. Shakespeare adapts the casket game from a medieval collection of stories, *Gesta Romanorum*, in a way that raises the stakes and transforms it into an instance of deep play. In the source, the game is devised for one person, the king's daughter, whose father sends her to marry the emperor's son. On her way, she is shipwrecked, swallowed by a whale and then rescued by a noble earl who brings her to the emperor. Unbeknownst to her, she must play the casket game and choose the correct casket if she hopes to marry the emperor's son. An incorrect choice will leave her unbetrothed. The consequences of failure are much more severe in *The Merchant of Venice* where an incorrect choice condemns Portia's suitor to a life of celibacy as he is henceforth forbidden from marrying. The competitive aspect of Shakespeare's casket game, where multiple suitors from different nations play before Bassanio even arrives, also introduces the threat of miscegenation. While the source text strongly suggests that divine intervention delivers the virgin to the king and his casket game, Shakespeare's play suggests it is the machinations of men, and men alone, that bring Bassanio to Belmont and into Portia's arms.

Shakespeare changes the suitor from a single woman to multiple men in his version, forcing Portia to assume the position of the helpless and dismayed. In terms of presence and personality, Shakespeare's clever and forthright Portia stands in stark contrast to the emperor's son, who notably remains absent and silent in *Gesta Romanorum*, and yet her fate is the same, if not worse, than his. She laments, 'I may / neither choose whom I would nor refuse whom I dislike; so is the will of a living daughter curbed by the will of a dead father' (1.2.22–4). Her dead father's 'will' refers to his desire, as well as to Portia's inheritance. Even as a dead man, his control over her inheritance ensures his control over her livelihood and 'living'. Though it is appealing to imagine Portia, as Caldwell does, as someone who 'exercises control, like Fortuna, over the livelihoods of those who risk and hazard for love and wealth', it is important to recall that her actions, which may appear heroic and even subversive, are circumscribed by her dead father's will (2014: 365). Moreover, Kim F. Hall's analysis of the play's gender and racial politics judiciously reminds us that Portia exercises her wit and acumen in the service of maintaining the status quo, which is not only male, but mandates the repulsion of aliens and outsiders (1992).

Portia's failed attempt to convince Bassanio to delay playing the casket game until she has a chance to teach him how to choose the correct one reveals her inability to take ownership of the risk that the caskets represent. It is true that Portia will eventually sing the rhymes-with-lead song that is supposed to guide Bassanio to her portrait, but whether he actually heeds her counsel, or chooses correctly on his own, is indeterminable. After all, Bassanio bluntly refuses Portia's direct assistance when it is offered to him, opaquely claiming that he is 'upon the rack' (3.2.25). Bassanio still has no idea that Antonio's ventures have failed, so the urgency cannot be tied to the impending forfeit of Antonio's bond. All Bassanio wants is for Portia to 'but let me to my fortune and the caskets' (3.2.39). If Antonio defends himself against fatefulness by asserting a false relationship between time and profit, Bassanio does the same by asserting a false relationship between his agency and fortune. This hailing of fortune recalls Bassanio's initial conversation with Antonio where he attempts to convince the merchant to finance his trip to Belmont. Bassanio is clearly aware of how self-interested it is for him to ask Antonio, who is in no position to lend him money, for help. Antonio states, 'Thou know'st that all my fortunes are at sea' and 'Neither have I money nor commodity / To raise a present sum' (1.1.177, 178–9). The first recorded use of the word 'fortune' to refer to an individual's collected possessions or 'wealth', as opposed to chance or luck, is in Spenser's *Faerie Queene* (1596). Shakespeare seems to be punning on the dual meanings of fortune here as Antonio has invested his entire fortune in this venture where his success is subject to the whims or waves of fortune. Despite Bassanio's intimate awareness of Antonio's dire financial straits, and the unlikelihood of his success in Belmont, he still confidently declares, 'I have a mind presages me such thrift / That I should questionless be fortunate' (1.1.175–6). The nature of fortune is that it is always questionable, and the fact that the word carries two meanings – wealth and chance – only adds to its dubiousness.[8] Nonetheless, Bassanio, unwilling and unable to await his fortune, rhetorically seizes it, turning it into the wealth he desires.

In debt we trust

It is telling that Portia identifies Bassanio, and not her father, herself or fortune, as the one who 'mak'st the fray' that causes her such dismay. Bassanio is not more fortunate, in terms of luck or wealth, than anyone who has played the casket game before him, but he is more favoured by Portia. There is something dismaying about the fact that Bassanio appears to be in such a hurry and is unwilling to take Portia's advice, even if these precautions would guarantee his success. Though he calls Portia his torturer, Bassanio only torments himself. One way to read Bassanio's rejection of Portia's offer for additional time and assistance is as a means to intensify the action. For action seekers, the intensity of the action may be more compelling than the action itself. While a desire for intensity drives Bassanio to play the casket game in the manner that he does, he, much like Antonio, also courts self-destruction because of the burden of his debt. While Bassanio professes to love Portia, he frames his plot to sail to Belmont as a means to 'get clear of all the debts I owe' (1.1.134). In order to convince Antonio to finance his risky trip to Belmont, where the odds of winning are against him, Bassanio tells the story of the two arrows.

Bassanio explains that his childhood strategy for finding a lost arrow was to shoot another one in the same direction, but with 'more advised watch' (1.1.142). By 'adventuring' or risking both arrows, he often found both (1.1.142). Recognizing that Antonio has lent him money several times already, Bassanio asks Antonio 'to shoot another arrow that self way' (1.1.148). Bassanio suggests that he will recover both arrows, which represent all the money he still owes Antonio, or at worst the second arrow, which represents the 3,000 ducats that he now requests.

Bassanio's story of the two arrows is a fantasy of self-determination that even Antonio, who asks Bassanio to declare what he wants in more plain terms, fails to grasp. Bassanio is asking Antonio for money, but he is also trying to promote an alternative attitude to take towards risk. Bassanio argues that one can manage the consequences of risk by taking even more risk. If you lose one arrow due to a lack of skill or recklessness, try to lose another one in the exact same way. It is irrational and self-interested for Bassanio to suggest that one should risk doubling one's losses in order to recover the sum that skill or thrift might have prevented one from losing in the first place. Langis notes that 'a reasonable person would not call this strategy "thrift" but rather "speculation" and even further, as the saying goes, "throwing good money after bad"' (2011: 23). Bassanio's bow becomes an instrument, not for hunting, sport or warfare, but for convincing Antonio to undertake a commercial venture that involves considerable financial risk on the chance of unusual profit. Following the logic of the insurance model, Bassanio tries to turn his attitude toward risk into a marketable, possessable commodity, but he seems to know his strategy is far from sound. He is careful to avoid affirming that he was always able to recover his arrows (just 'often' enough), or that he will ever fully repay his debt to Antonio. Bassanio's judgment and logic seems faulty, but in the end, the gamble does pay off. Bassanio's marriage to the fabulously wealthy and generous Portia allows him to repay all of his debts. Even Antonio eventually profits off of his seemingly disastrous overseas venture by waiting just a few more hours for the good news to roll in via post. The play does not suggest that success requires one to hazard all, but it does make an argument for the ubiquity of hazard, or what I have described as fatefulness, through the way in which it normalizes and even heroicizes insolvency. The nature of Antonio's and Bassanio's predicaments, and how they respond to them, shed light on a credit and legal system that exposes individuals to a host of new financial, emotional and physical risks that demand the development of new instruments, which includes attitudes, to manage them. Within such a system, success is not won by hazarding all, but by dulling one's alertness to the consequences involved in making a living.

The play positions men and women, as well as Venetians and non-Venetians, differently in relation to risk. Fatefulness is unavoidable, but only certain people get to own risk within the world of the play. Reserved for white Christian Venetian males, the ownership of risk, which I have defined as an attitude that rationalizes participation in deep play, is culture- and gender-specific, and yet conveniently manages to cut across geographic boundaries. Belmont is often read as the romantic, green world that stands in contrast to the crudity and crassness of commercial Venice, but the exceptionally charmed experiences of Antonio and Bassanio, as they deign to hazard all, blur the distinction between Venice and Belmont, and exacerbate the distinction between men and women, Venetians and non-Venetians.[9] The comparison between Antonio and Bassanio ultimately reveals how commercial life depends upon romantic notions of the relationship between risk and reward. Antonio imagines himself as a romantic hero because the merchant's logic is the same as the would-be lover's. R. Mark Benbow observes that the same language is used to describe Antonio's commercial activities and Bassanio's romantic adventures (1976: 4). He argues that a willingness to adventure one's self without respect to possible profits is merely an extension of the economy of the open heart, but this sort of statement risks reducing the complexity and crassness of what happens in

Belmont *and* Venice. Portia is an object of exchange in Venice, no more or less quantifiable or valuable than the cargo on Antonio's ships.

As a female character, Portia's orientation to risk is markedly different from that of her male counterparts. Portia is most free when she cross-dresses, an act that obscures her gender and her identity as a wealthy heiress. As someone who can flippantly offer to double, and then treble, the 3,000-ducat payment that is due to Shylock, Portia's seemingly unlimited wealth puts her in a position where it is impossible for her to lose more than she stands to gain in any financial situation. Thus, she disguises herself as a poor doctor of law who would beg her client's best friend, the unsuspecting Bassanio, for his gloves and his wedding ring. Her declaration, 'I will have nothing else but only this', is the closest she gets to approximating the resolve Bassanio and Antonio must possess before engaging in deep play (4.1.428). Her resolve, like her habit, gender and profession, are all feigned, as she proves to be deeply disappointed when Bassanio risks his life by breaking his vow to her and handing over the ring. It is Bassanio himself who, upon receiving the ring, says, 'But when this ring / Parts from this finger, then parts life from hence. O, then be bold to say Bassanio's dead' (3.2.183–5). According to Portia, the ring symbolizes the house, servants and Portia herself, the keeper of her dead father's wealth, and so a loss of the ring is indeed a loss of livelihood and life for Bassanio. And yet, all it takes to compel him after his initial refusal is Antonio's seemingly gentle urging: 'My Lord Bassanio, let him have the ring / Let his deservings and my love withal, / Be valued 'gainst your wife's commandement' (4.1.445–7). A homoerotic reading is certainly possible here where Antonio tries to ensnare Bassanio into a compromising love triangle, but within the context of deep play, a risk analysis seems more appropriate. Only Bassanio and Antonio could turn the doctor of law's arbitrary request for the ring into a deep-play scenario where Bassanio must weigh the value of Antonio's love against the value of his livelihood and life, which Portia's commandment represents. In the end, the price Bassanio pays for his wager is no more than Portia's displeasure and the comical threat of adultery as she claims she will 'have that doctor for my bedfellow' (5.1.233). The financial and bodily risk, at least for Bassanio, once again pays off.

Cohen observes that it is typical in comedies for protagonists to be confronted by improbable situations that symbolize uncertainty and insecurity, and preferred alternatives to the imposed constraints of daily life (1982: 782). He also notes, however, that *The Merchant of Venice* stands apart from Shakespeare's other comedies for its socio-economic emphasis and the gravity of its subject. These two distinct qualities of the play cannot be separated as one considers the 'improbable situations', which are recast as deep play, that Antonio and Bassanio must confront. The ubiquity of debt, debt bondage and the occurrence of default in early modern England suggests that Antonio's and Bassanio's predicaments, as well as Shylock's demand for flesh, were quite probable. In fact, the theatrical context may even enliven and make far more comprehensible the concerns *The Merchant of Venice* raises about the culture's attitude as it relates to risk. The early modern theatre, as an institution, was no stranger to debt bondage because of how embedded it was in the credit economy.[10] It was also a place where only English men were welcome to invest, write and perform. Playwrights Ben Jonson, George Chapman, John Marston, John Lyly, Cyril Tourneur, Thomas Middleton, Thomas Dekker and Philip Massinger all found commercial and/or artistic success in their own right, and all spent time in debtor's prison (Bailey 2013: 4).

The Merchant of Venice, a play about deep play written by a playwright who understood the complexities and risks of the theatrical venture, reveals that all individuals, whether landlocked or sea-bound, are perpetually at-risk, even if the ability to own risk is hardly equal opportunity.[11] At the hands of a skilled playwright, however, live theatre itself may function as a vicarious encounter with action for men and women alike because the events of a play, like the events of a cockfight, are problematic, consequential and wilfully encountered. In this exploration of the ways in which the theatre, in its representation of risk, can reveal something so vivid about the relationship between life and livelihood, it seems apt that Goffman would describe the kinds of vicarious experience that theatre, television and film provide audiences as 'living once-removed' (1967: 263). For a first-time audience to a given play, the results of the players' actions are yet to be determined, and the consequences of these actions will be felt over the duration of the play. One of the greatest pleasures of live theatre is the open invitation to the uncertainty at hand, and the knowledge that one, much like Antonio and Bassanio, has freely chosen to undertake that uncertainty. *The Merchant of Venice* is where the action is.

Notes

1 For example, see Skwire 2007; Moore 2012; Hunt 2014; Augustine and Adelman 1999.

2 See Byrnes, Miller and Schafer 1999; Collado, Risco, Banducci, Chen, MacPherson and Lejuez 2015.

3 Goffman (1967) defines fateful activities as 'problematic' (meaning that their results and consequences are not yet determined) and 'consequential' (meaning that the consequences of the activity will be felt over time).

4 For more on the lawfulness of Shylock's demands, see Garrett 2014.

5 Daniel (2010) offers an excellent survey of recent critical approaches to Antonio's sadness before presenting his own reading of Antonio as a character who shifts from melancholic to masochist.

6 Caldwell (2014) suggests that Antonio's generous backing of Bassanio's voyage might be read as wrongheaded, as mercantile prodigality was considered an ill-advised strategy by the mid-sixteenth century. While Antonio is well-meaning, he fails to exercise common sense or shrewd business skills in his generosity.

7 As Langis notes, in agreeing to stand surety for Bassanio, Antonio engages in unusually risky behaviour as a creditor. By lending money to someone who is already deeply in debt, Antonio goes against early modern moral instruction (2011: 23). Lim questions how prudent it is for Antonio to put himself at risk 'in a social world in which irresponsible acts and a culture of mistrust are perceived to be normative' (2010: 369).

8 Caldwell identifies Portia with Fortune, calling her Venice's Vanna White (2014: 365).

9 In studying the play's gift economy, Singh (2000) similarly argues that the play ultimately blurs all distinction between Belmont and Venice.

10 See Bailey 2013. Cerasano likewise argues that *The Merchant of Venice* is the most forceful demonstration of 'theatrical economics', in every possible sense of the term, that Shakespeare ever presented, given how the commercial setting of the play and the playhouse mirror one another in a multiplicity of ways (2004: 21).

11 Shakespeare's company, the Lord Chamberlain's Men, was the first playing company to become part-owners of the playhouse they used. Shakespeare's combined income from playwriting and investing made him rich. See Keenan 2016. The value of Shakespeare's and his partners' shares fluctuated as the original shareholders decreased or augmented their number. For example, when Kempe left the company in 1602, Shakespeare's share grew from 10 per cent of the whole to one-eighth of the total. His stake decreased to one-fourteenth by 1612, when more shareholders joined (Schoenbaum 1978: 210–12).

7

'Qualities of Breeding': Race, Class and Conduct in *The Merchant of Venice*

Patricia Akhimie

Introduction: Quality/qualities

The Merchant of Venice features competing vocabularies of valuation as measured by worldly wealth, moral worth and good conduct. Its visualizations of relative value include an odd assortment of distant argosies run aground; caskets of gold, silver and lead; and an astounding number of invitations to dinner parties. Shylock enters this minefield of contradictory valuation with a great deal of capital, as one capable of funding and thus fulfilling the aspirations of others to improve and to

---

This essay was completed with the support of the National Endowment for the Humanities. Any views, findings, conclusions or recommendations expressed in this publication do not necessarily reflect those of the National Endowment for the Humanities.

rise in the world, but he finds that his own aspirations are thwarted, that people 'like him' are despised. He discovers that where undesirable persons seem to possess worldly wealth, measures of moral worth and good conduct may be deployed to exclude them on other grounds. The contradictions inherent in the overlapping models for measuring relative value in the play reveal an underlying ideology of racial differentiation, a belief in the existence of innate differences between groups.

The Merchant of Venice upholds the belief that one's perceived inferiority may be overcome through the acquisition of new skills and the apprehension and practice of virtue. At the same time, the play presents Shylock as not only unsuccessful in, but also as inherently incapable of, such a transformation. The brutal punishment he receives for his misdeeds seems to penalize him not for his poor choices, but for his irredeemable and innate difference as a member of an undesirable group, his Jewish 'tribe'. The measure of Shylock's relative worth by various means in *The Merchant of Venice* is not ultimately an effort to evaluate his attempts at improvement or the nature of his aspirations, but instead a racialization of the inherent or inherited flaws he is imagined to share with a racial group.

I have organized my discussion of valuation and racial difference in this essay around the various meanings of a marvelously multifaceted word that recurs in *The Merchant of Venice*: 'quality'. At each iteration, the word 'quality' suggests the ways in which social and somatic differentiation intertwine in early modern conceptions of race. 'Quality' is one of a number of words available to early modern authors that participate in the production of racial differences (and often simultaneously in gender or class). Such words function to distinguish between groups, and lend themselves toward the hierarchization of groups, the naturalization of difference and the justification of bias or differential treatment. Such words distinguish between groups on the basis of attributes that are inherent or inherited, and those that are learned, providing a reasoning for existing inequalities of access and opportunity.

In *The Merchant of Venice*, the multiple meanings of 'quality' enable a new mode of social differentiation, locating racialism at the nexus of ideas about shared *ability* and about shared *belief* or *rank*. Shared ability is exemplified by the 'qualities of breeding' (2.7.33) of which the Prince of Morocco boasts, and shared belief or rank by Portia's 'quality of mercy', which 'droppeth as the gentle rain from heaven / upon the place beneath' (4.1.180–2). A particularly complex idea, the 'quality of mercy' may refer at once to a learned ability accessible to all, a shared characteristic of Christians alone, and an innate and/or natural and rank-related characteristic of social elites. Within this triangulated space, Shylock and his 'tribe' are exposed as not only lacking 'mercy' but as distinct in kind or 'quality' from a dominant group, not only incapable of achieving or acquiring the skill of mercy, but naturally deficient in this shared and heritable capacity. The multi-faceted concept of 'quality' contains within it the seeds of such divisions.

Throughout Shakespeare's plays, 'quality' is used to indicate differences on the basis of blood, rank, animal and plant species, hereditary traits, individual personality traits, shared political beliefs, shared military bonds and enemies, shared virtues and shared defects. In addition, the plays yield up many murky combinations of these meanings, especially when the word is employed euphemistically. When Hamlet commands one of the players to give a 'passionate speech' (2.2.369–70) – 'Come, give us a taste of your quality' (2.2.368–9) – he may be requesting a sample from the actor as representative of his entire cohort or 'quality', referring to the actor's high calibre or rank within the world of professional acting, referring to the actor's personal characteristic (his mettle, or pathos) or to his representation of the characteristic (passion) that he has been asked to display in performance. Because Hamlet imagines tasting this 'quality', the word might even be interpreted as a reference to the characteristics of an inanimate and edible plant or meat. 'Quality', here, may also refer to the actor's learned ability as a player on stage.

Often, 'quality' refers to innate and immutable characteristics. In the history plays, 'quality' is often used to refer to rank or family; in *Henry V*, for example, Henry reads in the report of the dead and injured that 'The rest are princes, barons, lords, knights, squires / And gentlemen of blood and quality' (4.8.90–1). Hotspur, in *1 Henry IV*, uses 'quality' as a reference to a military cohort or ally when he says to Sir Walter Blunt, 'you are not of our quality, / But stand against us like an enemy (4.3.36–7). Gloucester's apology to an impatient King Lear employs 'quality' as a personality trait or characteristic: 'My dear lord, / You know the fiery quality of the Duke, / How unremoveable and fixed he is / In his own course' (2.2.280–3). While Lear's response – 'What quality?' – seems to pun on the word in order to question not only the Duke of Cornwall's supposed characteristic quality of fieriness, but his very nobility (2.2.285). 'Quality' is a heritable trait related to rank and legitimacy in *King Lear*, as when Edmund rails that legitimate heirs may be favoured, but it is bastards who inherit 'fierce quality' as a result of the thrillingly illicit circumstances in which they are conceived (1.2.12). Quality may also denote the characteristic of an inanimate object or concept, as in Antonio's remark in *The Tempest* about the sudden drowsiness that overtakes the Italian courtiers: 'It is the quality o'th' climate' (2.1.200).

At the same time, 'quality' is often used to refer to skills or abilities that are possessed or may be learned, especially by men and women of rank. In *Troilus and Cressida*, Troilus invokes 'quality' as a learned skill, declaring, 'The Grecian youths are full of quality; / ... / and flowing o'er with arts and exercise' (4.4.75–7). In *As You Like It*, Orlando complains that his brother Oliver has prevented him from pursuing such exercises: 'You have trained me like a peasant, obscuring and hiding from me all gentleman-like qualities' (1.1.64–6). Similarly, in *Hamlet*, Claudius praises Laertes for his skill in swordsmanship, which is internationally renowned: 'You have been talked of since your travel much, / ... for a quality / Wherein they say you shine' (4.7.69–71).

Quality in the sense of an 'attainment' or 'accomplishment' (*OED*, 'quality, n. and adj.' A.2.b.) is now obscure and rarely used to describe such abilities. In the early modern period, however, the word is used frequently to describe the admirable attainment of skill in active sports for men: horseback riding, swordsmanship, falconry, hunting, etc., and sedate and attractive activities for women: singing, playing, silence, obedience, etc. Arcite in *Two Noble Kinsmen* gives the classic listing of gentlemen's accomplishments.

THESEUS
   What profess you?
ARCITE
   A little of all noble qualities.
   I could have kept a hawk and well have hallowed
   To a deep cry of dogs. I dare not praise
   My seat in horsemanship, yet they that knew me
   Would say it was my best piece; last, and greatest,
   I would be thought a soldier.

(2.5.9–15)

Arcite lists the learned skills of noblemen, those that single out elites and which pertain to the arts of war appropriate to knights. Henry VIII, meanwhile, holds up his first queen, Katherine of Aragon, as exemplary in her mastery of skills appropriate to women: 'rare qualities, sweet gentleness, / ... meekness saint-like, wife-like government, / Obeying in commanding' (2.4.133–5).

'Qualities' are indicative of virtues, and virtues are indicative of high rank. Thus those 'of quality' may also be possessed of 'qualities' appropriate to those of their rank or kind. The significance of these abilities is evidenced by the large number of works of conduct literature – how-to books on self-improvement – printed in the period. In conduct books, the word is used, confusingly, to describe both learned skill and innate ability. John Cleland urges the acquisition of exercises, but warns against excessive use in *Hero-paideia, or The institution of a young noble man* (1607): 'I tel you of those exercises, which are fittest for your qualitie, and how yee shoulde use them moderatlie for your recreation', describing his young male reader as distinct in kind from common men (Cleland 1607: Ee1). In his guide to horsemanship, William Cavendish, the Duke of Newcastle, urges readers to be diligent since 'good Qualities, come not by Instinct, but are got by great Labour, Study, and Practice' (Cavendish 1667: D). Later, however, he reminds readers of the innate ability that gentlefolk possess.

> Though *Horse-manship* be the Hardest of All, yet *Many* a *Gentleman* will Ride the *First Day* as well as the *Greatest Master*; but he is Deceived, as well as those that think to *Buy*, with their *Money*, any *Quality*: For if *Good Qualities* could be Purchased with *Money*, every *Rich Citizen* would be a *Fine Gentleman*. (1667: N2)

This combination is characteristic of works of conduct literature; the exhortation to learn, grow and better oneself is juxtaposed with reminders that such efforts will be fruitful for some, futile for others.

At its root (Latin *qualitat-*, *qualitas*), 'quality' references a belief in the possibility (necessity) of distinguishing between things on the basis of characteristics or natures that are understood as shared by all belonging to some group or 'kind' (Latin *qualis*). 'Quality' seems at once to distinguish between inherited, innate, essential or natural characteristics, and between the ranks that possess these representative characteristics. 'Qualities', meanwhile, may not be inherited traits but learned skills that nevertheless also seem to represent the rank/quality and character/quality of the agent who has learned them. It is the very confusion around the meanings of this term – 'quality/qualities' – that makes it valuable as an object of inquiry for early modern race studies. This paradoxical and conflated relationship between external evidence and internal essence, between learned skill and innate characteristic, all taken to be (sometimes) representative of group membership, lends itself to race thinking and to the association of race as kinship, race as the recognition of shared marks or traits that may be either, or at once, external and internal.

Quality and quantity

'Quality' (both innate and acquired) is contrasted with 'quantity' in proverbial and colloquial use but also in *The Merchant of Venice,* where the amount of wealth one has amassed is evaluated separately from the amount of worth of one has in society. In the dog-eat-dog mercantile capital of Venice, characters are constantly evaluated on the basis of their worldly wealth, and their moral worth, as well as their good conduct.

Worldly wealth is perhaps the most prominent method of evaluation on display in the play: Antonio is a wealthy merchant, but one whose monies are tied up in ventures and who must borrow against his credit; Bassanio is an insolvent prodigal with a generous friend in Antonio; Shylock is a well-connected usurer with a network of secondary lenders willing to supply him. Each man is an open balance book, and audiences are continually aware of the relation between their credit and debt. The spatial logic of the play allows audiences to visualize the assets and debts of merchants as ships floating on distant seas, 'argosies with portly sail' (1.1.8). Antonio's fortunes are 'bound to Tripolis ... the Indies ... Mexico ... and England' (1.3.17–19), and returning from 'Lisbon, Barbary, and India' (3.2.268), but all are lost to 'merchant-marring rocks' (3.2.270) far beyond the borders of the stage but visible in our mind's eye. Bassanio hopes to increase his assets by marrying a wealthy wife, joining the ranks of Portia's suitors, whom 'the four winds blow from every coast' (1.1.168) 'from the four corners of the earth' (2.7.39); indeed, the Prince of Morocco claims that so many suitors venture toward Belmont that 'the Hyrcanian deserts and the vasty wilds / of wide Arabia are as thoroughfares' (2.7.41–2). The distances traveled by ships and suitors are a measure of the great wealth at risk to be gained or lost.

Yet as Antonio's actual wealth evaporates with the loss of each ship, losses sharpened by the knowledge of his debt to Shylock, his estimation, his moral worth seems to increase. Where the ledger clearly indicates quantity of worth, quality is assessed by means of an examination of natural and acquired attributes. The merchants Salarino and Salanio laugh as they discuss Shylock's losses (his daughter, Jessica, has run away with large sums of money), but their tone changes when Salarino turns to news of Antonio's wrecked vessels. He eulogizes Antonio, saying, 'A kinder gentleman treads not the earth' (2.8.35). And, when Salarino reports the loss of yet another 'ship of good lading wrecked on the narrow seas' (3.1.3), Salanio is rendered speechless in his attempt to praise 'the good Antonio, the honest Antonio' (3.1.12–13). He laments, 'O, that I had a title good enough to keep his name company!' (3.1.13–14).

The casket game, too – the winner will gain Portia's hand – is designed to reveal that it is not the impermanent assets of worldly wealth or external appearances that matter most, but *virtue*. As Bassanio intones, 'So may the outward shows be least themselves: the world is still deceived with ornament' (3.2.73–4). Though the caskets of gold, silver and lead are described as a 'lottery', 'hazard' or game of chance by several characters, a chance to win great wealth or suffer great loss much like Antonio's mercantile adventures or Shylock's lending practices, it is not a game at all but a tool used to measure relative moral worth. The casket game is, for all intents and purposes, a game of three-card monte: anyone with sense should see at once that it's for suckers and pass by. Instead, Portia is inundated by droves of such marks, eager to try their luck and get rolled. The casket game is supposed to offer suitors the opportunity to choose right, thus proving themselves worthy. But players don't choose caskets in this game; caskets, as it were, choose them. The casket game identifies suitors as fools, braggarts, greedy idiots and so on.

While the play is structured in such a way as to suggest, predictably, that moral worth trumps worldly wealth and that goodness rather than glitz will be rewarded in the end with gold, conduct, the third system of valuation or differentiation, seems to disrupt and undercut the moralizing claims of the play. Conduct, as evidenced by the display of acquired skills, is believed to reflect inherent or natural attributes.

Qualities of breeding

The play offers passing references to archery, fishing, wrestling and other 'qualities of breeding', the term that the Prince of Morocco uses to describe his prowess in exercises or activities, highly coded forms of conduct, that set him apart from other men as better and more worthy of Portia's love (2.7.33). For some, these references function as a means to shore up their credit and to assure others of their ability to change, grow, learn and become more valuable as people and as socio-economic connections. Bassanio's attempt to persuade Antonio to invest in him again – despite the fact that he still owes Antonio a great deal of money, having previously squandered everything loaned him – tellingly involves an elaborate archery metaphor:

BASSANIO
  In my schooldays, when I had lost one shaft,
  I shot his fellow of the selfsame flight
  The selfsame way, with more advised watch
  To find the other forth, and by adventuring both
  I oft found both. I urge this childhood proof
  Because what follows is pure innocence.
  I owe you much, and like a wilful youth

> That which I owe is lost; but if you please
> To shoot another arrow that self way
> Which you did shoot the first, I do not doubt,
> As I will watch the aim, or to find both,
> Or bring your latter hazard back again
> And thankfully rest debtor for the first.
>
> (1.1.140–52)

This ludicrous proposition imagines that throwing good money after bad will yield a great return. We can only imagine that Antonio's infatuation with Bassanio allows him to overlook this nonsense. We might also note, however, that the invocation of archery here references a practice related to arms and hunting and reserved for social elites, a common language shared by gentlemen, the wealthy Antonio and Bassanio, who claims that though 'all the wealth [he has runs] in [his] veins' he too is 'a gentleman' (3.2.253–4). Conduct books on archery or 'shooting' like Roger Ascham's *Toxophilus, the schole of shootinge* (1545) and Gervase Markham's *The Art of Archerie* (1634), underscore such associations. As Cleland writes, in *Hero-paideia*, 'Al Noble men and Gentlemen, unto whom chieflie the honour or dishonour of warfaire redonndeth, shoulde entertaine this pastime of Shooting in the next place unto Riding of great horses' (1607: Ee2). Qualities of breeding serve to identify individuals as members of groups, to distinguish between groups on the basis of shared characteristics or attributes, and to rank those groups hierarchically. These again are the building blocks – the race concepts – that enable a recognizable racial ideology or racism.

To offer yet another example, I return to that odd fact I mentioned at the start of this essay: the inordinate number of dinner parties that fill *The Merchant of Venice*. There are, depending on how you count them, five or six dinner parties mentioned in the play. First, Antonio's friends are unable to console him, but they plan to meet together for dinner. Then Bassanio invites Shylock to possibly the same dinner, though Shylock refuses. Next Bassanio plans a blow-out feast in Venice before his departure for Belmont, which Shylock does attend. Meanwhile, Lorenzo and Jessica and Lancelot prepare for a wedding feast at Belmont. Later, the Duke invites Portia in her lawyer's disguise to dine with him. Even the Prince of Morocco gets an invitation. When he attempts to head straight for the casket game, Portia interrupts, saying, 'after dinner' (2.1.44).

These dinner plans are no trivial detail. Kim F. Hall has noted that this 'incessant eating' suggests 'Christian appetite[s] out of control' (1992: 93). Moreover, dinner is perhaps the most significant form of conduct and one of the first to be obsessively detailed in the earliest conduct literature published in England or on the continent. Norbert Elias's examination of the emergence of the concept of civilization as 'the transformation of human behavior' in *The Civilizing Process* focuses first and foremost on the evolution of table manners (1994: 42–67). To take one example, this evocative section written in dialogue from *The Mirror of Complements* (1634) demonstrates the very formal and formulaic nature of the dinner invitation:

A

Sir, you shall oblige me very much if you will do me the honour to come and take a poore dinner with me.

B

I thanke you with all my heart, I have not merited the favour of your courtesie, But I pray you excuse me for this time.

A

Why Sir, you shall do me a great favour if it please you, and for a requitall I shall serve you in all things where it may please you to imploy me.

B

Sir, you are too courteous and perswasive to be refused, and therefore I shall trouble you.

A

You cannot Sir, but you will do me a greater honour in it then I know how to deserve.

B

Sir, use me as your servant, I beseech you, for I do not affect ceremonies.

A

Truly Sir, it is not because I have any thing to dinner, that is worth your tarrying: But there is no remedie, you must a little exercise your patience with me, as a testimonie of your love.

(C6v)

If we compare this with Shylock's response to Bassanio's invitation, the difference is obvious.

SHYLOCK
I think I may take his bond.
BASSANIO
Be assured you may.
SHYLOCK
I will be assured I may; and, that I may be assured, I will bethink me. May I speak with Antonio?
BASSANIO
If it please you to dine with us.
SHYLOCK
Yes, to smell pork, to eat of the habitation which your prophet the Nazarite conjured the devil into. I will buy with you, sell with you, talk with you, walk with you and so following. But I will not eat with you, drink with you nor pray with you.

(1.3.25–34)

This response follows Shylock's discussion of Antonio's 'sufficiency' (1.3.16), in which it is revealed that Shylock is unable to judge others using any one of the three systems of valuation at work in the play. Bassanio says that Antonio is a 'good' (meaning moral) man, and therefore trustworthy, creditworthy, but Shylock is incapable of linking worldly wealth with moral worth. He is ignorant of the play's underlying, if hypocritical, message that a man's moral wealth must always trump his worldly wealth. Finally, he performs miserably according to the third system of valuation by means of conduct, by failing to accept a dinner invitation.

Shylock fails once again in adhering to the code of conduct when he imagines he will bait fish with Antonio's flesh:

SALARINO
> Why, I am sure if he forfeit, thou wilt not take his flesh. What's that good for?

SHYLOCK
> To bait fish withal; if it will feed nothing else, it will feed my revenge.
>
> (3.1.46–9)

In its reference to fishing, this gruesome metaphor points to a highly coded, much-lauded exercise, the topic of a full subgenre of conduct literature. In *The Secrets of Angling* (1613), John Dennys notes that the 'qualities of an Angler' are 'qualities of minde' which include – after, of course, Faith, Hope, and Love – Liberalitie, that essential willingness to give that eludes Shylock (D4v). You must give (time, care, ample fish food) to later receive (a good catch). Shylock imagines that, while he may not eat Antonio's flesh himself, he will never relinquish it. Instead he may use it as bait to catch the fish that is his revenge. The famous speech continues, and Shylock offers a litany of ways in which Jews and Christians are indistinguishable, but he has already distinguished himself as utterly unlike Salarino, for example, whose civilized sensibilities do not allow him to imagine an actual use for, let alone a hunger for, Christian flesh.

Conduct literature, with its didactic mode, is filled with corrections to failed attempts to behave appropriately. In an early anecdote in Della Casa's popular courtesy book *Galateo* (first English translation 1576), when a high-ranking and well-liked dinner guest breaches propriety by 'feeding ... vvith a certaine straunge noyes, vnpleasaunt to all men that heare it', his faux pas is addressed with the utmost discretion (C2v). Only once the offending guest, Count Richard, has taken his leave, is Galateo, the urbane titular servant, dispatched on horseback to ride a short distance with him and deliver a flattering speech containing a cleverly camouflaged suggestion that the count should 'endeuour [him] selfe to leaue it' (C2v). This incredibly mild chastisement – Galateo calls it 'louing admonition and councell' – allows all parties to save face, while educating the genteel reader about what not to do so that he or she may avoid such blunders and prevent any need for awkward 'councell' (C2v). This encounter carefully preserves Count Richard's dignity while emphasizing the idea that he, and the gentle reader, may improve themselves by improving their behaviour. The approach to correcting misbehaving dinner guests is easily contrasted with the correction Shylock will ultimately receive from the Duke of Venice. Where Count Richard can change, can mend and can return to polite society, Shylock will be marked as unwilling and even incapable of improvement and will be condemned for this failing.

The quality of mercy

Salarino has learned to behave according to a code of conduct. Shylock says he has learned something different: 'The villainy you teach me, I will execute, and it shall go hard but I will better the instruction.' This fearful hardening allows audiences to imagine that Shylock is something completely other. Moreover, as Tubal approaches moments after Shylock makes this pronouncement about the hardness his darker civilizing process has yielded in him, Salanio imagines that Tubal must be equally horrific in his attitudes; he says, 'Here comes another of the tribe; a third cannot be matched, unless the devil himself turn Jew' (3.1.70–1). As easily as this, a group, a tribe with an imagined shared trait of hardness, a lack of empathy, mercy or humanity, emerges and its absolute difference from an imagined Christian community is believed to be real. Earlier in the play, Shylock alone uses the term 'tribe', referring when he does so to others with whom he shares a religion, history and culture, as well as a business network of merchants and lenders. When Salanio co-opts the term, it is to describe a shared characteristic that marks all Jews as naturally and morally deficient, merciless as devils.

Where Shylock and his tribe are hard, Portia is soft, flexible, able to change, grow and improve. In a speech that closely echoes the Prince of Morocco's, Portia offers herself to Bassanio, describing herself as desiring to possess the qualities of breeding that would make her most desirable in the eyes of her beloved. She goes on to say that she is prepared to learn more, to better herself, to be something different, to rise:

PORTIA
> You see me, Lord Bassanio, where I stand,
> Such as I am. Though for myself alone
> I would not be ambitious in my wish
> To wish myself much better, yet, for you,
> I would be trebled twenty times myself,
> A thousand times more fair, ten thousand times more rich,
> That only to stand high in your account
> I might in virtues, beauties, livings, friends
> Exceed account. But the full sum of me
> Is sum of something: which, to term in gross,
> Is an unlessoned girl, unschooled, unpractised.
> Happy in this, she is not yet so old
> But she may learn; happier than this,
> She is not bred so dull but she can learn.
>
> (3.2.149–62)

This precious malleability is imagined to be a free and ample resource in a culture of conduct, yet in the play this kind of evolution is available only to some. Jessica, whose marriage and conversion save her from the condemnation that Shylock will receive, claims that she is 'a daughter to [Shylock's] blood' but not a daughter to his 'manners' (2.3.18–19), suggesting that her conduct, along with her newfound wealth, will prove her value.

Shylock, on the other hand, is condemned as unalterably unacceptable in his 'manners'. He does not possess and will not learn the quality of mercy which Portia in her lawyer disguise extols.

PORTIA
Then must the Jew be merciful.
SHYLOCK
On what compulsion must I? Tell me that.
PORTIA
The quality of mercy is not strained:
It droppeth as the gentle rain from heaven
Upon the place beneath. It is twice blest:
It blesseth him that gives and him that takes.
'Tis mightiest in the mightiest; it becomes
The thronèd monarch better than his crown.
His sceptre shows the force of temporal power,
The attribute to awe and majesty,
Wherein doth sit the dread and fear of kings.
But mercy is above this sceptred sway;
It is enthroned in the hearts of kings,
It is an attribute to God himself,
And earthly power doth then show likest God's
When mercy seasons justice. Therefore, Jew,
Though justice be thy plea, consider this:
That in the course of justice none of us
Should see salvation. We do pray for mercy,
And that same prayer doth teach us all to render
The deeds of mercy. I have spoke thus much
To mitigate the justice of thy plea,
Which, if thou follow, this strict court of Venice
Must needs give sentence 'gainst the merchant there.
(4.1.178–201)

In the phrase 'quality of mercy', 'mercy' is the possessive noun, it owns a 'quality'. But what is meant by 'quality' in this instance? Is it a measure of natural essence or a measure of skill, where that essence or skill is free-flowing abundance or generosity? Read as quality of a substance, the quality of mercy may refer to the specific characteristic of mercy which is its abundance, its free liberality, its 'twice blessedness' that benefits all parties. This is in contrast to the harshness of 'justice', which sentences one and rewards another. Mercy is heavenly where justice is earthly power. Read as a characteristic a person possesses, mercy might seem to be a quality belonging to members of a group with shared affinities or values; the implied group here is Christians. Portia's speech is a call to the audience of Christians, both onstage and off, to recognize themselves as belonging to this exclusive group that shares the characteristic or quality 'mercy', a group to which they imagine Jews like Shylock do not belong.

Portia indirectly calls mercy an 'attribute' and a 'deed' or 'deeds'. Thus, here, the 'quality of mercy' may mean the learned skill of mercy, acquired and practiced by Christians, by good people, by the virtuous. In the extended metaphor mercy is an exercise an 'attribute', or 'deed', that 'becomes' not just nobles but royals, a class of exercise far above and beyond, say, horsemanship or angling, and one at its greatest in those with the highest rank and greatest power in society (it is 'mightiest in the mightiest'). Portia describes it as an attribute in the 'heart' rather than a tangible physical feat of prowess, but one to which all people can aspire. The 'deeds of mercy' may be practiced by many and must be practiced by those who wish to receive God's mercy after death. Portia suggests that Shylock, too, may practice this quality. However, the effect of this scene seems to be to affirm that Shylock is incapable of possessing naturally, or acquiring through practice, this quality of mercy.

As Ian Smith has argued in his reading of Antonio's 'fair flesh', such subtle moves work to render whiteness an invisible norm, while racializing all that is not white as highly visible and somatically marked: 'Whiteness as invisible bears important ethical implications related to inattention. ... A silent, invisible racial majority can suspend direct, responsible involvement, rely on the privileges of being merely human, and redirect all things racial elsewhere' (Smith, forthcoming). Portia's disputation on Shylock's failures vis-à-vis the quality of mercy recognize him as racially 'other' while rendering a white Christian majority racially invisible, implicitly valued for its worldly wealth, moral worth and good conduct, improvable and always-improving, and somatically unmarked.

Shylock, meanwhile, is described incessantly in the trial scene as 'hard' – at once a bodily and psychological deformity – and thus unalterable. Antonio is resigned, saying, 'You may as well do anything most hard / As seek to soften that, than which what's harder – / His Jewish heart!' (4.1.77–9). The Duke calls him a 'stony adversary' (4.1.3) and claims he has seen more empathy plucked 'from brassy bosoms and rough hearts of flint, / from stubborn Turks, and Tartars never trained / to offices of tender courtesy' (4.1.30–2). Even Shylock damns himself, saying, 'I'll not be made a soft and dull-eyed fool, / To shake the head, relent, and sigh and yield / To Christian intercessors' (3.3.14–16); Salarino responds by calling him an 'impenetrable cur' (3.3.18). Gratiano manages a somewhat tortured, extended metaphor:

GRATIANO
> Not on thy sole, but on thy soul, harsh Jew,
> Thou mak'st thy knife keen. But no metal can,
> No, not the hangman's axe, bear half the keenness
> Of thy sharp envy. Can no prayers pierce thee?
>
> (4.1.122–5)

This eagerness to render Shylock hard and unyielding, impenetrable, essentially uncultivatable, strikes me as overkill to say the least. The excessive hardening of Shylock reflects another dilemma, the dilemma that faces any conduct culture then or now.

The Merchant of Venice is wrestling with the problem that in order to change, to learn new qualities of breeding, and to display them in such a way that one might gain social advancement and upward mobility, one must first have access, and access, in turn, requires capital. The culture of conduct purports to allow universal access to conduct and thus upward mobility, when in fact many are barred from competing by a lack of access to the wealth needed to compete. In this scenario, Shylock should then be a hero. After all, it is he who bankrolls Bassanio's rise from impoverished fancy boy to wealthy Portia's 'lord, ... governor, ... and king' (3.2.165). Instead, Shylock is imagined to be the one flaw in an otherwise healthy meritocracy in which the best man with the greatest virtue will win out. The play imagines that no one in the future will need the help of a willing lender to fund their personal ambitions when in fact, almost everyone, everywhere, requires such sponsorship. Shylock's unacceptability is thus an iteration of the dissatisfaction and the fear we all must feel when faced with the difficulty, the unlikelihood of success in a culture of conduct that favours only the Bassanios and Portias of the world.

8

Jessica, Sarra, Ruth: Jewish Women in Shakespeare's Venice

Shaul Bassi

Neighbours

Jessica and Sarra are two Jewish women from early modern Venice. They were born in the sixteenth century to prominent families in the Ghetto, the famous cosmopolitan area established by the Venice Senate in 1516 to include the Jews while simultaneously excluding them from the main body of the city (Davis and Ravid 2001; Katz 2017; Calabi 2017). Jessica was born into an Ashkenazi family and lived, like all German and Italian Jews (the only authorized moneylenders),

---

Thanks to Murray Baumgarten, Margaret Brose, M. Lindsay Kaplan, Carol Rutter, Tobias Döring and all the partners of the *Shakespeare in and beyond the Ghetto* Creative Europe Project (2016–19) for the events and conversations that enabled this essay.

in a house of the Ghetto Nuovo, the first and older Jewish quarter (the adjective 'new' referred to the pre-existing foundry or *geto*). Sarra belonged to a Sephardic family, and lived in the Ghetto Vecchio. Here lived Jews expelled from the Iberian peninsula and those of them who had temporarily relocated to the Eastern shores of the Mediterranean, returning in some cases to the faith they had been forced to abjure in Spain. Both women learned the laws, traditions and rites of their Jewish communities but were also irresistibly attracted to the broader cultural manners of Christian Venice. They both showed a talent for language and literature, producing elegant vernacular verses and showing a well-rounded erudition. Both had Christian suitors, men who tried to coax them out of the Ghetto and to persuade them that they should abandon the false belief of their forebears and embrace the truth of the New Testament. Their striking external beauty seemed at odds with their damning religious identity: Jessica is called 'Most beautiful pagan, most sweet Jew!' (2.3.10–11); Sarra is dubbed 'the beautiful enemy of Jesus' (Copia Sulam 2009: 515). They both received repeatedly the attribute of 'Gentle', where the homage to kindness barely conceals a less flattering pun on 'gentile'. This is where our analogies momentarily end and their destinies diverge: Jessica is eager to leave a house she perceives as a 'hell' and a father, a moneylender, who is stern and oppressive. Sadly, there is no maternal presence to compensate for his severity. Sarra is deeply affectionate to her parents and grateful to a father who has nurtured her literary talent; she is married to a moneylender. Jessica is said to have eloped with her Christian husband to Genoa, the ancient rival of Venice on the opposite coast of Italy, while Sarra defiantly rejects the invitation to join her unrelenting wooer in the same city. Both women entertain a Christian entourage of ambivalent associates and confidants, including a Moorish maid. Jessica conspires with them to rob her own house and steal her father's properties; Sarra falls victim to a scheme that will cause her house to be ransacked and a public scandal to ensue. They both have been subject, for centuries now, to malicious calumny by men. Of Jessica it is said that she squandered enormous amounts of money, and that she even bartered the ring of her deceased mother for a monkey. Of Sarra, it is insinuated that her published works cannot be her own making: how can a woman write poetry and philosophy so eloquently? It is even alleged that she denied in public conversation the immortality of the soul, a central tenet for both Christians and Jews. Ultimately, their common destiny is silence.

And now the crucial difference: the first Jewish Venetian woman is fictional, the second one is real; the comparison rests on a fantasy. Jessica, daughter of Shylock and Leah, and wife to Lorenzo, date of birth and death immaterial, is a character from Shakespeare's *The Merchant of Venice* (*c.* 1596), while Sarra Copia, daughter of Simon and Ricca (Rivka) Grassini, wife to Jacob Sulam, was born sometime around 1600, and died in 1641. The poetic license of my analogies is further encouraged by some tantalizing elements. Jessica is a name whose oldest written record is to be found precisely in *The Merchant of Venice*. Some commentators believe that the name is an anglicization of the biblical Iskah; the sage Rabbi Itz'hak states in the Talmud: 'By Iskah is meant Sarah'.[1] As Sarra Copia's correspondent Cebà joked about the fact that her family name meant 'Couple',[2] I pair off Jessica and Sarra, adopting and adapting the same associative method to explore the potential of this comparison for a reading of *The Merchant of Venice* in relation to the historical record.

What is the point of drawing together a fictional character and a historical author? The chronology of Sarra's public trajectory, spanning a few years immediately after Shakespeare's death and over two decades after the composition of *The Merchant of Venice*, places her at a safe distance from any temptation to seek evidence of direct contact, an activity best left to novelists, daydreamers and dilettanti. My interest lies instead in the manifold ways in which early modern subjects, whether real or fictional, travel in time and are translated and refigured, given new lives, identities and meanings by later narratives. I want to explore here how the afterlives of Shakespearean characters may revive interest in historical women, and, vice versa, the ways in which the history of real women can help us refocus Shakespearean characters and provide them with new backstories. To suggest that Sarra is an unacknowledged double of Jessica is to remark that facts bleed into fiction, fiction struggles with fact, myths vie with history, famous plots obscure untold stories and marginal biographies may inform our understanding of Shakespeare. Any modern interpretations and contemporary performances of *The Merchant of Venice* bring with them some sort of Jewish content and context, based on a combination of historical and ethnological research, creative re-imagining, cultural presuppositions, attachments and identifications on the part of critics, directors, actors and audiences. There is always a historical Jewish Venice in the backdrop of our theatrical or critical versions of the *Merchant*, and one should not delve into the history of Venetian Jews to mimic or reproduce a situation that had tenuous connections with the Venice of Shakespeare. Conversely, learning about the complexities of the Ghetto provides a wider range of options for reinventing Shakespeare's characters. Sarra Copia Sulam becomes another possibility, another identification, another subject position available in our constellation of modern Jessicas. The ultimate question this essay addresses is whether the life of Sarra Copia Sulam can suggest new visions of Jessica and her play.

Portrait of the Jewish woman as still life and dangerous beauty

The tropes orienting the representation of Jessica as well as actual Jewish women may be usefully contextualized in the phenomenon defined by Zygmunt Bauman as 'allosemitism', a more capacious term than antisemitism, which has the merit of alerting us to the fact that even positive and sympathetic representations of Jews are often guided by the assumption that the Jew is always an irreducible 'other' (Bauman 1998: 143–56). Gender further complicates this perception: 'The Jewess ... is a sign that signifies different cultural and gendered constructs for different times and different places. A heuristic model, the Jewess cannot be fully controlled or domesticated. Therein ultimately lies her threat, her offense, and her perpetual ability to reveal the fault lines in cultural, disciplinary, and religious borders' (Levine 1997: 155). If the beautiful Jewess, a trope that Efraim Sicher has persuasively demonstrated predates by centuries its success in French and British Romantic culture, is an insidious threat even in its apparent passivity, other Jewish women are represented as unruly and dangerous (Sicher 2017). The archive of figurations of Jewish women in Western culture seems to favour these two specular tropes. They could be defined as the 'Jewish woman as still life', namely, as beautiful, passive, silent object of contemplation and curiosity, and the 'Jewish woman as dangerous', namely, as endowed with remarkable and unpredictable agency. The first trope is found in *Merchant*, when Shylock reacts to his daughter's betrayal by envisioning her as an inert, adorned idol: 'I would my daughter were / dead at my foot, and the jewels in her ear!' (3.1.80–1). In 1608 the Englishman Thomas Coryat visited the Ghetto of Venice and, unlike Shakespeare, had first-hand contact with the local Jews. His received negative stereotypes about Jewish ugliness were partially reversed at the view of Levantine women:

> In the roome wherin they celebrate their divine service, no women sit, but have a loft or gallery proper to them selves only, where I saw many Jewish women, whereof some were as beautiful as ever I saw, and so gorgeous in their apparel, jewels, chaines of gold, and rings adorned with precious stones, that some of our English Countesses do scarce exceede them. (Whittaker 2013: 78)

Coryat seems to pit his first-hand testimony against his own prejudice, and yet another stereotype may be lurking there. Dana Katz and Efraim Sicher have both described the Jewish woman as a silent and ostensibly passive object of contemplation as a figuration of the dangerous lure of *synagoga* to the Christian man (Katz 2017: 106). The tenacity of these tropes and the uncertain boundaries between fact and fiction, are demonstrated by another sixteenth-century Jewish woman from Venice. Madonna Bellina appears as the addressee of a love letter penned around 1550 by the Venetian actor and playwright Andrea Calmo:

> To the pillar of music, the Jewess M.[adonna] Bellina: Even though we are separated from one another by [the distance from] your Jewish belief to our certain Christian knowledge, [....] no young woman has been more genteel (gentile) than you among all those born in the descent of the Jewish people. [...] If Esther with her gallantry, beauty, and ability saw to it that captive Mordecai be freed and that the scribes, Pharisees, and Levites be spared and their dominion restored, you, on the contrary, bind men, inflame hearts, and enslave whoever hears, sees, and visits you. [...] you gladden festivities, honour comedies, astound listeners, and stupefy women. [...] And if I love you so much and, with the grace of God, were a young man with many [youthful] faculties, bind and hide yourself, [for] should I go as far as Colchis, I'd want to abduct and take you for my legitimate wife, first having you baptized; you understand? (Harrán 2008: 36–7)

Starting from her name, Madama Bellina embodies the paradox of the representation of Jewish women. She stands for the ultimate impossibility of realism, the difficulty of disentangling fact from mythology, the inextricable knot between the lives of Jewish women and certain allosemitic tropes and paradigms: in short, the inescapable allegorical dimension attached to the figurations of Jews both before and after Jewish emancipation, which made Jews, at least in principle, equal citizens. Bellina may have been a real person, but for Calmo, her Jewishness became more relevant than her individual musical and artistic worth and he felt obligated to place her in a theological framework. Or, alternatively, Bellina may have been just a figment of Calmo's imagination conjured up to make a specific point in his satirical production. Unless new documents are discovered and give at least (in the high improbability of ever hearing her own voice) different perspectives on her identity and life, this undecidability is irrevocable. And sure enough, Bellina – whether she lived a life on this planet – exists only through the textual creation of a male author. We can have no direct access to her words and music, which, in an ironical historical counterpoint to Jessica's discomfort with this art, was one of the few professional activities allowed to Venetian Jews. But through Bellina we have a glimpse of a different tradition, a counternarrative to that of the Jewess as silent object of contemplation, one where being Jewish and a woman are not mutually exclusive identity components, and where the Jewish woman is more subject than object, steeped in the reality of Jewish Venice, and endowed with an artistic agency. Madama Bellina, then, reminds us that Jessica is a fictional character who is nevertheless fleshed out and continuously reinvented in relation to the changing conditions of real (Jewish) women, and that Sarra was an actual person whose biography has come to us through a set of representations structured by powerful Christian (and to a lesser extent) Jewish tropes.[3]

Portrait of the Jewish woman as rebel

Every age picks its favourite character from *The Merchant of Venice* – James Shapiro observes – and after Antonio, Portia and Shylock, the protagonist for our times is Jessica (Shapiro 2019). Jessica is part of a structural polarity: 'the duality of the ugly, wicked Jew and his desirable beautiful Jewish daughter', a 'binary relation ... with the mother as effaced or at best a "shadowy background figure"' (Sicher 2017: 1, 11) that has developed since the late Middle Ages, countering the assumption that this symbolic construct originated in the nineteenth century.

> The pairing of the wicked Jewish father (who represents the Jews' collective refusal to accept the Christian messiah) with his beautiful Jewish daughter (who rejects the Law of the father and can be converted to Christianity) repeatedly allegorizes the tension between Old and New Testaments, spirit and flesh, law and dispensation, obedience and rebellion, and, in a problematic way, morality and erotic desire. (Sicher 2017: 1)

History has made Jessica even more of an ambivalent presence in this constellation, her character overdetermined by both her cultural antecedents and her afterlife, especially after the Holocaust. She has recently become the arena where a philosemitic reading of the play, aimed at redressing the classic interpretation of her conversion as a good thing and redeeming her Jewish identity, enters in critical tension with a feminist interpretation. Can Jessica represent the redemption of the Jew through her conversion? Is Jewishness a racial marker indelibly inscribed in her body? Does her escape make her a hero of women's liberation or a cynical traitor to her widowed father and the faith? Scholars, directors, actors, and fiction writers have long struggled with these interrelated questions.

Janet Adelman sees her as the irreducibly alien 'other', calling our attention to the fact that while her father is devastated by her conversion and betrayal, the Christian characters remain deeply suspicious of her outsider status.

> In the face of continued designation of her as an infidel and stranger, she appears to absorb the lesson implicit in Lancelot's pun – and as though in response, she fantasizes a radical separation from her father's blood and nation as the price of inclusion in the social club to which her husband belongs, and as the only way to cast off her status as a Jew. (2008: 140)

M. Lindsay Kaplan, on the other hand, uses a different framework to portray Jessica as the perfect convert, fully assimilated into a reconstituted Christian identity. Reading the character through medieval theories of body and gender, she argues that, in light of a combination of the Aristotelian model of sexual reproduction and of Christian theology, '[w]hile male Jews may possess an immutable racial identity, their daughters' status, as imperfect versions of their father and impressionable material for a Christian husband's formative seed, makes them ideal vehicles for effecting a successful conversion of Jews' (Kaplan 2007: 16). In other words, the inferiority of woman and her role as a vessel of the male seed makes her more susceptible to a successful assimilation: 'Jessica serves to solve the "problem" of converting racially Jewish men as represented by Shylock' (Kaplan 2007: 30).

However, in spite of references to a quasi-biological difference between Shylock's flesh and hers (3.1.34–5), Jessica remains the potential vehicle of an ineffaceable Jewish identity: if her children will be baptized as Christian, matrilinearity will render them Jewish by the norms of Halakha, Jewish religious law. It is noteworthy that Sarra Copia Sulam belonged to a community including many marranos who had been authorized by the pragmatic Republic of Venice to return to Judaism after their forced conversion in the Iberian peninsula to take advantage of their trade networks.

The modern rehabilitation of Shylock has also triggered a parallel vilification of Jessica, who 'attracts a modern odium' (Middleton 2015: 294): she becomes the ruthless daughter who betrays her father and her faith, not hesitating to steal his money and to barter her dead mother's ring for a monkey. More positive interpretations still read her as an impregnable shape-shifter, inviting opposite feelings of anxiety or aspirations of independence (Middleton 2015: 294). Heinrich Heine's famous pronouncement enables the feminist reading of Jessica as the young woman who wants to escape an authoritarian father and a suffocating cultural world:

> Did Shakespeare here mean to sketch a Jewess? Indeed no; what he depicts is only a daughter of Eve, one of those beautiful birds, who, when they are fledged, fly away from the paternal nest to the beloved man. So Desdemona followed the Moor ... That is woman's way. [...] The genius of Shakespeare rises still higher over the petty strife of two religious sects, and his drama shows us neither Jews nor Christians, but oppressors and oppressed, and the madly agonised cries of exultation of the latter when they can repay their arrears of injuries with interest. (Heine 1895: 134)

An abstract, universal womanness is posited that is separable from Judaism, an idea that to be human and to be a woman is somehow at odds with being Jewish, not only from the point of view of Christian theology but also from a certain model of liberal, secular thinking. Heine's rhetoric of dissociation, typical of the age of emancipation and of an assimilated Jew, will enjoy a great fortune and will become a dominant mode in many twentieth-century interpretations eager to disentangle Shakespeare's Venetian plays from their political and religious implications.[4]

Against both her cultural neutralization and denigration, a number of modern authors and directors have tried to recast Jessica as a good Jewish daughter; Jewish feminist writers, in particular, have tried to rescue her even from early rewrites where her Jewish redemption coincided with sacrificial death (see both Coodin and Gilbert in this volume). As Michelle Ephraim argues:

> feminist writers embrace *The Merchant* as an opportunity to collapse Shakespeare's dichotomy of oppressive Jewish father/miserable Jewish daughter and to explore how the play can generate the interpretive possibility of a daughter who ultimately values her Jewish identity as fundamental to her conception of selfhood. (2017: 343)

These feminist novels 'reclaim [the] linguistic control from both the Christian man and the Christian woman who assumes a male guise and whose skillful manipulation of words and meaning originally banished Jewish identity from Shakespeare's play' (Ephraim 2017: 358). Giving (Jewish) voice to Jessica in fiction is an important strategy, one that has interesting parallels in modern stagings of the play, where she is frequently given a prominent role in the ending, either as a silent but suffering witness to her father's sentencing or even as a repentant worshiper, who invokes the God of Mercy in Jewish prayer (as in the successful Globe production of 2016) when she attends Shylock's forced conversion. The paradox is that to salvage Jessica's Jewish identity, progressive directors, critics and authors have to restore her devotion and loyalty to the (law of) the father and disable her potentially feminist subversiveness. A parallel, more nuanced, move can be found in literary criticism. Sarah Coodin has recently considered Jessica's trajectory in the light of the biblical narratives of Dinah and Rachel, an intertextual and hermeneutic gesture that allows the reader to endow Shylock's daughter with a sense of moral agency and to understand her as a Jewish character (Coodin 2017).

In the last analysis, these interventions cannot elude the fact that in the *Merchant*'s final act there are no famous last words for her. As Michael Neill cogently argues: 'Whatever the ultimate cause of Jessica's sadness, it seems to render her mute' (2018: 108). However, it is precisely 'Jessica's unspeaking' (108) that has also opened up a vast space for the widely discrepant interpretations of the characters and her intentions, motivations and feelings. They will now be compared to the documented speaking and unspeaking of Sarra, in the context of the specific conditions of the Ghetto of Venice.

Portrait of the Jewish woman as author

An intermittent presence in Italian literary histories, Sarra Copia Sulam lived in the Ghetto of Venice in the first half of the seventeenth century and entertained Jewish and

Christian intellectuals in her famous literary academy. Modern scholarship, especially that of Umberto Fortis and Don Harrán, the editors of previous critical editions respectively in Italian and English, has provided a rich picture of Sarra's life, time and works (Fortis 2003; Copia Sulam 2009). At a time when Italian Jewish culture was promoting a very traditional model of a family-oriented *eshet chayil* (woman of valour) (Fortis 2015; Adelman 2001), Sarra received from her father the gift of an education in both Jewish and Italian cultures. Harrán summarizes thus her exceptional accomplishments:

> She knew languages: beyond Italian, Venetian, *giudeo-veneziano*, basic Hebrew, and possibly Latin, she read and may have written and conversed in Spanish and French and is said to have composed poetry in Venetian. Aside from philosophy, her interests ran the spectrum from literature to theology and astrology. (Copia Sulam 2009: 33)

On 19 May 1618 the young Sarra wrote a letter to the Genoese writer and cleric Ansaldo Cebà, over thirty years her senior, whose poem on Queen Esther she had profoundly appreciated. Struck by the identity of this unlikely fan, Cebà responded with equal admiration but, like Calmo, could not help framing Sarra in the usual tropes. In a correspondence that lasted for four years – he died in 1622, six months after the last communication – he ended each and every letter inviting her to convert to Christianity. Sarra was consistent in the content of her response, and quite creative in its formal variants: she would accept baptism if he underwent circumcision; she preferred the Mount Parnassus waters over that of the font; and with all the canals they had in Venice, what use were the baptismal waters?

Her audacity came at an expense. Sarra was embroiled in two major controversies that ultimately forced her to abandon her public role. In the first she defended herself in a published manifesto from the accusation of having denied the immortality of the soul in her academy. In the second, she was the victim of a robbery by her preceptor Numidio Paluzzi, aided and abetted by her servants (including her maid Arnolfa), who stole her money, jewelry and household objects, in a situation oddly reminiscent of Shylock's. The controversies continued after her death. By being Jewish and female she was not easily accommodated to mainstream Italian literary criticism, which even in its more secular expressions remained influenced by a Christian and androcentric orientation (Copia Sulam 2009: 76). While Italian scholarship has made her at best an object of curiosity (and occasionally doubted her authorship and identity), for exponents of the *Wissenschaft des Judentums* interested in combining Jewish tradition and secular culture, Sarra became the pioneer of the intellectual circles of nineteenth-century Germany that propelled Jews into the mainstream. Giuseppe Veltri quotes the unusually enthusiastic praise of Heinrich Graetz: 'Young, charming, with a noble heart and keen intellect, striving for great things and a lover of the Muses, Sara Sullam enchanted both old men and young boys. ... She basked in a realm of beauty, exuding her enthusiasm in a moderated, soft and delicate work' (2009: 228).

However, for the fourteen poems and the manifesto that have survived after Cebà apparently destroyed all the letters and poems he received from her, the terms '[s]oft and delicate' do not reflect the combative tone of her extant repertoire. As Harrán puts it:

> Her correspondence with Cebà and Bonifaccio put her on the defensive; hence the proliferation of militant vocabulary (gladiator, warrior, weapons, darts, arrows, spears, blows, stabs, wounds, shields, war, combat, arena, trophy, slaughter) – 'I gird myself for defense.' One can only speculate on the kinds of themes Copia would have emphasized in her poetry if she had not been pressured on all fronts to explain, justify, and 'fight' for her rights. (Copia Sulam 2009: 71)

A lawsuit filed against her robbers led to the publication of a satirical pamphlet titled *Sareide*, whose slanderous content was read in public places, including the Jewish quarters: 'at the end of the following month, August, the infamous libels were seen, the *Sareide* were read in the ghetto, insults were exchanged, abuses were shouted, threats of both passion and fury were hurled' (Copia Sulam 2009: 410).

If Jessica is irresistibly attracted to Lorenzo's Christian world and wishes to escape from the claustrophobic environment of Shylock's house, the story of Sarra paints a very different cultural picture, illuminating a more fluid and dynamic relationship between Jews and Christians. Post-Holocaust narratives, as shown by Mitchell Duneier, tend to read the prototypical Venetian Ghetto in the light of the genocidal and segregationist policies of twentieth-century ghettoes that inherited its name (Duneier 2016). The seventeenth-century Ghetto was a far more ambivalent space, one where Sarra had built her Belmont and proudly defended her right to be part of the larger intellectual world while protecting her identity. Cebà wrote to Sarra that he hoped her soul would be one day 'refined in the furnace of Christian charity' (Fortis 2015: 296), but, at least for a few years, she thrived semi-autonomously in the Jewish foundry (*geto*) of the Ghetto in the face of repressive and critical forces. Her academy contributed to making the Ghetto a very porous contact zone, where Jewish culture was produced and disseminated throughout Europe, and where incipient forms of Christian Judeophilia paved the way for philosophical skepticism that we consider one of the breeding grounds of modernity (Veltri 2009). Without suggesting any anachronistic view of interfaith dialogue and Enlightenment tolerance, the Ghetto should be considered not only as a place of separation, but as a contact zone and a contested space, a site of interrogation and conflict, one where, even in an undeniable unbalance of power, Christians and Jews met, fought and traded insults, and where the Jews, locked in, curfewed and periodically threatened with expulsion as they were, also felt culturally empowered. We agree with Harrán that in this peculiar environment, Sarra Copia Sulam, as a Jewish woman, spoke in 'another voice' in both the societies she inhabited.

> For non-Jews any religion other than Christianity was regarded as deviant, and in their male-dominated society women were seriously marginalized. The same holds for the Jewish minority, which in its own male-dominated community assigned a subordinate role to women and expected them to abide by the norms defined by Jewish religious law and indigenous social custom. Both non-Jews and Jews usually imposed silence on women. But Copia broke the rules: she did not limit the sphere of her activity to her family and household, nor did she stay in the background or guard her tongue. Rather she read, wrote, studied, and speculated; she opened her house to Jews and Christians; she sounded them out for their views on poetry, philosophy, and religion; she conversed and corresponded with them, forcefully arguing her own views; and she defended her person against slanderers and her faith against scoffers. (Copia Sulam 2009: 3)

Parallel portraits

By writing primarily for a Christian audience and defensively in response to specific polemical readers, Sarra occupies a liminal subject position, a middle ground where she advocates her right to be a woman writer and to maintain her Jewish identity by speaking a predominantly non-Jewish literary language. This suggests a last analogy between Jessica and Sarra, based on their textual strategy of appropriation of the dominant discourse.

At the crucial moment, when she has just escaped and has not yet fully transitioned to the Christian side, Jessica voices some lines that Gilberto Sacerdoti, ascribing to her the intention of gaining some credit with her new community, interprets as if she 'pretends to remember something which is both true and false' (Sacerdoti 2018: 148).

> When I was with him I have heard him swear
> To Tubal and to Cush, his countrymen,
> That he would rather have Antonio's flesh
> Than twenty times the value of the sum
> That he did owe him.
>
> (3.2.283–7)

Sacerdoti glosses that while it is true that Shylock is now bent on revenge over any financial compensation, it is unlikely that Jessica may have heard him swear anything since her elopment. The critic compares her attitude to that of Jewish apostates keen to score points with the Christian majority by denouncing other Jews to the inquisitors. But he also notices the peculiar intertextual nature of her scriptural reference:

> the extraordinary thing is that Jessica, while ostensibly trying to separate herself from her father, has picked out the names of her father's 'countrymen' from the Book of Genesis (10:2–6), where Tubal and Cush are the sons of Shem's two brothers, Japheth and Ham. [...] Shem is the ancestor of the Semites, Japheth of the Gentiles and Ham of the Hamites. Which means that in the Bible the sons of the three brothers are not only all cousins and grandsons of Noah, but, in the Semite Jessica's words, all 'countrymen' of one country which happens to be the world itself. And of course, in a world where all are cousins and countrymen nobody would be an alien, nor ashamed to be his father's child. Such might have been the brave old world of the origins, and *inshalla* such might be the brave new world of the future, but for the time being this is only the half-conscious cosmopolitan dream, or *lapsus*, of the apostate daughter of a Jew who, being countryless, can have 'countrymen' only in his daughter's fancy. (2018: 147)

Sacerdoti is quick to recall that the dream of a global cosmopolis envisioned in Genesis 10 has already been undermined by the curse of Ham in Genesis 9, a curse associated with the Jews in Augustine and with black Africans since the Middle Ages, especially after the onset of the slave trade referenced by Shylock (see also Kaplan 2019b: 103–28). In Act 5, Jessica turns to a different source, this time evoking the Greco-Roman mythology of Ovid; 'In such a night / Medea gathered the enchanted herbs / That did renew old Aeson' (5.1.12–14). Sacerdoti suggests: 'The barbarous Medea stands to Athens as the Jewess Jessica to Venice' (2018: 158). Like Jessica, Medea abandoned her father, God and land to follow her lover to embrace a superior civilization. Tellingly, the specific episode refers to Jason asking Medea to gather magic herbs that will produce a 'boyled juice' capable of rejuvenating his father. The mythical vision of a potion working as a blood transfusion amounts for Sacerdoti to a solution to Jessica's conversion, made imperfect by Shylock's blood. Is this a humanist image of regeneration or a concession to the protoracial thinking inaugurated by the laws of *limpieza de sangre* that expelled Sephardic Jews (like Sarra's family) from Spain a century earlier? Caught between a possible 'cosmopolitan dream' and an ambiguous mythical reference, Jessica ends as a suspended, unresolved character who ultimately 'unspeaks'.

Her final speech finds a parallel in one of Sarra's last-known poems, where we can finally listen to her own voice, even if not properly her words. *Notices from Parnassus* was a collection of texts that were published in defense of Sarra against the slanderous *Sareide*. She personally contributed four sonnets that gratefully echoed as many supportive poems by Christian literati, and in the specific case of this response to Alberto dei Magni, she reproduced eleven of his end words in different order, in a significant homage and display of virtuosity.

Quel desio di saper ch'in cor gentile
Sovente alberga ad ingannevol luce
Mi trasse; indi, seguendo infido duce,
Tardi di cor vilan scorgei lo stile.

Fummi il costui disagio qual focile
Ch'ognhor colpiami il cor; ma chi m'induce
A dir quali esche ardesse se riluce
Pur anco illustre l'oprar mio virile?

Mi tacio donque e m'ascrivo a la schiera
De' Melciadi Focioni se non lece
Ch'un empio ingrato altro premio m'apporte,

Di cui non so qual inferna megera
L'alma ingombrassi che d'honore in vece
Danno mi procurasse, oltraggio e morte.

That desire to know things, which often lodges
In a genteel heart, drew me
To the deceptive light: there, following a faithless leader,
I later perceived the ways of a boorish heart.

His discomfort was, for me, like a flint
That struck my heart every hour; but who induces me
To say what kinds of tinder ignited it
If my courageous actions shine as ever illustrious?

I keep quiet, then, and I enroll in the company
Of those like Melchiades and Photius if it is impermissible
For an impious ingrate to show me another reward;

I do not know what infernal Megaera
Would so encumber his soul as to cause me not honor,
But harm, offense, and death.

(Copia Sulam 2009: 460–1)

Sarra starts by describing her humanistic hankering for knowledge thwarted by the conspiracy of one of her persecutors, even as she declares a certain degree of empathy with his 'discomfort' (a probable allusion to Numidio Paluzzi's illnesses). She reprises Dei Magni's appellative 'alma gentile' ('genteel soul', with the possible pun on 'gentile' that we observed in both Calmo's Bellina and Shakespeare's Jessica) by calling herself 'genteel heart', in contrast with her former friend and now offender's 'boorish heart'. Don Harrán identifies the characters to whom Alberto had compared Sarra as the Roman pope Melchiades and the Constantinople bishop Photius, 'two figures who suffered persecution, yet outlived it to be recognized for their achievements' (Copia Sulam 2009: 460). However, it is more likely that, as observed by Umberto Fortis, 'Melciadi e Focioni' are actually the Greek leaders Miltiades and Phocion, the victims of Athens' ingratitude (Fortis 2003: 134). By accepting the association with two famous statesmen who acquired great public prominence and later fell from grace, meeting with violent death in prison, Sarra achieves several goals. In the context of a prolonged Jewish-Christian dispute, both personal and theological, she deploys, like Jessica, the tertium of Greek culture (possibly through Machiavelli's poem *Ingratitude*), where classical virtue is disarticulated from theology. Like Jessica, Sarra was misled by the 'deceptive light' of a 'faithless leader' but chose instead to keep her faith. But while inscribing herself one last time in the 'cosmopolitan dream' represented by her desire to know and embodied in her interfaith academy, she resolves, like Jessica, to 'keep quiet'. This is the fate that befell Sarra, whose public persona disappeared until her death in 1641. In that year she is celebrated by the epitaph penned for her gravestone by her old mentor Leon Modena: 'A lady of exquisite taste ... wise was she among women'. Jessica and Sarra end their lives as good, 'unspeaking' wives.

Jessica is a textual creation that Shakespeare dramatized by elaborating the trope of the Jewish daughter. Sarra was a real person who fashioned her literary persona through a strenuous negotiation between the legal restrictions of the Ghetto, the social dictates of her Jewish community, the cultural conventions of Counter-Reformation Italian society and her personal vicissitudes. When Sarra was born, probably Jessica had already begun her afterlife. Since then, the Shakespearean character has been reimagined multiple times by actors, critics and writers. Each reimagining of *The Merchant of Venice* brings necessarily with it a direct or indirect representation of its

Jewish Venetian setting, running the full spectrum of positions from antisemitic stereotype to philologically correct historical reconstruction. In this light, the story of Sarra is offered here as another possible con-text and co-text for Shakespeare.

Jessica and Sarra are two bold go-betweens, two liminal women who attempt to bridge separate social and cultural worlds but are ultimately condemned to silence. And yet, while relegated to their condition of 'still life', their words still have the power to provoke us.

Coda: Portrait of the Jewish woman as judge

I wish to conclude with a third Jewish woman acting on the Venetian stage. In 2016 Ruth Bader Ginsburg, Associate Justice of the Supreme Court of the United States, presided over a moot court that retried Shylock, Antonio and Portia in a special event connected to the first performance of *The Merchant in Venice* in the Ghetto. Ginsburg led the five judges to rule unanimously that the question of the pound of flesh was 'a merry sport' that no court would enforce; Shylock was restored the 3,000 ducats and the demand of his conversion nullified; Portia was declared 'an impostor' and sentenced to study law in Padua. This ruling was read by some as misogynistic and by others as a source of empowerment that aligned her ideally with path-breaking figures such as Sarra Copia Sulam; Elena Lucrezia Cornaro Piscopia, the Venetian aristocrat who became, in 1678, the first woman in Europe to receive a PhD; and Ruth Bader Ginsburg herself. In the sumptuous School of San Rocco, the authority and charisma of a Jewish woman and legal giant of our times, ruling under Tintoretto's imposing ceiling paintings of the Old Testament as harbinger of the New, offered a touch of poetic justice for two pioneering Jewish women from another era, Jessica and Sarra.

Notes

1 The full passage reads: 'Yisca is Sarah; and why was she called Yisca? Because she discerned by means of the holy spirit, as it is said, In all that Sarah said to you, hearken to her voice (Genesis 21.12). Another explanation is: because all gazed [*sakin*] at her beauty' (Megillah 14a). As Stephen Orgel has convincingly demonstrated, Jessica, far from being a Jewish or Biblical name, 'is in fact a common enough name in Scotland, a diminutive of the woman's name Jessie. If Shakespeare knew any Jessicas they were Scottish' (Orgel 2003: 152).

2 There are two accepted spellings for her name. In Italian editions she goes by Sara Copio Sullam. The early modern spelling sanctioned by Don Harrán's critical edition 'Copia' also means 'copy' in Italian, with another ironical twist on resemblance.

3 The fact that Bassanio also mentions Colchis with regard to the suitors who travel to win Portia (1.1.170) is a tantalizing coincidence that there is no room to explore here. I thank M. Lindsay Kaplan for this observation.

4 However, as Stephen Greenblatt has recently reminded us, to be a 'daughter of Eve' means everything but to be simply a universal woman, irrespective of the theological pronouncements and cultural beliefs of Christians and Jews (Greenblatt 2017a).

9

'Marvellously Changed': Shakespeare's Repurposing of Fiorentino's Doting Godfather in *The Merchant of Venice*

Thomas Cartelli

The sad part Antonio plays

I begin this leap into 'the elephant's graveyard of literary study' with a series of close readings that may seem to lead only to a restatement of the 'critical commonplace' – or to some, anachronistic claim – that Shakespeare's merchant, Antonio, is homoerotically inclined (Greenblatt 1985: 163).[1] I indulge this move to demonstrate how radically Shakespeare has altered the configurations of character and relationship he found in his likeliest source, Giovanni Fiorentino's late fourteenth-century *Il Pecorone* (1558 p.d.), and how these alterations contribute to Shakespeare's repurposing of a story centred on a callow youth's pursuit of a wealthy widow into a darker drama underwritten by the face-off between a Jewish moneylender who hates Christians and a Christian merchant who hates Jews.

The Merchant of Venice has for so long been identified with Shylock, Portia and the casket scenes at Belmont that hardly anyone thinks too hard about the play's titular merchant, Antonio, who was arguably more central to Shakespeare's designs than he has been in the play's stage history. Although the play was initially listed in the 1598 Stationers Register as *The Jew of Venice* – suggesting that before making its move from stage to page the play had already been hijacked by Shylock – in its first printing the title page reads, *The most excellent Historie of the Merchant of Venice, With the extreme cruelties of Shylock the Jew towards sayd merchant*, with the heading on its first page of text – *The Comical History of the Merchant of Venice* – further remarking Antonio's centrality. No one, of course, leans very heavily on Shakespeare's titles for evidence of anything. And perhaps E. K. Chambers was right to surmise no special dramatic pertinence in the play's early fastening on Antonio's sadness, doubting 'whether this particular point in the play was intended for the audience at all, and is not rather the intrusion of a personal note, an echo of those disturbed relations in Shakespeare's private life of which the fuller but enigmatic record is to be found in the *Sonnets*' (1925: 117). But by the time we return to Chambers's musings at the end of this chapter, we may consider the emergence of this 'personal' note pertinent to a fault.

That Shakespeare wants us to take Antonio seriously is clear from the play's first lines, which establish the mystery of the melancholy Antonio experiences but claims to be unable to explain:[2]

ANTONIO
    In sooth I know not why I am so sad.
    It wearies me; you say it wearies you;

But how I caught it, found it or came by it,
What stuff 'tis made of, whereof it is born,
I am to learn; and such a want-wit sadness makes of me,
That I have much ado to know myself.

(1.1.1–6)

Antonio presents his sadness as a disease that has come upon him inconspicuously, unannounced – whose source, occasion and significance he has yet to learn: a phrase which, as Paul Hammond notes, constitutes 'a gesture of demurral; [a] question [that] cannot be answered; [a] line [that] cannot be completed' (2002: 91). This sombreness or melancholy (if we can name it thus when the play never does) appears even to subvert his established knowledge of himself; as he concludes, 'I have much ado to know myself'.[3]

Although Antonio claims he cannot fathom the source of his sadness, he insists that it is not caused by his shipping ventures, and, with a dismissive 'Fie, fie', rejects love as the cause, words sounding more like 'a reproach [...] than a denial' (Hammond 2002: 91). Whether Antonio does or does not know himself is a live issue. That he does know himself and is hiding something may be the case; he could be using the fashionable show of melancholy to cover a less acknowledgeable mood or predilection.[4] He may even – as Salanio, Salarino and Lars Engle suggest – be hiding the fact that he *is* actually 'sad to think upon his merchandise' (1.1.39).[5] But it is also possible that Antonio's emotional turmoil unsettles an idea of himself on which he has founded his personal and social identity. If so, he may be having difficulty coming to terms with feelings clearly legible to onlookers like Salarino, who describes Antonio's eye so 'big with tears' as he bid farewell to Bassanio that he turned his face away, 'put his hand behind him, / And, with affection wondrous sensible, / [...] wrung Bassanio's hand', prompting Salanio to conclude, 'I think he only loves the world for him' (2.8.46–50).[6]

This assessment of Antonio's despairing response to Bassanio's departure is given pre-emptive ocular proof in

Michael Radford's representation of Antonio looking out his window and seeing Bassanio disembark from a gondola in the first scripted scene of his 2004 film (see Cartelli 2009). As we witness Jeremy Irons's Antonio visibly brighten at the sight of the feckless young man (goblet of wine in hand), it becomes plain that Antonio has been anticipating this all along, and that what both he and his auditors took for sadness may rather have been unacknowledged anxiety about Bassanio's arrival. In both playtext and film, this anxiety breaks to the surface in the question Antonio asks as soon as they are alone:

> Well, tell me now, what lady is the same
> To whom you swore a secret pilgrimage,
> That you today promised to tell me of?

(1.1.119–21)

This question has clearly been eating away at Antonio for some time. But why should this disclosure prove so urgent to a man whose response to the idea of his loving anyone is a peremptory 'Fie, fie'? Traditional criticism answers that it is merely the loving concern for a friend that motivates him. Skeptics, however, may wonder why one friend would become so preoccupied with the marital possibilities of another that sadness would make a 'want wit' of him? More cynical minds might ask why, if his love for Bassanio is erotically motivated, would Antonio be so eager to offer everything he has to finance Bassanio's quest for Portia? Why promise to do his all to drive his beloved away and make himself miserable in the process? Is he really that loving, that self-sacrificing – that much like the all-forgiving fairy godfather Ansaldo in the Fiorentino source story? If so, why – unlike the older but considerably more complacent Ansaldo – does he say that his lot in life is to play 'a sad part', portray himself as 'a tainted wether of the flock' and invite Shylock to do his worst?

The crucial business this scene transacts dramatizes the kind of intimate relationship between men that has been variably defined on a continuum beginning with friendship and ending with something more sexually charged.[7] Many who have bowdlerized, repressed or happily confessed the scene's homoerotic implications generally fail to explore, or stress, its one-sidedness: the extent to which it places Antonio in the position of the doting, older, would-be lover/patron of a younger, free-spending gentleman who responds to him with affection but also recognizes (and acts on) his power to exploit that affection. Paul Hammond (again) proves the exception when he contextualizes this 'older man in love with younger' schematic in terms of the love the ancient Greek '*erastes* [shared] with his *eromenos*, though in this instance with a young man who seems not fully to reciprocate' (2002: 90).[8]

But like Hammond, my effort to reckon with the disproportion in this relationship – focused in part on the young man's desire to profit as well as on his failure to reciprocate – prompts me to take a somewhat more modern approach to the play's first scene, where Antonio's demurrals, denials and incomplete phrasings sound symptomatic of that performance of 'Closetedness', which, as Eve Sedgwick writes, is 'initiated as such by the speech act of silence', 'a silence that accrues particularity by fits and starts' (1990: 3). Whereas Salanio and Salarino fasten on Antonio's alleged preoccupation with business concerns, Gratiano focuses on the 'marvellously changed' face Antonio now shows to the world:

GRATIANO
You look not well, Signior Antonio;
You have too much respect upon the world:
They lose it that do buy it with much care.
Believe me, you are marvellously changed.
ANTONIO
I hold the world but as the world, Gratiano,
A stage, where every man must play a part,
And mine a sad one.

(1.1.73–9)

Gratiano's comment prompts a candid admission from Antonio, calling into question the earlier admission that he has 'much ado to know myself'. This is a very different way of reckoning with that sadness, which, by his own admission, had seemed to come upon Antonio for no reason obvious enough to own or identify. It indicates, rather, a confirmed belief that the sad part that Antonio says he 'must play' in the drama of his life is not reflective of the mood of a moment or some fashionable affectation but fixed in his mind as destiny.[9]

Late in the play, as he becomes persuaded that Bassanio cannot save him from giving Shylock the pound of flesh, we hear Antonio describe himself in a way that further deepens and darkens the nature of this belief and the hold it has on him:

> I am a tainted wether of the flock,
> Meetest for death; the weakest kind of fruit
> Drops earliest to the ground, and so let me.
>
> (4.1.113–15)

It is understandable that Antonio should begin to set his course toward death, but puzzling that he should liken his condition to that of a castrated ram, unsuited for breeding and endurance, and also 'to the weakest kind of fruit', as if destined to live a damaged, unproductive life and die a premature death.[10] What could he – or better, Shakespeare – mean to suggest by such comparisons? If, as one critic has baldly contended, Antonio is making a 'veiled admission' here 'that he deserves to die because he is a sodomite' (Kleinberg 1983a: 120), how legible would that admission have been to Antonio's auditors? And if it proves as obvious to them as it does to Antonio, how do we explain their continued respect and admiration for a man whose sexual self-characterization makes him so unloving to himself? If *they* have no particular moral objection to same-sex love, why should he?

The marginalization of such a character in performances and discussions of a play whose title suggests his primacy may well speak to the successful closeting of the character himself in discourses of friendship and melancholy that render strict identification – of role and intention – ambiguous and unsettled. Something like this coyness characterizes the movement of mind and verse at the close of Shakespeare's Sonnet 20 – 'But since she pricked thee out for women's pleasure, / Mine be thy love and thy love's use their treasure' – where 'a gesture of demurral' becomes a performance of denial (see Auden 1948: 230). Alan Sinfield has argued convincingly that 'The fact that the text of *The Merchant* gives no plain indication that the love between Antonio and Bassanio is informed by erotic passion does not mean that such passion was inconceivable' and 'may well mean that it didn't require particular presentation as a significant category', adding that 'the early modern organization of sex and gender boundaries is different from ours and the ordinary currency of that culture is replete with erotic interactions that strike strange chords today' (1996: 134, 139). These comments offer powerful correctives to readers and critics who deny both the visibility and viability of same-sex love relations in early modern England and who consider arguments like Sinfield's anachronistic. But I am, in the end, claiming something different in speaking to the uncannily *modern* mix of *ex*pression and *re*pression, of affirmation and self-loathing that Shakespeare brings to his characterization of Antonio and to the self-characterization of the speaking voice of the sonnets. Like that speaking voice, Antonio seems to be a character who does and does not know himself, who denies what he knows because he lacks the courage or conviction to be the self he knows he is in a world *that might well allow him to be that self* but cannot offer him any guarantee of acceptance or satisfaction. Visible as his affections may be to his associates and friends, and viable as they may be in attracting a needy gentleman to his side, they remain currency too suspect to the merchant himself to trade freely and shamelessly on the open market. Ironically, as Janet Adelman contends, 'if what Antonio's silence in 1.1 defends him against is knowledge of his desire for Bassanio, that desire everywhere leaks out, not only in [...] his melancholy insistence that he does not mind dying as long as Bassanio is present at his death [...] but also in plot elements that provide a displaced and unacknowledged language for what is concealed within: a language of ships and blood and wounds to the heart' (2008: 116).

Fiorentino repurposed

This is a good place to consider both how closely Shakespeare modeled this scenario on – and how radically he altered it from – its primary known source in the first story told on Day Four of *Il Pecorone* by the nun, Sister Saturnina, to her beloved friar, Brother Auretto. In Fiorentino, relations between the Bassanio and Antonio prototypes, Giannetto and Ansaldo, are free of any incursion from sexuality or modern psychology. Giannetto is the youngest of three sons of a Florentine father who, close to death, wills his entire estate to his two elder sons, bidding Giannetto to seek his fortune with his childless godfather, Ansaldo, described as the wealthiest merchant of Venice. Ansaldo immediately adopts Giannetto as son and heir; repeatedly puts Giannetto's pleasure and well-being ahead of his own; and is only too willing to sacrifice his considerable fortune to give Giannetto whatever he wants or thinks he needs (see Hammond 2002: 89). This proves to be quite a lot as Giannetto loses almost all that Ansaldo possesses in an effort to win the hand of a rich widow whose success at outlasting her suitors contributes greatly to the wealth of Belmonte, the city over which she presides: a pattern implicitly replicated in Bassanio's explanation of why he is going back to the well that is Antonio yet another time, and in Antonio's willingness to serve as Bassanio's self-sacrificing enabler.[11]

Richly furnished with costly merchandise and a splendid ship by Ansaldo in order to pursue a trading venture to Alexandria, Giannetto is diverted by news of the widow's wealth and beauty to try his hand at possessing her. But failing to perceive that the drink he is offered at her bedside is drugged, he wakes to discover the loss of his ship and all his goods. Although he is furnished with even costlier merchandise and a better ship on his second attempt, events follow the same pattern, this time resulting in the loss of almost all Ansaldo's worldly possessions. Financed a third time by a loan of 10,000 ducats Ansaldo secures from an unnamed Jewish usurer who, as in *The Merchant*, seeks a pound of flesh in return if the debt is not made good, Giannetto manages to succeed at last, thanks to the advice of the widow's waiting-woman, who tells him the secret to success that he should have easily deduced on his own. The tale then unwinds much as the play does: the Jew threatens Ansaldo with death once the date of the bond comes due; alerted to Ansaldo's plight, Giannetto belatedly offers the Jew ten times the amount borrowed and is refused; and the widow arrives in disguise to save the day and Ansaldo's life, much as a more polished, self-aware and sophisticated Portia does in *The Merchant*.

A late plot turn in the Italian story – which has Giannetto give the widow's waiting-woman in marriage to the elderly Ansaldo – is pointedly altered in Shakespeare's adaptation where Nerissa is married to the opportunistic Gratiano, leaving Antonio the odd man out in every sense of the word. Although this change may seem negligible, it seems indicative of Shakespeare's effort to 'heteronormalize' the play's marriage plot while isolating Antonio out as a comparatively asocial, same-sex-directed older man consigned to spend the rest of his days in commercial pursuits on the Rialto. As Auden notes, 'Shakespeare could have followed the *Pecorone* story in which it is Ansaldo [...] who marries the equivalent of Nerissa', but instead 'portrays Antonio as [...] incapable of loving a woman': a difference that is 'registered in his lack of a partner in the play's conclusion' (Auden 1948: 229; O'Rourke 2003: 391).

These are not the only changes Shakespeare makes to Fiorentino's tale, which is almost entirely Giannetto's story, with Ansaldo, the Jew and the widow effectively serving as his respective underwriter, enabler and objective. In *The Merchant*, the drama of Antonio's gloomy expectation is highlighted from the start, with succeeding scenes concentrating on Portia and Shylock in ways that triangulate the play's interests and plot around the subject positions of victim, victimizer and redeemer or saviour. Bassanio, for his part, serves less as a focus of dramatic interest than as a linking device that brings Antonio into the orbit of Shylock to finance the venture for Portia, and then prompts Portia's journey to Venice to save Antonio's life. There are, however, several intriguing correspondences that can be drawn between Giannetto and Bassanio, who differ mainly in terms of the one character's simplicity and the other's sophistication. For example, where Giannetto gracelessly concocts baseless lies to explain how he lost his ships and why he wants to engage in additional voyages, Bassanio is so practiced in the art of dissimulation that he is able to forgive his own prodigality in the act of proclaiming it. In tune with the non-judgemental mode of address that often characterizes Fiorentino's *novelle* and those of Boccaccio, Giannetto is matter-of-factly described as so caught up in pursuit of the widow that the only shame he feels is fear of failure: a feature that Shakespeare translates more flatteringly into Bassanio's hazarding all to achieve fair Portia.

As one of the *novelle's* happy innocents who blunders into good fortune, Giannetto is also the opposite of the calculating Bassanio, who proves capable not only of insinuating himself into Antonio's affection and cashbox alike but of winning the golden fleece that is Portia by betting on the lead casket on his first try. Whereas Bassanio is, in this and other respects, every bit the well-bred gentleman, Giannetto comes from a decidedly mercantile Florentine background and moves within similar mercantile circles in Venice, such that when his friends consider a recreational adventure, it is a lucrative shipping venture to Alexandria that they fasten on. Belmonte itself, unlike Shakespeare's Belmont, is firmly rooted in an economic reality, its wealth generated by a form of sex-tourism that draws wealthy young men to its shores to seek to possess the widow. As opposed to the glittering spectacle of the three caskets and of princes drawn from four corners of the globe to venture like latter-day Jasons for the 'richly left' Portia, we find at the climax of Giannetto's quest a tawdry trick not unlike the kind that are played on would-be lovers in Boccaccio's more lurid stories. Shakespeare notably transports this intra-mercantile fantasy of great riches gained through persistence, risk-taking and insider information into a social and cultural surround that separates the noble pairing of the aristocratic Bassanio and Portia from the workaday commercial trafficking of Antonio and Shylock, relieving them of soiled association with the sources of their wealth and prestige.

More dramatically consequential than any of this is, of course, Shakespeare's adaptation of Fiorentino's nameless Jew, who seeks Ansaldo's life merely 'so that he might boast that he had slain the chief of the Christian merchants' (Fiorentino 2006: 94), into the richly individuated Shylock. But Shakespeare's transformation of Fiorentino's selfless, all-forgiving elderly father-figure into the seemingly selfless, self-pitying bachelor Antonio is arguably as radical. The changed nature of the new relationship between the surrogates for the old Giannetto/Ansaldo configuration emerges, as noted above, from the nuanced exchanges Shakespeare presents in the play's first scene, and then from the way Antonio represents himself to his associates and to Bassanio as the conflict with Shylock intensifies. Related changes follow from the fact that Antonio's relations with Bassanio are those of a chosen, and choosing, friend, lover and sponsor as opposed to those of a godfather evolved into an adoptive, surrogate father. Instead of a doting, elderly man who lives in a state of prosperous semi-retirement, Antonio is a vigorous player on the Rialto, with four argosies at sea at once. And apart from once being called Bassanio's 'most noble kinsman' – a connection Shakespeare fails to explain or develop – Antonio and Bassanio seem to be free agents who hail from different social and economic strata, however closely implicated they may be in each other's lives.

Antonio also occupies a position that places Bassanio in a situation of co-dependency similar to Giannetto's on Ansaldo.

The dialogue that governs the interaction between Antonio and Bassanio in the play's first scene describes a relationship in which the client is of nobler blood but slimmer resources than the patron and has not necessarily been given but has borrowed the funds he has chronically failed, and may never be required, to repay. This fiction of indebtedness is underwritten by a deeper implied bond between the two that approximates the boundlessness of Ansaldo's generosity to Giannetto and Giannetto's boundless need for that generosity to continue but lacks that relationship's aura of disinterestedness. Indeed, the assumption that Antonio's investment will be repaid upon Bassanio's return could be read as a cover story that allows both parties to disguise the unscripted but assumed *emotionally* usurious promise to sustain bonds of affection after the monetary debt's satisfaction.

This is another place where Shakespeare's play and Fiorentino's story part ways and do so in an unusually 'homoeconomic' manner. As Jody Greene writes in relation to gift-giving in *Timon of Athens*, a play whose title character resembles Antonio in several particulars:

> Sodomy both defined and realized the 'brotherly love' to which Elizabethan rulers and their followers were constantly adjured. It paradoxically bound the community ever closer together by offering a category against which even the most intimate relationships between men could define themselves [...]. In a similar way, as Marcel Mauss and Shakespeare himself systematically demonstrate, usury enabled the alliances formed by Renaissance patronage by providing the solvency necessary for elaborate gift-giving while ensuring a duration to the relationships among members of any patronage network. The possibility of disinterested gift-giving was a powerful and necessary but ultimately empty cultural fiction. ([1994] 1999: 257)

René Girard elaborates on the same subject with specific application to *The Merchant of Venice*, indicating the extent to which the lender's pose of disinterestedness masks the figurative compounding of the borrower's interest: 'The generosity of the Venetians is not feigned. Real generosity makes the beneficiary more dependent on his generous friend than a regular loan. In Venice a new form of vassality prevails, grounded no longer in strict territorial borders but in vague financial terms. The lack of precise accounting makes personal indebtedness infinite' (1980: 115). The interdependence of sodomy, usury and patronage of which Greene writes is not synonymous with the power dynamic Girard describes and the emotional usury that Antonio exacts, but helps explain why Antonio makes use of a usurer in the first place and how he can respond so incautiously to Shylock's substitution of a pound of flesh for interest. As Adelman writes, 'spending his wealth appears to be the only form of spending himself that [Antonio] can articulate, and unlocking his purse the only form of unlocking his person' (2008: 118). 'No wonder Antonio embraces the bargain so willingly' (120).

Like Chambers, Adelman detects a narrative not unlike the narrative embedded in the Sonnets in Antonio's efforts to make use of the only resources he has in order to have Portia 'judge / Whether Bassanio had not once a love' (4.1.273–4). Adelman observes, for example, of the play's first words and of its trajectory to the trial scene, that 'the play seems […] to express the deep pathos of a man who cannot fully know his own desires and cannot allow others to know them, for whom being known would be tantamount in fantasy to being excruciatingly opened up to view – and who nonetheless wants nothing more than to be known' (2008: 121). And she follows this up with a reading of the trial scene that sees it as a 'slow striptease' in which 'the man who would not disclose himself in 1.1 stands half-naked on stage for at least seventy long lines while Shylock prepares to make incision on him' (120): a punishment that 'would be tantamount to his own confession', inscribing 'his inside on his outside, making his desire and his shame visible to all' (121). Nothing comes close to this in

Fiorentino, where the self-sacrificing Ansaldo has no interest in anything apart from enabling Giannetto.

There is a final, revealing way in which Shakespeare differentiates Antonio, not only from Ansaldo but from virtually all the other Christians in his play. Although none is well-disposed towards Jews, only Antonio aggressively 'spurns with [his] foot' and 'spits' on Shylock while actively making interest-free loans to his fellow Christians in a manner that resembles the practices of Venice's *monte di pietà*.[12] Like the singular position he maintains as Bassanio's older friend, lover and benefactor, the unusual hostility Antonio shows Shylock in their first dramatic encounters, and the back-story supplied for it in references to their past relationship, are Shakespeare's invention, and have little basis in the primary sources he consulted, possibly apart from Silvayn's *Orator* (1581) and Marlowe's *Jew of Malta* (1589/90), whose governor Ferneze, however, sermonizes in a self-consciously bombastic vein compared to which Antonio's sermonizing comes off as pietistic Christian cant:[13]

>   Mark you this, Bassanio,
> The devil can cite Scripture for his purpose.
> An evil soul producing holy witness
> Is like a villain with a smiling cheek,
> A goodly apple, rotten at the heart.
> O, what a goodly outside falsehood hath!
>
> (1.3.93–8)

It is difficult to understand why Shakespeare, in transforming the gracious Ansaldo into the censorious Antonio, would choose to inject so deforming a disposition as race-hatred into Antonio's characterization. Would taking aggressive stands against usury and its practitioners make Antonio seem more virtuous still, evincing a commitment to Christian morality deeper than his predictably Venetian devotion to profit? Did Shakespeare invest Antonio with this bias to supply Shylock with a more defensible reason to insist on his bond? Or did

Shakespeare want his audience to consider Antonio's animosity to Jews in general and Shylock in particular expressive of Antonio's moroseness, possibly even of frustrated sexual desire?

The mere number of such questions indicates how deeply Shakespeare has complicated his source material. Seeing Antonio's animosity as virtue is no doubt harder for us today than it would have been for Shakespeare's contemporaries: a problem that makes it difficult to determine whether or not *The Merchant* is – or was – a bluntly antisemitic play.[14] Contending that Antonio's animosity supplies Shylock with a motive absent from Shakespeare's original does something different; it individualizes the contention between Christian and Jew, making it less a struggle of theologies or ideologies than of persons and personalities. Connecting Antonio's aggressive antisemitism to his sexual frustration or unexplained melancholy, while it may seem altogether too modern, has the effect of returning the titular *merchant* of Venice to the foreground, bringing him into even closer alliance, psychologically speaking, with Shylock, who is also alienated, angry and as extreme in his hatred of Christians as Antonio is in his hatred of Jews. Indeed, linking Antonio's sadness (however defined) and hatred of Jews to his frustrated same-sex desire, and identifying how prevailing antisemitic biases were often grounded in associations of Jews with sodomy, psychoanalytic critic Seymour Kleinberg goes so far as to consider Antonio 'the earliest portrait of the homophobic homosexual' (1983a: 120).[15] Perhaps because I cannot imagine a virtuous practice of Christianity as intolerant and as inhumane as Antonio's, I am missing Shakespeare's point here. But perhaps Shakespeare himself could not fully account for his character's compulsive turn to cruelty every time he encounters his Jewish other, and Kleinberg is right to pursue more subterranean tracks of connection, leading him to claim that Antonio 'hates himself in Shylock: the homosexual self that Antonio has come to identify symbolically as the Jew' (120).

'Marvellously changed'

Few of the points I have made here about Antonio's same-sex desire and antisemitism are new. I elaborate on them because both characteristics are so foreign to the warm-hearted paternalism of Fiorentino's Ansaldo as to prompt renewed attention to what is effectively unsourced and thus unique and purposive in Shakespeare. In the introduction to his chapter on *The Merchant of Venice* in the second volume of *Narrative and Dramatic Sources of Shakespeare*, Geoffrey Bullough writes that 'Nothing was lost in Shakespeare's experience. Traces of his reading remained below the surface of his mind, waiting for an opportunity to float up as images or names or ideas maybe years later' (1957–74: 453–4). Why or how such traces helped re-shape Fiorentino's Ansaldo into a character whose closest analogues in Shakespeare's work arguably are the speaker of Shakespeare's same-sex sonnets, the ardent 'second Antonio' in *Twelfth Night* and the twinned protagonists of *Measure for Measure* is a mystery I have insufficient space to explore.[16] But Kenneth Gross has opened up a promising path of inquiry, observing that

> If Antonio becomes, in Angus Fletcher's words, 'a psychopath of the business world', it is not because he's a merchant or even because he can't quite separate commerce from usury, but rather because he wants his money to do what it cannot. [...] He wants to stand apart from what he also wants to make use of; he wants to make of his isolation the one stable, absolute form of fate outside the world of time [...]. In this his isolation takes on a life of its own; his defense becomes a symptom, a mask that possesses him, fixates him. With a kind of pathological generosity, he isolates himself from a merchant's ordinary fears, refusing to acknowledge the reality of the chances, gifts, and exchanges of which the world of international commerce is only the most extravagant emblem (2006: 48–9).

Gross notes here how Antonio's isolation is enforced by a fixation on principles that are not only unsustainable in the mercantile world of Venice but inconsistent with the circulation and acquisition of wealth. One wonders whether Antonio's tendency to see himself standing above the fray of Venetian mercantile commerce betrays an aspirational wish to position himself as Bassanio's social equal despite Bassanio's repeatedly making use of him for the expertise he has demonstrated in finding '[w]here money is' (1.1.184). As Steve Patterson persuasively contends, there's nothing terribly innovative in Shakespeare's depiction of Antonio's same-sex desire within a same-sex friendship: 'indeed, homoerotic desire [...] had long distinguished the protagonists of the friendship genre'. Rather, 'What *is* striking is how the amorous pursuit of a gentleman seems both strange and unproductive when risked by a merchant' (1999: 24). If it is true, as Adelman writes, that 'Dramatic characters are all to some extent partial authorial projections, insofar as they give satisfyingly concrete outer expression to internal phenomena, externalizing the theater of the inner world' (2008: 122), then we should not be altogether surprised that the disproportion in status relations between Antonio and Bassanio echoes the similar disproportion that obtains in the love-longing expressed by an aspirational gentleman for an unachievable aristocrat in Shakespeare's sonnets.

The sources of Shakespeare's plays are seldom singular and, even when they are, usually serve more as starting points than as fully fleshed-out maps faithfully followed in dramatic terms. In this respect, however, sources become crucial resources for isolating what the playwright has chosen to add, subtract, intensify, suppress or transform – and for speculating about why such choices were made in the first place. Most sources are, in the act of recycling, divorced from their original cultural surround and repurposed to serve recontextualized afterlives in Shakespeare's plays. It isn't, in this respect, just the source Shakespeare may be mining, adapting and transforming when he takes another's story and makes it his own; it is also what, in the playwright's compositional present, impinges on, informs, helps shape the way the source-story is (re)composed. And this includes not only such obvious influences as the power of censors, the preferences of patrons, the tastes of audiences, the news of the day and the whims of a queen, but the playwright's own enduring preoccupations – all of which are put on prominent display the greater the discernible distance there is between a character in his flat initial emergence and in his later, more rounded rewriting.

Notes

1 Cf. Janet Adelman: 'it has become a critical commonplace that his sadness is a consequence of his homoerotically charged feeling for Bassanio, who is about to leave him, trading in their relationship for marriage' (2008: 115).

2 This is unavoidably the first of many times I use the word 'melancholy' in place of Shakespeare's preferred term, 'sadness'. I do so because of the difficulty of finding other words to match what we discover is not only Antonio's mood of a moment but avowedly permanent disposition, and because – as Mote the Page promises to demonstrate at the start of *Love's Labour's Lost* 1.2 – they are not necessarily the same thing; meanings of the term at the time tending more towards 'seriousness' or even 'sorrow' than to the humorally charged 'melancholy'. Of course, Mote initially claims that 'looking sad' is a 'great sign' that a 'man of great spirit grows melancholy' (*LLL* 1.2.1–3), a position that also informs Gratiano's injunction that Antonio 'fish not with this melancholy bait / For this fool gudgeon, this opinion' (*MV* 1.1.101–2). Quotations from *The Merchant of Venice* are drawn from John Drakakis's Arden 3 edition (2011). Quotations from Shakespeare's other works are taken from *The Norton Shakespeare* 3 (Greenblatt 2016).

3 Adelman observes that 'Antonio may, like Hamlet, have that within which passes show, but unlike Hamlet […] Antonio takes no delight in self-analysis […] he interrupts his contemplation of [his sadness'] origins with an extraordinary three beat silence (l. 5), as though he would like to curtail scrutiny – or perhaps as though there is nothing within him to scrutinize […]. And for the

most part, the play respects Antonio's silence ..., terminating the conversation about his sadness and removing him from center stage for most of the play' (115). Arthur Little, Jr., incisively claims that 'This is an extremely important instantiation of queer mourning (and speaking). Within the aggressively heteronormative worlds of Venice, and especially Belmont, queer speaking seems almost necessarily an act of not only speaking about but performing queer "suffering", articulating and performing *lack* as a constitutive part of queer desire' (2011: 217).

4 The word 'melancholy' is uttered only when Gratiano accuses Antonio of making a show of it, 'With purpose to be dress'd in an opinion / Of wisdom, gravity, profound conceit' (see Hurrell 1961: 330–1). Hurrell further observes that 'while the slightly ambiguous "sad" is used by and of Antonio several times in the play, the more obvious "melancholy" is [...] avoided – though it is used freely by most critics of the play', concluding that 'Shakespeare's Antonio is a man mentally depressed, not a conventional melancholic' (331). By contrast, Drew Daniel (2010), relying on the recent resurgence of 'humours' criticism, takes Antonio's melancholy as a given and makes a strong case for the play's saturation in masochistic fantasies and satisfactions.

5 Engle reads Antonio's sadness as 'a market-linked phenomenon' (1986: 22).

6 As Hammond observes: 'When Salerio describes Antonio's "affection", he is using a word which was much stronger in Elizabethan English than it is today. As well as "kind feeling, fondness" it also meant "passion", especially sexual passion, and the disturbance of the mind's equanimity by violent feelings which it cannot control' (2002: 92–3). The feelings that motivate Antonio here have less to do with any imminent threat from Shylock than from the imminent loss of Bassanio to a love different in kind from anything Antonio can offer in return.

7 Leo Rockas is one of the few to speak decisively, if reductively, of this matter in claiming that when Antonio 'calls himself "a tainted wether of the flock" [...] he must mean he is impotent or homosexual' (1973: 346). Steve Patterson offers a considerably more nuanced assessment of the subject in 'The Bankruptcy of Homoerotic Amity' (1999).

8 W. H. Auden deploys a different schematic in claiming that Shakespeare 'deliberately avoids the classical formula of the Perfect Friends by making the relationship unequal' (1948: 229).

9 This sense of destiny may derive from the emergence in Antonio of a culturally specific homosexual subjectivity, informed by his estrangement from a heteronormative order that defines his difference from that great mass of others for whom the world works. Sinfield finds 'enticing' the thought 'that the development of the modern subject is in some ways dependent on the development of the gay subject' (1994: 14).

10 This passage has generated considerable interpretive debate. As James O'Rourke writes, 'Antonio's self-identification as the "tainted wether" invokes both the roots of the sacrificial Christ-figure in the Jewish Bible and the Christian mythology of predatory Jewishness [...]. But as a "*tainted* wether" [...] Antonio becomes not the lamb "without blemish" called for in Leviticus [...] but the scapegoat who has, in Tyndale, "all the iniquities of the children of Israel, and all their transgression in all their sins" put upon his head so that they can be carried off' (384–5).

11 So void of psychological interest is Fiorentino's story that the widow can say 'All is well' when she thinks she has foiled Giannetto for a third time and, in the next breath, account herself 'well content' when she discovers it is she who has been foiled (Fiorentino 2006: 93).

12 Initially funded by philanthropic contributions and maintained by the moderate interest they charged borrowers, *monte di pietà* were established in the fifteenth century to offer loans to the poor in exchange for pawned property. Their avowed purpose was to compete with, and ultimately eradicate, the practice of usury dominated by Jews.

13 One other place where we find evidence, and echoes, of the kinds of arguments Antonio brings to bear against Shylock – and, particularly, of those Shylock brings to bear against Antonio – is in the undervalued source/analogue *The Orator* (1581) by Alexandre Silvayn, which was 'Englished' from the French in 1596, probably by Anthony Munday. The Jew in this unresolved debate draws a much more secure contract than Shylock does, requiring the merchant in question to 'give' a

carefully weighed pound of his flesh to the Jew instead of having the Jew do his own carving.

14 Apparently, it was just as hard nearly a hundred years ago: 'To the modern *ethos* Antonio spitting upon the usurer's gabardine is almost a more distasteful figure than the usurer himself, and the notion that even a proven criminal may justly be compelled to change his religion as the price of his life is intolerable. But one is to suppose that the Elisabethan audience saw things after this kind' (Chambers 1925: 114).

15 Cf. O'Rourke: 'The strength of Kleinberg's interpretation of Antonio's character is that it both makes the extremity of Antonio's bigotry explicable (there is no mention of any other Venetians routinely assaulting Shylock on the Rialto), and shows the play giving coherent form to a pressing social issue' (2003: 380).

16 Initially claiming that 'the dribbling dart of love' can never 'pierce a complete bosom' (*Measure for Measure* 1.3.2–3), Duke Vincentio later proposes marriage to the novice, Isabelle, as she recoils from the threat of sexual assault. The Duke also describes Angelo as someone who 'scarce confesses / That his blood flows or that his appetite / Is more to bread than stone' (1.3.51–3). For an incisive assessment of the 'two Antonios' in *Merchant* and *Twelfth Night*, see Pequigney 1992.

10

Balthazar's Beard: Looking (Again) Into the Merchant's Closet

A. Eliza Greenstadt

Antonio, the titular merchant of Venice, opens the comedy by proclaiming himself a tragic character. 'In sooth I know not why I am so sad', he muses (1.1.1). We soon learn that he expects this very day to hear details of his friend Bassanio's plan to woo the heiress Portia. It seems Antonio fears Bassanio will abandon him for this new love.[1] Yet Antonio never gives a reason for his mood.

Since the mid-twentieth century, critics have claimed that the merchant is unable to explain his sadness because he's in the closet. In 1960 Graham Midgley contended that 'Antonio is an unconscious homosexual in a predominantly, and indeed blatantly, heterosexual society' (125). In 1983, Seymour Kleinberg presented a more self-aware depressive: 'Antonio is ... in despair because he despises himself for his homosexuality, which ... fills him with sexual shame' (113). Written over the course of gay liberation's major assault on the closet, these interpretations portray the merchant as a modern homosexual desperate to hide his pathologized sexuality from society's homophobic gaze. Criticism since the 1980s, however, has questioned this transhistorical view of gay identity. Inspired by Eve Kosofsky Sedgwick's claim that before the invention of modern homophobia, male same-sex desire existed on a homosocial continuum spanning formal, businesslike associations and deeply felt erotic attachments, scholars have envisioned a Renaissance homoeroticism free from Modernity's 'male homosexual panic' (1990: 185). So in contrast to earlier critics, for recent *Merchant* interpreters the point has been, in Jeffrey Masten's words, 'not to bring the Renaissance out of the closet, but rather to bring the closet out of the Renaissance' (1994: 302). Alan Sinfield's provocative 1996 reading of the play offered the reminder that just because today 'male-male relations, and hence male-female relations, are held in place by fear of [male] homosexuality, … we should not assume it for other times and places.... An intriguing thought, therefore, is that in early modern England same-sex relations *were not terribly important*' (1996: 130–1). Steve Patterson followed in 1999 by contending that homoeroticism was 'implicit between inseparable male companions' (10); and in the 2011 anthology *Shakesqueer*, Arthur L. Little, Jr. goes further to argue that Renaissance men could engage in marriage-like unions. Unlike earlier critics who assumed Antonio would need to hide his love for another man, this generation of *Merchant* interpreters depict a Renaissance when men could freely express their love through a rich vocabulary of public gestures. Yet they still think Antonio is closeted.

To justify what now appears to be an anachronistic view of the merchant as trying to hide a shameful sexual identity, these critics read Shakespeare's play as an allegory in which Portia's eventual victory over Antonio in their rivalry over Bassanio presages the larger historical transition Sedgwick describes, in which a premodern 'continuum of male homosocial bonds' became 'brutally structured by a secularized and psychologized homophobia' (1990: 185).[2] While according to Sedgwick this transformation began with the British Restoration, *Merchant*'s recent interpreters cite the play's proto-capitalist milieu to explain the precocious modernity of its sexual politics. According to Sinfield, 'Portia's centring of the matrimonial couple and concomitant hostility towards male friendship manifests an attitude that was to be located as "bourgeois"' (1996: 137). For Patterson, the play 'is a dramatization of the failure of male friendship in a radically shifting mercantile economy ... that seems better regulated by a social structure based on marital alliance and heterosexual reproduction' (1999: 10). Little understands *Merchant* 'as situated at a critical cultural point where the valuation of same-sex coupling is under siege by an encroaching heterofantasy world of marriage, capitalism, (re)production, and homophobia' (2011: 216). Mapping *Merchant*'s dramatic plot onto a larger historical narrative, these readings portray Portia as an enforcer of heteronormativity who uses 'tricks to prevent men from acting on desires that have been suppressed, not erased' (Patterson 1999: 31). Yet if Portia pushes Antonio into the closet, then it is difficult to explain why the merchant seems so repressed at the start of the play, before he's even met her. For Patterson, at the drama's opening Antonio 'speaks as a man at odds with the changing values of his culture' whose role 'as amorous lover seems sadly outmoded, himself a kind of anachronism' (1999: 9, 14), while Little's Antonio 'mourns. To be sure, he mourns the impending loss of Bassanio, but he mourns, too, a loss of an affirmative language and knowledge of his social and institutional place' (2011: 217). As Lara Bovilsky observes, these critics' Antonio is 'awkwardly poised temporally', as if he is 'proleptically embodying an identity whose time has not yet come' (2016: 127).

What if, in contrast, we view Antonio as both closeted and of his time? I ask because I've grown increasingly dissatisfied when I talk to students about the merchant's desire. Like Sinfield, I suggest that the sex life of Bassanio's 'dearest friend' (3.2.291) and 'bosom lover' (3.4.17) may be more interesting to us than it was to Shakespeare's audience: perhaps we're trying to open a closet that wasn't there. I describe how the words 'lover' and 'friend' were often used interchangeably; I tell them that unlike today male friends kissed and caressed in public, declared their undying love – and even slept in one bed. Then I share Sinfield's shrug: 'Whether Antonio's love is what we call sexual is a question which ... is hard to frame, let alone answer' (1996: 125). Yet even Sinfield acknowledges that Antonio's feelings are 'certainly ... intense', motivating his 'desperate bond with Shylock' as a strategy for 'holding on to Bassanio'. Sinfield admits that the play carries an 'air of homoerotic excess, especially in the idea of being bound and inviting physical violation' (1996: 125–6). Antonio's extreme decision to risk a pound of his flesh to loan Bassanio money hardly seems in keeping with a society in which 'same-sex relations were *not terribly important*'. Unimportant to whom? By drawing a historicist curtain across Antonio's exorbitant expressions of love, are we ignoring his carnal passion and unwittingly keeping him in the closet?

In what follows I interpret Sinfield's observation that *Merchant* 'allows us to explore a social arrangement in which ... same-sex passion ... appears not to have attracted very much attention' (1996: 139) as describing not the characters' lack of interest in these erotic possibilities, but rather their ability to *appear* uninterested. From this angle, we can perceive the drama as a social commentary that asks how violently destructive Antonio's passion must be before he and those surrounding him will stop studiously ignoring it. This reading entails viewing the closet in *Merchant* not as a hiding place for an individual's secret sexual identity but as the shared code by which a community maintains certain erotic relationships as open secrets. Recent work on Renaissance friendship has reflected the towering influence of Alan Bray, who has shown that male intimate relationships were vulnerable to imputations of 'filthiness' if they crossed lines of social class or appeared openly mercenary (1994: 48). Others have demonstrated that the crucial guarantee of friendship's respectability was the perception of likeness – whether of class, wealth, age or gender. From this evidence it has seemed reasonable to conclude, with Masten, that 'alongside the condemned homoeroticism of sodomy (with its attendant discourses of "disparitie" and social disruption), there was the sanctioned homoeroticism of male friendship' (1997: 36–7). Yet writers on amity did not openly approve sex between men; instead, they contrasted the mutual and steady love between similar friends with the carnal desire that drove disparate lovers to seek bodily gratification. As Laurie Shannon observes, inequality between partners may itself have been the 'trigger' for articulating male-male eroticism (2000: 190). In this representational environment, men could pass off otherwise dubious desires behind the virtuous cloak of friendship's similitude.

In *Merchant*, Antonio uses the pretence of friendship's likeness – what the play calls *kindness* – to disguise and advance his own passionate ends.[3] The bargain he strikes with Shylock pretends to the friendly terms of an interest-free loan but risks an erotically laden sacrifice of flesh. Although the characters surrounding Antonio treat the merchant's manipulative displays of self-denial as if they're exemplary acts of friendly generosity, this charade becomes more difficult to sustain as the bond's tragic consequences become unavoidable. Portia heightens the tension with her sarcastic jabs at friendship's lofty rhetoric, which some interpret as homophobic taunts intimidating the merchant into silence. But Portia doesn't create the play's closet – she attacks it. Her disguise as the 'learned doctor' Balthazar (4.1.104) perverts the homosocial structure suppressing both her and the merchant's desires. After saving Antonio and Bassanio from Shylock's bond, Balthazar enters a new pact with them via the 'ring trick' that grants Portia masculine privilege but only by ironizing it. When in the play's final scene Bassanio realizes he has entered into a mock contract with a simulated man, he jokingly invites the 'doctor' to bed. This is the first time a character acknowledges desire for a member of his own sex. Moreover, by highlighting what Bruce R. Smith describes as the 'eroticized ... power distinctions that set one male above another' in Renaissance society (1991: 194) – specifically the oppositions stranger/lover, boy/man –

Bassanio's quip pierces the bland cover of amity's homosocial continuum to reveal the hidden desire for the friend. Instead of entering a closet, *Merchant* ends by prying one open.

* * *

While Antonio's pronouncement of his sadness may provoke questions about his individual personality, his behavior also invokes established stereotypes of homoerotic melancholy reaching as far back as the shepherd Corydon, who in Virgil's Second Eclogue laments that his rustic gifts have failed to win the boy Alexis's favours. By the time of *Merchant*, several would-be Corydons had already graced the verse of Elizabethan England. Edmund Spenser's 1579 *Shepheardes Calender* featured Hobbinol's unrequited yearning for the boy Colin; a decade later Christopher Marlowe ventriloquized Virgil's swain in his 'The Passionate Shepherd to His Love' (*c*. 1588); and in 1594 Richard Barnfield published the shepherd Daphnis's versified attempts to seduce the reluctant Ganymede. When a few years later Antonio opened *The Merchant of Venice* by admitting his sadness, his situation too resembled Corydon's. Like the lovelorn shepherd courting his master's favourite boy, Antonio is divided from his beloved by social difference: he is a wealthy merchant while 'Lord Bassanio' (1.1.69) is a moneyless aristocrat. Like Corydon, in the past Antonio has plied his beloved with gifts. And like Corydon, he now finds that his offerings have failed to bind his beloved to him. Yet unlike Corydon – and unlike his Renaissance copies – Antonio does not name the cause of his misery. When his companions ask him if love has provoked his sadness, he replies only, 'Fie, fie' (1.1.46). Compared to the era's volubly pining shepherds, the merchant seems repressed. Though this opacity makes him appear presciently modern, Antonio is less likely reacting to an impending homophobic regime than to his own period's taboos. While Spenser, Marlowe and Barnfield safely cast their homoerotic lovers in an irrecoverable pastoral world, Antonio instead occupies the contemporary landscape of Renaissance Venice. This environment may inhibit him from speaking the cause of his sorrow. But by invoking, then choking, a homoerotic literary tradition, *Merchant* does not portray Antonio as mourning an impossible, outmoded love. Rather, his passion simmers, unacknowledged, as the drama unfolds. This creates the possibility that he could fulfil his desire in the present.

In its early modern setting, this homoerotic potential appears less elegiac than symptomatic. This is because it manifests as a distortion of the Renaissance code of friendship. Desiderius Erasmus explained this code in his *De ratione studii*, where he used Virgil's Second Eclogue as an example to advise schoolmasters on how to expose their charges to classical texts that 'may corrupt the young'. To avoid harming students' morals, Erasmus advises, teachers should frame Virgil's poem – a mainstay of the English grammar school curriculum – as a negative example to prove that 'friendship can only exist among similar people, for similarity promotes mutual good will, while dissimilarity on the other hand is the parent of hatred and distrust'. The conscientious instructor should emphasize not only the difference in age between the shepherd and the boy, but other distinctions as well: 'Corydon is from the countryside; Alexis is from the city. Corydon is a shepherd; Alexis is a courtier. … Corydon is ugly, while Alexis is handsome. … In short, they differ in every respect'. Attachments between such disparate types can only achieve what Plato described as a 'terrestrial' love grounded in 'the transience of earthly things or even filthiness [*turpibus*]'. Companions who are similar, in contrast, may aspire to Plato's 'celestial' love, 'rooted in the goods of the soul', producing 'true and honourable affections'. So the schoolmaster should teach that 'among the good, love is always mutual, while among the common [*vulgares*] it is common for one to love, the other to hate, one to pursue, the other to flee' (1978: 683–6). Erasmus frames differences between partners – in attributes and hence levels of interest – as signals that their relationship, rather than being rational, friendly and good, is rather passionate, carnal and filthy.

This code explains the extravagant way Antonio embellishes familiar Renaissance tropes of amity. When Bassanio asks him for a loan to pursue his courtship of Portia, the merchant lavishly offers, 'My purse, my person, my extremest means / Lie all unlocked to your occasions' (1.1.138–9). By lending Bassanio money at no interest and with little expectation of return, Antonio pledges to share his wealth in accordance with Aristotle's famous dictum that friends were 'one soule in two bodies' and so, as Michel de Montaigne explained, everything was 'by effect common betweene them' (1603: I.93–4). The merchant's offer, however, implies carnal as well as spiritual merger: *purse* was slang for vagina (Williams 1994: 1116–19), and the sexual meaning of unlocking becomes unmistakable when in the next scene Portia reveals that the man with the key to the right casket will gain entry to her own purse and person. Antonio literalizes his bodily investment when he hazards a pound of his flesh to secure the loan from Shylock. According to Patterson, Antonio becomes the 'prototype of the passionate friend' who 'risk their lives for one another, swoon when parted, publicly proclaim their love, and make hyperbolic vows of eternal devotion' (1999: 10–11). Yet unlike the friend in exemplary tales who endangers himself to save his companion from the brink of death, Antonio gruesomely wagers his flesh merely to finance Bassanio's mercenary plot to wed 'a lady richly left' (1.1.161). The merchant secures the exorbitant sum of 3,000 ducats to provide his friend with luxuries such as 'rare new liveries' (2.2.102–3) that allow him to 'hold a rival place' (1.1.174) with Portia's other suitors, even though she's attainable by a test that could be won by a penniless stowaway. And when Antonio must face his seemingly pointless (self-)immolation, he insists that Bassanio witness his death, hammering home the enormity of his sacrifice. In Antonio's hands, the friend's hyperbolic proclamations of love appear attempts to bribe and manipulate. Antonio acts less like a friend obeying the call of selfless devotion and more like a lover in the throes of a greedy obsession. While even critics who see the merchant as a stereotypical friend recognize his behaviour as 'excessive' (Patterson 1999: 23; Sinfield 1996: 126), others interpret Antonio symptomatically, viewing his self-destructiveness as a psychological drive toward self-exposure, masochism or nihilism.[4] Maybe, but we should also notice that his desperate violation of friendship conventions is itself conventional. As Montaigne put it, 'In true friendship, [love] is ... equally tempered, a constant and setled heate, all pleasure and smoothnes, that hath no pricking or stinging in it', whereas 'lustfull love ... is ... but a ranging and mad desire in following that which flies us' (1603: I.91). According to this formula, Antonio's love for Bassanio can only rise to heights of carnal passion if it is unfulfilled. The merchant himself signals the performative nature of his emotions when he describes the world as a 'stage, where every man must play a part, / And mine a sad one' (1.1.78–9). By acting the part of a jilted and grasping lover even as he protests friendship, Antonio signals that the merger he seeks with Bassanio is one of not only souls, but also flesh.

This means Antonio can only express his desires by transgressing the amity ideal that offers them moral cover. Shakespeare's play resists fully psychologizing this transgression by formalizing the bond of friendship in the loan agreement Antonio seals with Bassanio and Shylock. At first it seems the merchant will emphasize his selfless generosity by contrasting himself with the usurer to whom he is forced to appeal. Antonio translates the biblical prohibition against charging interest to 'brother[s]' as opposed to 'stranger[s]' (Deut. 23.20) into the language of amity when he directs Shylock to lend the money 'not / As to thy friends, for when did friendship take / A breed for barren metal of his friend?' (1.3.127–9). By accusing the usurer of breeding money, Antonio highlights the distinction between self-interested moneylending and interest-free friendship. Shylock surprises the men, however, by offering, 'I would be friends with you and have your love, / ... / Supply your present wants, and take no doit / Of usance for my moneys' (1.3.134–7). By promising to forego interest, Shylock recasts the loan as a pledge of friendship. He adds, 'This is kind I offer', and Antonio agrees, declaring 'Content, in faith: I'll seal to such a bond / And say there is much kindness in the

Jew' (1.3.138, 148–9). Emphasizing *kindness*'s connotations of both generosity and sameness, Antonio portrays the Jew's gesture as uncharacteristically charitable and therefore less alien. To underscore that the bond is a pact of friendship based in similitude, *kind* and *kindness* together appear six times in the scene, with Antonio exclaiming at its conclusion, 'The Hebrew will turn Christian, he grows kind' (174). But belying this apparent harmony is the forfeit Shylock proposes: a pound of the merchant's flesh. Once Antonio defaults on the loan and the usurer demands the penalty, their bond forms shackles of subjection rather than ties of affinity.

Because it ostensibly fulfils a contract of friendship, Shylock's vindictiveness threatens not just Antonio's life but the pretence of *kindness* that sanctifies bonds among Venice's elite Christian men. So as it increasingly seems that the merchant will endure the contract's violent penalty, his Christian companions don't seem curious about why he and Bassanio would enter such a grizzly bargain in the service of their supposedly equal and mutual love. When the barely distinguishable Salarino and Salanio decide they must warn Antonio that Shylock may try to exact his bloody forfeit, Salarino says of the merchant, 'A kinder gentleman treads not the earth' (2.8.35) and then recounts how Antonio reacted to Bassanio's departure to woo Portia:

> Bassanio told him he would make some speed
> Of his return. He answered, 'Do not so,
> Slubber not business for my sake, Bassanio,
> But stay the very riping of the time;
> And for the Jew's bond, which he hath of me,
> Let it not enter in your mind of love.
> Be merry, and employ your chiefest thoughts
> To courtship, and such fair ostents of love
> As shall conveniently become you there.'
>
> (2.8.37–45)

In his farewell, Antonio behaves as a model friend who puts the other's happiness above his own. Yet compare the words Salarino reports with those he brings to Belmont in a letter from Antonio requesting Bassanio's return to Venice:

> Sweet Bassanio, ... my bond to the Jew is forfeit, and, since, in paying it, it is impossible I should live, all debts are cleared between you and I if I might but see you at my death. Notwithstanding, use your pleasure; if your love do not persuade you to come, let not my letter.
>
> (3.2.314–20)

In contrast to Salarino's earlier report that the merchant did not want the bond to enter Bassanio's 'mind of love', Antonio's letter reminds Bassanio that he still owes him a debt that will only be cleared by witnessing his death.

Such possessive manipulation clearly violated the friendship code. Erasmus distinguished letters honestly attempting to solicit friendship (*amicitia*) from 'filthy' (*turpem*) or 'amatory' (*amatoriae*) letters which, in contrast, attempt to arouse a 'spirit of mutual love' by means of 'two main instruments of persuasion: praise and pity'. The latter 'demonstrate intense love joined to deep despair', even threatening that if our love is not granted 'we are resolved to cut short a cruel life by whatever means possible' (1985: 331–2). Although Antonio doesn't threaten suicide, following his letter's delivery he confides to Salanio,

> These griefs and losses have so bated me
> That I shall hardly spare a pound of flesh
> Tomorrow to my bloody creditor.
> ... Pray God Bassanio come
> To see me pay his debt, and then I care not.
>
> (3.3.32–6)

Antonio's need to dramatize his own suffering hardly jives with Bassanio's description of him moments before as

> The dearest friend to me, the kindest man,
> The best-conditioned and unwearied spirit
> In doing courtesies; and one in whom
> The ancient Roman honour more appears
> Than any that draws breath in Italy.
>
> (3.2.291–5)

These set pieces attesting to Antonio's virtue prime us to gloss over passive-aggressive behaviour that would otherwise threaten his friendship with 'amatory' disgrace. If his inability to name the source of his feelings at the play's beginning makes him appear a victim of false consciousness, by the third act we can understand why he has 'much ado to know' himself (1.1.6). Both Antonio and everyone surrounding him describe him in ways that are completely out of line with his actual behaviour.

Shylock helps support the impression of Antonio's virtue by taking the role of avenging villain and assigning the merchant the part of innocent victim. But Portia disrupts this reassuring dynamic. Although she intervenes to save Antonio from Shylock she also replaces the usurer as the drama's sardonic commentator on amity's pieties. When Bassanio is forced to admit to her that he is not only penniless but has 'engaged' himself to a 'dear friend' (3.2.260), she reassures him she has no problem sending him to the rescue with her money: 'since you are dear bought, I will love you dear' (312). Implying that Antonio purchased Bassanio with his loan, Portia transforms the stock epithet 'dear friend' into a statement of financial worth, crassly exposing the material basis for the men's supposedly spiritual bond. She more directly takes aim at friendship's pretences when Lorenzo praises her for her 'godlike amity' in sending Bassanio to rescue 'so dear a lover' of her husband (3.4.3, 7). As she did earlier, Portia twists Lorenzo's 'dear' into a measure of economic value, reasoning that there must be likeness between companions

> Whose souls do bear an equal yoke of love.
> Which makes me think that this Antonio,

Being the bosom lover of my lord,
Must needs be like my lord. If it be so,
How little is the cost I have bestowed
In purchasing the semblance of my soul
From out the state of hellish cruelty.

(3.4.13–21)

Drawing on the trope of amity's similitude, Portia assures Lorenzo of her faith that, as her husband's friend, Antonio 'must needs be like' him. But then she undercuts friendship's fantasy of communalism by assuring Lorenzo that she knows exactly how 'dear a lover' Antonio is of her lord, and that he is well worth the investment.

Amplifying Lorenzo's 'dear ... lover' to 'bosom lover', Portia anticipates the moment when Antonio will fulfil the bond by exposing his 'bosom' to be penetrated 'Nearest the ... heart' (4.1.241, 229). Presiding over the court proceedings in her disguise as Balthazar, Portia provokes this crisis by luring Shylock to the cusp of penetrating the merchant's flesh – revealing not only the usurer's murderous intentions, but also the merchant's amorous ones. Grasping Bassanio's hand, Antonio speaks what he believes are his last words:

Commend me to your honourable wife;
Tell her the process of Antonio's end,
Say how I loved you, speak me fair in death,
And, when the tale is told, bid her be judge
Whether Bassanio had not once a love.
Repent but you that you shall lose your friend
And he repents not that he pays your debt.
For if the Jew do cut but deep enough
I'll pay it instantly with all my heart.

(4.1.269–77)

Antonio is at last staging the scene when Bassanio will bear witness that 'your friend / ... pays your debt'. Grotesquely literalizing the conceit of 'bosom lovers', Antonio offers his disembowelled heart as proof of 'how I loved you' not only to Bassanio, but to his 'honourable wife'. By paying the ultimate price, Antonio will prove that her husband 'had ... once a love', ensuring that Portia will never surpass this gesture of devotion. What Antonio doesn't realize is that, as Balthazar, Bassanio's wife is already present to 'be judge' of this pledge of faith. The irony increases when Bassanio rises to Antonio's heights and goes higher:

> Antonio, I am married to a wife
> Which is as dear to me as life itself;
> But life itself, my wife and all the world
> Are not with me esteemed above thy life.
> I would lose all, ay, sacrifice them all
> Here to this devil, to deliver you.
>
> (4.1.278–83)

Witnessing Bassanio offer up not only his own life but hers in exchange for Antonio's, Portia quips, 'Your wife would give you little thanks for that / If she were by to hear you make the offer' (4.1.284–5). The wife, supposedly waiting silently offstage to be disposed of, voices her protest at being treated as moveable goods.

Portia forces her husband to choose between the bonds of amity and matrimony when, as Balthazar, after the proceedings she asks Bassanio for her betrothal ring as recompense for saving Antonio from Shylock. One line of critics reads this 'ring trick' as Portia's strategy to defeat Antonio as her romantic and ideological rival. So Jonathan Goldberg claims that Portia's 'power as boy is directed against and serves to police Antonio and Bassanio and to separate them; ... the boy-girl figures a triumph for the patriarchy' (2010: 142). For Sinfield, Portia 'does not disguise herself ... to evade hetero-patriarchal pressures', but to advance a strategy that 'is purposefully heterosexist' (1996: 127); and Little likewise views Portia as 'patriarchally and homophobically empowered' (2011: 222). For these interpreters, Portia may attack the patriarchal institution of friendship that would position her as chattel to be exchanged, but only in the service of a new heteronormative regime of monogamous wedlock.[5] Not all critics have been so ready to label Portia a homophobe, however. Edward J. Geisweidt contends that by giving the ring to Antonio to return to Bassanio, Portia 'indicates her intentions to include Antonio as a necessary component of her matrimony, of her desire, and Bassanio's desire' (2009: 350). And according to Will Stockton, 'The strange path of the ring through three hands signal[s] not an obvious victory for heterosexual marriage over queer friendship' but 'a conjunction of marriage and friendship ... in which husband and wife, husband and friend, and friend and wife, are all one flesh' (2017: 56).[6]

Whether they view Portia's actions as punishing or inclusive, these interpretations underplay the challenge her gender masquerade poses to the patriarchal structure supporting both friendship and marriage. As Karen Newman observes, Portia's disguise as Balthazar is a simulation that, 'by denaturalizing gender-coded behaviors[,] ... perverts authorized systems of gender and power'. Newman argues that Portia's performance 'short-circuits' a homosocial system that depended on the exchange of women to secure male bonds (1987: 33, 26). This 'hetero-patriarchy', I would add, functioned by refusing to recognize that the men who bought, exchanged or possessed female bodies were capable of being placed in similarly eroticized states of subjection. Antonio courts such subjection by commodifying his body. In the courtroom Shylock claims he has as much right to his 'dearly bought' (4.1.99) pound of the merchant's flesh as the Venetians do to their 'purchased slave[s]' (4.1.89). Balthazar disallows the Jew's claim by invoking a law prosecuting Shylock as an 'alien' threatening the life of a 'citizen' (4.1.345–7), a move that reasserts tribal affiliation over wealth by reserving 'the freedom of the state' (3.2.277) for Christians and bondage for strangers. Returned to his social standing,

Antonio wins his freedom but apparently loses the ability to showcase his passion by subverting his own patriarchal privilege. But while Balthazar restores order, the judge's identity is itself disordered. Not only a woman pretending to be male, the 'young doctor of Rome' (4.1.151–2) is an outsider who assumes the supreme authority of Venice and a youth who precociously takes a man's role. Crossing the lines separating female and male, stranger and citizen, boy and man, Balthazar exposes the traits distinguishing those subjects with the patriarchal right to exchange the bodies of others from those whose bodies were subject to such exchanges. Though Balthazar enforces the law, by assuming masculine privilege from a critical distance, Portia's cross-dressed performance comes to represent the possibility of forging relations of *kindness* not in a haze of false consciousness, but under the spell of a conscious fiction. Through Balthazar, *Merchant* find alternative ways to express desires that would otherwise either appear as denigrated difference or disappear in the silence of indifference.

* * *

Just when Balthazar releases Antonio and Bassanio from Shylock's power, the judge commits them to a new bond of ostensible friendship. Like the pound of flesh, the pledge securing this bond of *kindness* – Portia's betrothal ring – has a carnal weight in vast excess of the value it supposedly carries in the exchange. Portia makes the trinket's symbolism explicit when she bestows it on Bassanio after he passes the casket test designed to select her husband. Portia reclaims 'the right of voluntary choosing' (2.1.16) denied her by her father's will, announcing to Bassanio,

> Myself, and what is mine, to you and yours
> Is now converted ...
>   even now, but now,
> This house, these servants, and this same myself,
> Are yours, my lord's. I give them with this ring
> Which, when you part from, lose or give away,
> Let it presage the ruin of your love,

And be my vantage to exclaim on you.

(3.2.166–74)

If her father materialized the 'prize' (2.9.59) of her fortune, virginity and vagina in the lead casket, Portia instead embodies them in her ring. As she gives the jewellery to Bassanio, she ritually converts 'myself, and what is mine' to her husband, acting simultaneously as bride and the father giving her away. But as if she doesn't trust her father's test to try her suitor's mettle, she makes the gift conditional: her legalistic language of having a 'vantage' to 'exclaim on' Bassanio suggests that the ring's loss might constitute a breach of contract annulling their union. Since the ring represents what she calls the 'full sum of me' (3.2.157), her fear that he'll lose it reads less as sexual jealousy than anxiety that Bassanio will reduce her body, like the jewellery itself, to fungible goods.

This fear would seem to be realized when, in the courtroom, her husband offers to trade her life for Antonio's. Although Portia's joking 'little thanks' recognizes Bassanio's lavish gesture as unenforceable, she tests his sincerity when, as Balthazar, she asks for her ring. Since the couple have not consummated their marriage, the request tests not just Bassanio's personal commitment but the match's very validity. Antonio adds his own emotional stakes to the decision when, after Bassanio at first refuses to break his oath to Portia, he beseeches,

My lord Bassanio, let him have the ring.
Let his deservings and my love withal
Be valued 'gainst your wife's commandement.

(4.1.445–7)

As Lawrence Hyman observes, Bassanio's 'opportunity to give and hazard all that he has comes about when his friend and his wife, from different motives, both act to make him give up the ring' (1970: 115). Hyman refers to the demand emblazoned on the winning casket: 'Who chooseth me must give and hazard all he hath' (2.7.9). Whether Bassanio took that risk is debatable;

however, when he at last agrees to give the ring to Balthazar, he endangers the fortune he just achieved in Portia. Bassanio has weighed Portia's full sum against Antonio's purse and person and made his choice.

Critics typically view Bassanio as facing a decision between his commitments to Antonio and Portia and hence the competing demands of same-sex and cross-sex bonds. But in the choice Antonio offers, two different kinds of male bonding occupy one side of the scales. The merchant asks his friend to weigh *both* the judge's 'deservings *and* my love' against his wife's 'commandement'. As in the bond with Shylock, this triangular arrangement deflects attention from Antonio's desire by embedding it within a more general pledge of *kindness*. Bassanio offers the gift after the Duke prompts Antonio to 'gratify' Balthazar, 'For in my mind you are much bound to him' (4.1.402–3). When Antonio and Bassanio then ask the judge to 'Take some remembrance of us as a tribute' (4.1.418), their offer represents what Lorna Hutson describes as 'a particular institution of the gift' in which 'the exchange of rings, knives, and caps' becomes a '"pledge" or "wager" of the good faith and honour of friends to one another' (1994: 5). To this pledge of gratitude for Balthazar's 'deservings', Antonio adds the emotional weight of his 'love withal'. He can do so because friendship's homosocial continuum allowed the same gestures to signify both the superficial courtesy owed a legal functionary and the deep devotion compelled by a 'bosom lover'.

Portia puts pressure on this indifference when she chastises her husband for returning to Belmont without the ring. Recounting that he at first refused to part with Portia's gift even to the man who had saved 'the very life of my dear friend', Bassanio explains

> I was enforced to send it after him,
> I was beset with shame and courtesy,
> My honour would not let ingratitude
> So much besmear it.

(5.1.216–19)

Bassanio fails to mention that it was Antonio's ultimatum that 'enforced' him to change his mind, for fear of 'ingratitude' toward the merchant's sacrificial gesture of love. The eroticized violence of Antonio's act disappears into the coercive force of a generalized system of 'honour' among male peers. But Portia will have none of it. She counters Bassanio's excuse by threatening that if he really gave the ring to a 'worthy doctor', then 'I will become as liberal as you; / I'll not deny him anything I have, / No, not my body, nor my husband's bed' (5.1.226–8). As Geisweidt points out, Portia's threat of cuckoldry highlights 'the latent desire between Antonio and Bassanio' (349). By insisting on the ring's amorous significance, Portia disallows the alibi of Balthazar's 'deservings' that conceals Bassanio's actual reason for parting with the precious gift: Antonio's love.

The scene shifts toward resolution when Bassanio, browbeaten, attempts to make a fresh vow to Portia, swearing 'by my soul, ... / I never more will break an oath with thee'. Antonio characteristically inserts himself, declaring,

> I once did lend my body for his wealth,
> Which, but for him that had your husband's ring,
> Had quite miscarried. I dare be bound again:
> My soul upon the forfeit, that your lord
> Will never more break faith advisedly.
>
> (5.1.247–53)

Antonio rewrites Bassanio's vow as a three-way bargain structured like the agreement with Shylock, in which he stands surety for Bassanio's oath by offering himself as forfeit. Although he appears to cleanse this new arrangement of the original's carnal taint by pledging his soul rather than his flesh, he not only invokes but also presses the earlier debt by taking Bassanio's oath to 'never more break' faith and adding the legalistic proviso 'advisedly'. This recalls the moment when Gratiano chased after the departing Balthazar, explaining, 'My lord Bassanio, upon more *advice*, / Hath sent you here this ring' (4.2.6–7; emphasis added). By adding 'advisedly' to Bassanio's oath, Antonio hints that it was he – not some fussy honour code – that 'enforced' Portia's husband to part with her ring. Now acknowledging that he is 'the subject of these quarrels' (238), he promises to respect Bassanio's mended faith to Portia, but only by asserting his prior claim to her husband's loyalty. Declaring 'Then you shall be his surety', she appears to accept Antonio's terms, honouring his role as go-between by handing him a ring to give to Bassanio, directing, 'Bid him keep it better than the other' (5.1.254–5).

Whether they believe Portia ultimately excludes or includes Antonio when she gives him the ring to return to her husband, critics agree that the final passing of the jewellery symbolically resolves these characters' rivalry – and hence the conflict between marriage and friendship. In fact, rather than resolving the comedy in a vision of social harmony, the ring exchange ends it on a note of festive inversion. Bassanio accepts the ring from Portia, but then the ritual breaks down. He never swears the proposed oath. When he recognizes that the jewellery Antonio has handed him is 'the same I gave the doctor', Portia mock-apologizes: 'Pardon me, Bassanio, / For by this ring the doctor lay with me' (257–9). Learning that she was Balthazar all along, Bassanio reframes this threat as a solicitation: 'Sweet doctor, you shall be my bedfellow. / When I am absent, then lie with my wife!' (284–5). The lovers' final passing of the rings is not sealed with a vow but crowned with a punchline.

Bassanio's solicitation owes its bawdiness to the tension that has been building throughout the scene between casual and passionate friendship. On its face his invitation for the 'doctor' to be his bedfellow is entirely in keeping with the period's spiritualized notions of amity. The ménage he imagines is not unlike the one reportedly enjoyed by the playwrights Francis Beaumont and John Fletcher, who 'lived together, … both batchelors; lay together … had one wench in the house between them, which they did so admire' (Aubrey 1898: 96). As Masten observes, 'There seems to be nothing to cover, no need for closet space in this shared household' (1993: 303). Shielding the playwrights' sleeping arrangements from licentiousness is the biographer's assurance that they shared a 'wonderfull consilimity of phansey ..., which caused the dearnesse of friendship between them' (Aubrey 1898: 95). For Montaigne, such perfect similitude distinguished 'those we ordinarily call friendes and amities, [who] are but aecquaintances and familiarities' from 'perfect and true' friends who, 'being no other than one soule in two bodies' hold 'All things ... by effect common betweene them. Wils, thoughts, judgements, goods, [and] wives' (1603: I.92–4). When Bassanio solicits the 'sweet doctor' to share his bed and wife, he treats him as such a 'perfect and true' second self. Yet moments before, this same doctor threatened him with cuckoldry. Portia could taunt, 'I'll have that doctor for my bedfellow' (233) because Bassanio has just been at pains to depict Balthazar as 'but those we ordinarily call friendes ..., [who] are but aecquaintances'. When Bassanio insisted that the doctor was a mere casual friend, far from regarding the civil servant as deserving intimate privileges he feared him as an interloper in the marital bed. Bassanio's solicitation gains its erotic charge by suddenly addressing the formerly 'worthy' doctor as 'sweet', creating a kind of comic persistence of vision: the impression lingers that he is inviting a stranger to bed. Beaumont and Fletcher 'lay together' in apparent innocence, but Bassanio's 'bedfellow' euphemisms are tainted. As a result, his fantasy acknowledges that some husbands want to be cuckolded and – for the first time in the play – that some friends want to have sex with each other. Rather than resolving the tensions between friendship and marriage, the 'doctor' releases erotic energies that violate both.

Onstage, of course, Bassanio directs his solicitation to the wife he is about to bed for the first time. This marital frame gives him cover to finally express the desire for the friend that has been building throughout the play. But so does the fact that Portia's male alter-ego is a pubescent boy. As Stephen Orgel observes, in the period 'boys were, like women – but unlike men – acknowledged objects of sexual attraction for men' (1996: 70). Bassanio's joking invitation to the doctor couches desire for the friend within a display of lust for acknowledged objects of sexual attraction – the wife and her pubescent male doppelgänger. But if the sudden onset of Bassanio's interest in the 'sweet' doctor troubles the boundary between stranger and lover, it also exploits the gap between boy and man. In this space there opens the possibility of carnal friendship. Certainly, like other Shakespearean husbands, Bassanio reacts with delighted relief upon learning that the pretty youth he's grown so fond of is actually a woman he can marry. Yet unlike these grateful spouses, Bassanio has had no opportunity for flirtatious banter with his cross-dressed wife; he treats Balthazar in the courtroom as a mere functionary. This makes his abrupt attraction to Portia's male alter-ego appear unmotivated.[7] Lacking an emotional explanation, we are encouraged to notice that the doctor's change in status from stranger to lover involves a shift from man to boy. In the play this is a demotion not necessarily in age but in social class. In Shakespeare's time *boy* maintained its original meaning as a young servant or rogue (Smith 1991: 194), and Portia's disguise highlights the status difference between boys and men. In contrast to Shakespeare's other cross-dressed heroines, when disguised as a male youth she does not take the servile occupations of page or peasant but instead wields the patriarchal authority reserved for manhood. We are reminded of the judge's precociousness when the esteemed Doctor Bellario introduces him to the court with the recommendation: 'I beseech you, let his lack of years be no impediment to let him lack a reverend estimation, for I never knew so young a body with so old a head' (4.1.158–60). Shylock finds biblical precedent for the legal prodigy when he praises Balthazar as 'A Daniel come to judgement; yea, a Daniel!' (219) – a reference to the Apocrypha's story of how the 'yong childe' Daniel's forensic acumen saved Susannah (Susanna 45). Such reminders prompt the audience to notice the youth of the boy actor playing the man's part of the sombre judge. Within the theatrical world, Balthazar's age difference reads as sex difference. When Portia first envisions her disguise, she imagines how she will 'speak between the change of man and boy / With a reed voice' (3.4.66–7): her voice's high pitch signals the change of not only 'man and boy' but woman and boy, stressing that 'the Elizabethan ideal ... of aristocratic womanhood', as Orgel points out, 'was what we would call boyish' (1996: 70). This perception of physical resemblance reflected women and boys' shared subordination since, Orgel observes, both were 'treated as a medium of exchange within the patriarchal structure' (1996: 103). It makes little difference whether beneath the judge's robes we perceive Portia or the boy actor playing her. Either way we're witnessing a simulation of patriarchal authority by someone who is, by definition, excluded from it. In the courtroom Bassanio is indifferent to Balthazar because he takes the 'worthy doctor' at face value: as a patriarchal authority inappropriate for lascivious interest. But when Portia reveals the woman behind the judge, she brings the 'sweet doctor' down to her subordinate, eroticized level. The doctor – who traverses the boundaries between male and female, lover and stranger, man and boy – is like the merchant, who crosses the line between privilege and denigration. In the absence of any other motivation, Bassanio's desire seems trained on that transgression itself.

As the final word on the ring ritual, Bassanio's joke enacts a new, ironic contract. Addressed to Portia, his jesting invitation is a command to remain chaste: she must share his bed and, when he is 'absent', sleep with his wife – i.e., alone. But the domestic arrangement he actually describes is what the ring exchange appears already to have solemnized. Portia's banter established that the trinket grants sexual access to its recipient. If so, then Antonio gained this access to her when she gave him the ring, and he offered his own person to Bassanio by in turn handing the ring to him. Although Bassanio addresses his solicitation to Portia, the ring dumbshow puts Antonio in the position of the 'sweet' friend, who can both be Bassanio's bedfellow and lie with his wife. The joke's humour – and meaning – arises from its refusal to decide the doctor's ultimate identity. Thus the transition from Portia's 'the doctor lay with me' to Bassanio's 'doctor, ... / lie with my wife' is similar to the ironic resolution of Shakespeare's Sonnet 138, when the speaker describes how he 'lie[s]' with his mistress, 'and she with me, / And in our faults by lies we flattered be' (138.10–14). When Portia confronts Bassanio with his loss of the ring, she mockingly encourages him to 'swear by your double self' (5.1.245). But exposing her own double self gives them both the option to lie with the doctor. This lie acknowledges Portia's ownership of her body by envisioning her in a sex act that is and is not cuckoldry and so evades a code of womanhood that would force her to either be objectified as a wife or vilified as a whore. The lie allows Bassanio to be bedfellows with a man who both is and is not a friend and so evade a code of manhood that would force him to either be celebrated as a virtuous companion or condemned as a filthy sodomite.

Personifying *kindness* itself in the doctor, *The Merchant of Venice* ends by giving the lie to any notion of absolute equivalence, any chance that one could even the scales without taking into account the added weight of the instrument constructed to achieve the balance. Shakespeare's play exposes the libidinous excess that such balancing acts simultaneously produce and deny. While Antonio lent his body to make this excess tragically visible, ultimately the boy actor becomes the theatrical rather than sacrificial surrogate for surplus desire. By self-consciously assuming various patriarchal roles, the boy democratically offers the potential to valourize this desire through the shared willing suspension of disbelief – whether in a marriage, a friendship or a theatre. The unreachable boy of pastoral elegy, glimpsed obliquely in Antonio's opening lament, returns in the final act looking more like the gender-fluid protagonist of pastoral romance, wandering through a landscape outside the patriarchal law. At the same time, Portia/Balthazar maintains an ironic distance from the roles s/he assumes only if we continue to recognize certain categories of human as denied the right to own and exchange the bodies of others. While the doctor is able to move seamlessly among the positions of wife, mistress, boy, friend and judge, the same cannot be said for all the characters in this play. Several are conspicuously missing from the final picture of community gathered onstage. The rejected foreign suitors, including the Moroccan prince whose dark 'complexion' (1.2.125; 2.7.79) Portia finds repellent, have left Belmont after vowing never to marry, effectively reducing themselves to lifelong boyhood. Shylock, too, has been denied his patriarchal rights when Antonio forces him to bequeath his fortune to 'the gentleman / That lately stole his daughter' (4.1.380–1). When Balthazar invokes the law against aliens to threaten Shylock's life, *kindness*'s logic is so strained that the Jew must flee the stage, never to return. But when, at the play's conclusion, Portia reveals she is Balthazar, she conjures the ghosts of such strangers and boys who, by virtue of age, class, religion, nation or race have been excluded from the drama's happy ending.

Perhaps the closest we come to knowing whether Antonio joins in Portia and Bassanio's plan to embrace a fabricated manhood and 'lie with the doctor' is when, learning from her that his ships have 'safely come to ground', in his final line Antonio addresses Portia as 'Sweet lady' (5.1.286) – an endearment echoing Bassanio's solicitation to the 'Sweet doctor'. The epithet suggests an intimacy that can be glimpsed earlier when, after the court proceedings, Balthazar reluctantly accepts the men's offer of gifts:

> You press me far, and therefore I will yield.
> Give me your gloves; I'll wear them for your sake,
> And, for your love, I'll take this ring from you.
>
> (4.1.421–3)

One assumes that the gloves are begged of Antonio and the ring of Bassanio. The internal rhyme 'your gloves'/'your love' links Antonio's love to the ring, presaging Bassanio's ultimate motive for parting with the gift. At the same time Balthazar promises to wear the gloves for the merchant's 'sake', becoming the site where the symbol of Bassanio's desire touches Antonio's second skin. As objects penetrated by human fingers, gloves and ring held similar vaginal and anal connotations.[8] Their interplay with the lovers' hands traces a complex erotic circuit that hopelessly confuses roles: does the gloved hand slip inside the ring, or the ringed hand inside the glove?

Critics and directors often chart Antonio's level of social inclusion by deciding where he ends up when the characters take their final exit from the stage. After a parade of three married couples enter Portia's house, does the merchant stand alone? Or does he stride in arm-in-arm with Bassanio, Portia or both? Perhaps, whatever the arrangement, directors might consider leaving the door open behind them. The ending of *The Merchant of Venice* acknowledges the confines of the closet, but also multiplies possibilities for kindness, kinship and kink. Unlocked to all occasions, Belmont's open door would allow anyone inside the house to indulge a sudden whim to lie with the doctor.

Notes

1 For an overview of early twentieth-century interpretations of Antonio's melancholy, see Hurrell 1961. For an early reading of Antonio as homosexual, see Auden 1962.

2 See also Sedgwick 1985: 83–93. On Portia as winning the rivalry with Antonio, see Hyman 1970; Geary 1984; and Berger 2010.

3 This is the third of a trilogy of essays I have written on *kindness* in *Merchant*. See Greenstadt 2013 and Greenstadt 2017.

4 See Adelman 2008; Daniel 2010; Bovilsky 2016.

5 On Portia as enforcer of heterosexuality, see also O'Rourke 2003.

6 For another recent reading of the ending as non-monogamous, see Garrison 2014.

7 Space doesn't permit me to discuss the ways the contrasting relationship between Nerissa and Gratiano heightens this effect.

8 On this symbolism of the ring, see Shannon 2000; Geisweidt 2009; and Stockton 2017. On gloves, see Jones and Stallybrass 2001.

WORKS CITED

Abella, I., ed. (1977), 'Portrait of a Jewish Professional Revolutionary: The Recollections of Joshua Gershman', *Labour/Le Travail*, 2: 184–213.

Adelman, H. T. (2001), 'Jewish Women and Family Life, Inside and Outside the Ghetto', in R. C. Davis and B. Ravid (eds), *The Jews of Early Modern Venice*, 143–65, Baltimore: Johns Hopkins University Press.

Adelman, J. (2008), *Blood Relations: Christian and Jew in* The Merchant of Venice, Chicago: University of Chicago Press.

Akhimie, P. (2018), *Shakespeare and the Cultivation of Difference: Race and Conduct in the Early Modern World*, London and New York: Routledge.

Alexander, B. (2015), 'A Merchant of Many Faces' [unpublished conference paper], The Shylock Project, Venice, 29 June.

Andreas, J. R., Sr. (2002), 'The Curse of Cush: Othello's Judaic Ancestry', in P. C. Kolin (ed.), *Othello: New Critical Essays*, 169–87, New York: Routledge.

Antler, J. (1997), *The Journey Home: Jewish Women and the American Century*, New York: The Free Press.

Aristotle (1984), *The Politics*, trans. C. Lord, Chicago: University of Chicago Press.

Ascham, R. (1544), *Toxophilus the schole of shootinge*, London.

Astington, J. (2015), 'Pastoral Imagery in *The Merchant of Venice*', *Word & Image*, 31 (1): 43–53.

Aubrey, J. (1898), *Brief Lives, Chiefly of Contemporaries*, vol. 1, ed. A. Clark, Oxford: Clarendon.

Auden, W. H. (1948), 'Brothers and Others', in *The Dyer's Hand*, London: Faber & Faber.

Auden, W. H. (1962), *The Dyer's Hand and Other Essays*, ed. E. Mendelson, London: Faber & Faber.

Augustine, N. and K. Adelman (1999), *Shakespeare in Charge: The Bard's Guide to Leading and Succeeding on the Business Stage*, New York: Hyperion.

Bailey, A. (2011), 'Shylock and the Slaves: Owing and Owning in *The Merchant of Venice*', *Shakespeare Quarterly*, 62 (1): 1–24.
Bailey, A. (2013), *Of Bondage: Debt, Property and Personhood in Early Modern England*, Philadelphia: University of Pennsylvania Press.
Baker, R. (1659), *The Marchants Humble Petition and Remonstrance to his Late Highnesse*, London.
Barth, J. (2016), 'Reconstructing Mercantilism: Consensus and Conflict in British Imperial Economy in the Seventeenth and Eighteenth Centuries', *The William and Mary Quarterly*, 73 (2): 257–90.
Barton, J. (1984), *Playing Shakespeare*, London: Methuen.
Bassi, S. (2011), 'Barefoot to Palestine: The Failed Meetings of Shylock and Othello', in L. Tosi and S. Bassi (eds), *Visions of Venice in Shakespeare*, 231–49, Surrey, England: Ashgate.
Bauman, Z. (1998), 'Allosemitism: Premodern, Modern, Postmodern', in B. Cheyette and L. Marcus (eds), *Modernity, Culture and 'the Jew'*, 143–56, Cambridge: Polity Press.
Benbow, R. (1976), 'The Merchant Antonio, Elizabethan Hero', *Colby Library Quarterly*, 12 (4): 156–70.
Bentham, J. (1839), 'The Rationale of Reward', in J. Bowring (ed.), *The Works of Jeremy Bentham*, 189–266, Edinburgh: William Tait.
Bentham, J. (1882), *Theory of Legislation*, trans. R. Hildreth, London: Trubner.
Berger, H. (2010), 'Mercifixion in *The Merchant of Venice*: The Riches of Embarrassment', *Renaissance Drama*, 38 (1): 3–45.
Berger, J. (2011), 'Triangle Fire: Clinging to Scraps of Memories', *The New York Times*, 25 March. Available online: https://cityroom.blogs.nytimes.com/2011/03/25/triangle-fire-clinging-to-scraps-of-memories/
Berry, L. E. (2007), *The Geneva Bible: A Facsimile of the 1560 Edition*, Peabody, MA: Hendrickson Publishers.
Biberman, M. (2004), *Masculinity, Anti-Semitism, and Early Modern English Literature: From the Satanic to the Effeminate Jew*, Aldershot, Hampshire, England: Ashgate.
Billington, M. (2011), 'The Mercy of Quality: Magnificent Shylock Meets Vegas: *The Merchant of Venice*. Royal Shakespeare Theatre, Stratford-on-Avon 4/5', *The Guardian*, 20 May.
Boehrer, B. (1999), 'Shylock and the Rise of the Household Pet: Thinking Social Exclusion in *The Merchant of Venice*', *Shakespeare Quarterly*, 50 (2): 152–70.

Boehrer, B. (2010), *Animal Characters: Nonhuman Beings in Early Modern Literature*, Philadelphia: University of Pennsylvania Press.

Boldt, E. (2015), 'Change of Perspective with a Danse Macabre', *Goethe Institut*, July. Available online: https://www.goethe.de/en/kul/tut/gen/tup/20561753.html (accessed 15 August 2017).

Bovilsky, L. (2008), *Barbarous Play Race on the English Renaissance Stage*, Minneapolis: University of Minnesota.

Bovilsky, L. (2010), '"A Gentle and No Jew": Jessica, Portia, and Jewish Identity', *Renaissance Drama*, 38: 47–76.

Bovilsky, L. (2016), '"Racked … to the Uttermost": The Verges of Love and Subjecthood in *The Merchant of Venice*', in M. Frank, J. Goldberg and K. Newman (eds), *This Distracted Globe: Worldmaking in Early Modern Literature*, 121–41, New York: Fordham University Press.

Bray, A. (1994), 'Homosexuality and the Signs of Male Friendship in Early Modern England', in J. Goldberg (ed.), *Queering the Renaissance*, 40–61, Durham: Duke University Press.

Brenner, R. (1993), *Merchants and Revolutionaries: Commercial Change, Political Conflict, and London's Overseas Traders, 1550–1653*, London: Verso.

Britton, D. (2014), *Becoming Christian: Race, Reformation, and Early Modern English Romance*, New York: Fordham University.

Bullough, G. (1957–75), *Narrative and Dramatic Sources of Shakespeare*, vol. 2, London: Routledge & Kegan Paul; New York: Columbia University Press.

Bulman, J. (1991), *Shakespeare in Performance: The Merchant of Venice*, Manchester and New York: Manchester University Press.

Burnett, M. T. (1991), 'Apprentice Literature and the "Crisis" of the 1590s', *The Yearbook of English Studies*, 21: 27–38.

Burton, T. (1828), *Diary of Thomas Burton, Esq*, London.

Byrnes, J., D. Miller and W. Schafer (1999), 'Gender Differences in Risk Taking: A Meta Analysis', *Psychological Bulletin*, 125 (3): 367–83.

Calabi, D. (2017), *Venice and Its Jews*, Roma: Officina Libraria.

Caldwell, E. (2014), 'Opportunistic Portia as Fortuna in Shakespeare's *Merchant of Venice*', *SEL Studies in English Literature*, 54 (2): 349–73.

Calvin, J. (1578), *A commentarie of Iohn Caluine, vpon the first booke of Moses called Genesis*, London: Henry Middleton.

Cappa, F. (2016), *Perché Shylock?*, documentary, RAI TV.

Cartelli, T. (2009), 'Redistributing Complicities in an Age of Digital Production: Michael Radford's Film-Version of *The Merchant of Venice*', in N. Levine and D. Miller (eds), *A Touch More Rare: Harry Berger, Jr. and the Arts of Interpretation*, 58–73, New York: Fordham University Press.

Cartwright, J. and E. Cartwright (1649), *The Petition of the Jewes for the Repealing of the Act of Parliament for their Banishment out of England*, London.

Cavendish, W., Duke of Newcastle (1667), *A New Method, and Extraordinary Invention, to Dress Horses, and Work them According to Nature*, London.

Cerasano, S. P., ed. (2004), *A Routledge Literary Sourcebook on William Shakespeare's* The Merchant of Venice, New York: Routledge.

Chakravarty, U. (2018), 'Race, Natality, and the Biopolitics of Early Modern Political Theology', *Journal for Early Modern Cultural Studies*, 18 (2): 140–66.

Chambers, E. K. (1925), *Shakespeare: A Survey*, London: Sidgwick & Jackson.

Charry, B. (2008), '"(T)he Beauteous Scarf": Shakespeare and the "Veil Question"', *Shakespeare*, 4 (2): 121–36.

Chaver, Y. (2011), 'Writing for the Jews, Writing for the Goyim: Twentieth-Century Adaptations of "The Merchant of Venice"', *Jewish Social Studies*, 17 (2): 28–47.

Cleland, J. (1607), *Hero-paideia, or The institution of a young noble man*, Oxford.

Cohen, J. (1999), *Living Letters of the Law: Ideas of the Jew in Medieval Christianity*, Berkeley: University of California.

Cohen, W. (1982), '*The Merchant of Venice* and the Possibilities of Historical Criticism', *ELH*, 49 (4): 765–89.

Collado, A., C. Risco, A. Banducci, K. Chen, L. MacPherson, and C. Lejuez (2015), 'Racial Differences in Risk-Taking Propensity on the Youth Version of the Balloon Analogue Risk Task (BART-Y)', *The Journal of Early Adolescence*, 37 (2): 222–35.

Collier, T. (1656), *A Brief Answer to Some of the Objections and Demurs made against the Coming in and Inhabiting of the Jews in this Commonwealth*, London.

Conti, B. (2015), 'Shylock Celebrates Easter', *Modern Philology*, 113 (2): 178–97.

Coodin, S. (2017), *Is Shylock Jewish?: Citing Scripture and the Moral Agency of Shakespeare's Jews*, Edinburgh: Edinburgh University.

Copia Sulam, S. (2009), *Jewish Poet and Intellectual in Seventeenth-Century Venice*, (ed. Don Harrán), Chicago: University of Chicago Press.

Crome, A. (2015), 'English National Identity and the Readmission of the Jews', *Journal of Ecclesiastical History*, 66 (2): 280–301.

Crouch, N. (1695), 'The Proceedings about the Jews in England in the year 1655', in *Two Journeys to Jerusalem*, 167–71, London.

Daniel, D. (2010), '"Let me have judgment, and the Jew his will": Melancholy Epistemology and Masochistic Fantasy in *The Merchant of Venice*', *Shakespeare Quarterly*, 61 (2): 206–34.

Daniel, D. (2013), *The Melancholy Assemblage: Affect and Epistemology in the English Renaissance*, New York: Fordham University.

Darcy, R. F. (2003), 'Freeing Daughters on Open Markets: The Incest Clause in The *Merchant of Venice*', in Linda Woodbridge (ed.), *Money and the Age of Shakespeare: Essays in New Economic Criticism*, 189–200, New York: Palgrave.

Davis, R. C., and B. Ravid (eds) (2001), *The Jews of Early Modern Venice*, Baltimore: Johns Hopkins University Press.

Della Casa, G. (1576), *Galateo: Galateo of Maister Iohn Della Casa, Archebishop of Beneuenta. Or rather, A treatise of the ma[n]ners and behauiours*, trans. R. Peterson, London.

Dennys, J. (1613), *The Secret of Angling*, London.

Doerry, M., and K. Wiegrefe (2016), 'Book of Hate: The Bold Attempt to Demystify Hitler's *Mein Kampf*', *Spiegel Online*, 15 January. Available online: http://www.spiegel.de/international/germany/new-annotated-mein-kampf-offers-insight-into-hitler-a-1072032.html (accessed 15 August 2017).

Donoghue, J. (2013), *Fire under the Ashes: An Atlantic History of the English Revolution*, Chicago: University of Chicago Press.

Doran, G. (1993), 'Solanio', in R. Jackson and R. Smallwood (eds), *Players of Shakespeare 3*, 68–76, Cambridge and New York: Cambridge University Press.

Döring, T. (2015), 'Shylock, the German' [unpublished conference paper], The Shylock Project, Venice, 7 July.

Dössel, C. (2015), 'Angekommen', *Süddeutsche Zeitung*, 19 October. Available online: http://www.sueddeutsche.de/kultur/theater-mit-fluechtlingen-angekommen-1.2699162 (accessed 15 August 2017).

Drakakis, J. (2011), 'Introduction', *The Merchant of Venice*, Arden Shakespeare, Third Series, London and New York: Bloomsbury.

Duneier, M. (2016), *Ghetto, The Invention of a Place, the History of an Idea*, New York: Farrar, Straus & Giroux.

Elias, N. (1994), *The Civilizing Process*, Oxford and Cambridge: Blackwell.

Engle, L. (1986), '"Thrift Is Blessing": Exchange and Explanation in *The Merchant of Venice*', *Shakespeare Quarterly*, 37 (1): 20–37.

Engle, L. (1993), *Shakespearean Pragmatism: Market of His Time*, Chicago and London: University of Chicago Press.

Enstad, N. (1999), *Ladies of Labor, Girls of Adventure: Working Women, Popular Culture, and Labor Politics at the Turn of the Twentieth Century*, New York: Columbia University Press.

Ephraim, M. (2005), 'Jephthah's Kin: The Sacrificing Father in *The Merchant of Venice*', *Journal for Early Modern Cultural Studies*, 5 (2): 71–93.

Ephraim, M. (2008), *Reading the Jewish Woman on the Elizabethan Stage*, Aldershot: Ashgate.

Ephraim, M. (2017), 'Jessica's Jewish Identity in Contemporary Feminist Novels', in E. Nahshon and M. Shapiro (eds), *Wrestling with Shylock: Jewish Responses to The Merchant of Venice*, 337–58, Cambridge: Cambridge University Press.

Erasmus, D. (1534), *Opus de Conscribendis Epistolis*, Basilea.

Erasmus, D. (1978), *On the Method of Study / De Rationi Studii ac Legendi Interpretandique Auctores*, in C. R. Thompson (ed.) and B. McGregor (trans.), *The Collected Works of Erasmus*, vol. 24, 661–92, Toronto: University of Toronto.

Erasmus, D. (1985), *On the Writing of Letters / De Conscribendis Epistolis*, in J. K. Sowards (ed.) and C. Fantazzi (trans.), *The Collected Works of Erasmus*, vol. 25, Toronto: University of Toronto Press.

Erne, L. (2013), *Shakespeare and the Book Trade*, Cambridge: Cambridge University Press.

Espinosa, R. (2009), '"Can no prayers pierce thee?": Re-imagining Marian Intercession in *The Merchant of Venice*', *Explorations in Renaissance Culture*, 35 (2): 172–93.

Fiorentino, S. G. (2006), [*The Merchant of Venice*], in L. Marcus (ed.), *Norton Critical Edition of William Shakespeare, The Merchant of Venice*, 84–99, New York: W.W. Norton.

Fletcher, J. and W. Shakespeare (2015), *Two Noble Kinsmen*, rev. ed., ed. L. Potter, London: Bloomsbury.

Fortis, U. (2003), *La bella ebrea: Sara Copio Sullam, poetessa nel ghetto di Venezia del'600*, Torino: Zamorani.

Fortis, U. (2015), *L'attività letteraria nel Ghetto (Venezia 1550–1650)*, Livorno: Salomone Belforte.

Freccero, C. (2015), 'A Race of Wolves', in M. Senior, D. Clark and C. Freccero (eds), *Animots: Postanimality in French Thought*, special issue of *Yale French Studies*, 127: 110–23.

Freinkel, L. (2002), *Reading Shakespeare's Will: The Theology of Figure from Augustine to the Sonnets*, New York: Columbia University Press.

Gardiner, S. R. (ed.) (1906), *Constitutional Documents of the Puritan Revolution 1625–1660*, Oxford: Oxford University Press.

Garrett, L. (2014), 'True Interest: The Dangers of Lawful Lending in *The Merchant of Venice*', *Journal of Early Modern Cultural Studies*, 14 (1): 32–62.

Garrison, J. S. (2014), *Friendship and Queer Theory in the Renaissance: Gender and Sexuality in Early Modern England*, New York: Routledge.

Geary, K. (1984), 'The Nature of Portia's Victory: Turning to Men in *The Merchant of Venice*', *Shakespeare Survey*, 37: 55–68.

Geertz, C. (1972), 'Deep Play: Notes on the Balinese Cockfight', *Daedalus*, 101 (1): 1–37.

Geisweidt, E. J. (2009), 'Antonio's Claim: Triangulated Desire and Queer Kinship in Shakespeare's *The Merchant of Venice*', *Shakespeare*, 5 (4): 338–54.

Giesbrecht, J. (2010), 'Accommodating Resistance: Unionization, Gender, and Ethnicity in Winnipeg's Garment Industry, 1929–1945', *Urban History Review/Revue d'histoire urbaine*, 39 (1): 5–19.

Gilbert, M. (2002), *Shakespeare at Stratford: The Merchant of Venice*, London: Thomson Learning.

Gilbert, M. (2017), 'Jewish Directors and Jewish Shylocks in Twentieth-Century England', in E. Nahshon and M. Shapiro (eds), *Wrestling with Shylock: Jewish Responses to The Merchant of Venice*, 291–316, Cambridge and New York: Cambridge University Press.

Gildon, C. (1710), 'Remarks on The Plays of Shakespeare', in N. Rowe (ed.), *The Works of Mr. William Shakespear*, vol. 7, 257–464, London.

Girard, R. (1980), '"To Entrap the Wisest:" A Reading of *The Merchant of Venice*', in E. W. Said (ed.), *Literature and Society: Selected Papers from the English Institute, 1978*, N.S. 3, 229–63, Baltimore and London: Johns Hopkins University Press.

Glaser, E. (2007), *Judaism Without Jews: Philosemitism and Christian Polemic in Early Modern England*, Basingstoke: Palgrave Macmillan.

Goffman, E. (1967), 'Where the Action Is', in *Interaction Ritual: Essays on Face-to-Face Behavior*, 149–270, New York: Doubleday Anchor.

Goldberg, J. (2010), *Sodometries: Renaissance Texts, Modern Sexualities*, New York: Fordham University.

Gordon, A. (1909), 'William Kiffin', in S. Lee (ed.), *Dictionary of National Biography*, vol. 31, 98–100, London: Smith, Elder, & Co.

Granville, G. (1701), *The Jew of Venice*, London.

Green, M. A. E. (ed.) (1875), *Calendar of State Papers Domestic: Commonwealth, 1655–6*, London: Longman and Company.

Greenblatt, S. (1985), 'Shakespeare and the Exorcists', in P. Parker and G. Hartman (eds), *Shakespeare and the Question of Theory*, 229–63, New York: Methuen.

Greenblatt, S. (2017a), *The Rise and Fall of Adam and Eve*, New York: Random House.

Greenblatt, S. (2017b), 'Shakespeare's Cure for Xenophobia', *The New Yorker*, 10 July. Available online: https://www.newyorker.com/magazine/2017/07/10/shakespeares-cure-for-xenophobia (accessed 15 August 2017).

Greenblatt, S. (gen. ed.) (2016), *The Norton Shakespeare* 3, New York: W. W. Norton.

Greene, J. ([1994] 1999), '"You Must Eat Men", The Sodomitic Economy of Renaissance Patronage', in S. Orgel and S. Keilen (eds), *Shakespeare and Gender*, 229–63, New York and London: Garland.

Greenstadt, A. E. (2013), 'The Kindest Cut: Circumcision and Queer Kinship in *The Merchant of Venice*', *ELH*, 80 (4): 945–80.

Greenstadt, A. E. (2017), 'Strange Insertions in *The Merchant of Venice*', in G. Stanivukovic (ed.), *Queer Shakespeare: Desire and Sexuality*, 197–226, London: Bloomsbury.

Gross, K. (2006), *Shylock Is Shakespeare*, Chicago: University of Chicago Press.

Hall, K. F. (1992), 'Guess Who's Coming to Dinner? Colonization and Miscegenation in *The Merchant of Venice*', *Renaissance Drama*, n.s. 23: 87–111

Hammond, P. (2002), *Figuring Sex Between Men from Shakespeare to Rochester*, Oxford: Clarendon Press.

Harrán, D. (2008), 'Madonna Bellina, "astounding" Jewish Musician in Mid-Sixteenth-Century Venice', *Renaissance Studies*, 22 (1): 16–40.

Harris, J. G. (2004), *Sick Economies: Drama, Mercantilism, and Disease in Shakespeare's England*, Philadelphia: University of Pennsylvania Press.

Harris, J. G. (2006), *Foreign Bodies and the Body Politic: Discourses of Social Pathology in Early Modern England*, Cambridge: Cambridge University Press.

Harris, J. G. (2007), 'The Time of Shakespeare's Jewry', *Shakespeare Studies*, 35: 39–46.

Harris, J. G. (2010), 'Shakespeare and Race', in M. De Grazia and S. Wells (eds), *The New Cambridge Companion to Shakespeare*, 201–16, Cambridge: Cambridge University Press.

Hart, B. W. (2018), *Hitler's American Friends: The Third Reich's Supporters in the United States*, New York: Thomas Dunne Books.

Hawkes, D. (2004), 'Materialism and Reification in Renaissance Studies', *The Journal For Early Modern Cultural Studies*, 4 (2): 114–29.

Heine, H. (1895), *Heine on Shakespeare*, Westminster: A. Constable and Co.

Helms, M. W. and J. P. Ferris (1983), 'John Frederick (1601–85) of Old Jewery London', in B. D Henning (ed.), *The History of Parliament: History of Commons, 1660–1690*, London: Secker & Warburg Limited. Available online: http://www.historyofparliamentonline.org/volume/1660-1690/member/frederick-john-1601-85 (accessed 7 November 2017).

Henriques, H.S.Q. (1905), *The Return of Jews to England: Being a Chapter in the History of Law*, Clark, NJ: The Lawbook Exchange Ltd.

Hessayon, A. (2011), 'Jews and Crypto-Jews in Sixteenth- And Seventeenth- Century England', *Cromohs*, 16: 1–26.

Hillman, R. (2018), 'Mercy Unjustified: A Reformation Intertext for *The Merchant of Venice*', *Shakespeare Jahrbuch*, 154: 92–105.

Hirsch, B. D. (2006), '"A Gentile and No Jew": The Difference Marriage Makes in *The Merchant of Venice*', *Parergon*, 23 (1): 119–29.

Hirsch, B. D. (2009), 'Counterfeit Professions: Jewish Daughters and the Drama of Failed Conversion in Marlowe's *The Jew of Malta* and Shakespeare's *The Merchant of Venice*', *Early Modern*

Literary Studies, 19: 37 paragraphs. Available online: http://extra.shu.ac.uk/emls/emlshome.html

Hirschfeld, H. (2005), 'Compulsions of the Renaissance', *Shakespeare Studies*, 33: 109–14.

Hirschfeld, H. (2006), '"We All Expect a Gentle Answer, Jew": *The Merchant of Venice* and the Psychotheology of Conversion', *ELH*, 73 (1): 61–81.

Hirschfeld, H. (2010), '"And He Hath Enough": The Penitential Economies of *The Merchant of Venice*', *Journal of Medieval and Early Modern Studies*, 40 (1): 89–117.

Höbel, W. (2015), 'Schiff der Träume: Wenn Flüchtlinge die deutsche Bühne entern', *Spiegel Online*, 6 December. Available online: http://www.spiegel.de/kultur/gesellschaft/schiff-der-traeume-im-hamburger-schauspielhaus-a-1066232.html (accessed 15 August 2017).

Holland Festival Programme (2014), *Die Schutzbefohlenen*. Available online: https://www.hollandfestival.nl/nl/programma/2014/die-schutzbefohlenen/ (accessed 15 August 2017).

Holmer, J. (1985), '"When Jacob Graz'd His Uncle Laban's Sheep": A New Source for *The Merchant of Venice*', *Shakespeare Quarterly*, 36 (1): 64–65.

Horowitz, D. (1998), *Betty Friedan and the Making of The Feminine Mystique*, Amherst: University of Massachusetts Press.

Hulse, L. (2008), 'Jordan, Thomas (*c*. 1614–1685), actor, poet, and playwright', *Oxford Dictionary of National Biography*, Oxford: Oxford University Press. Available online: http://www.oxforddnb.com.ezproxy.lib.uwf.edu/view/10.1093/ref:odnb/9780198614128.001.0001/odnb-9780198614128-e-15122 (accessed 7 November 2017).

Hundley, T. (1994), 'Much Ado About Shakespeare', *Chicago Tribune*, 17 June. Available online: http://articles.chicagotribune.com/1994-06-17/features/9406170021_1_jewish-prism-gentile-world-unsubtle-reminder (accessed 15 August 2017).

Hunt, B. (2014), 'What Most People Get Wrong about Investment Diversification', *Business Insider*, 25 February. Available online: http://www.businessinsider.com/what-people-get-wrong-on-diversification-2014-2 (accessed 31 May 2019).

Hurrell, J. D. (1961), 'Love and Friendship in *The Merchant of Venice*', *Texas Studies in Literature and Language*, 3 (3): 328–41.

Hutson, L. (1994), *The Usurer's Daughter: Male Friendship and Fictions of Women in Sixteenth-Century England*, London: Routledge.

Hyman, C. A. (1988), 'Labor organizing and female institution-building: The Chicago Women's Trade Union League, 1904–24', in R. Milkman (ed.), *Women, Work & Protest: A Century of U.S. Women's Labor History*, 22–41, Boston: Routledge.

Hyman, L. W. (1970), 'The Rival Lovers in *The Merchant of Venice*', *Shakespeare Quarterly*, 21 (2): 109–16.

Jajja, M. A. (2014), 'The Stereotype Representation of Non-Whites/Non-Christians as Others in Shakespearean Plays: *The Merchant of Venice* and *Othello*', *ELF Annual Research Journal*, 16: 157–70.

Jessey, H. (1656), *A Narrative of the Late Proceeds at White-Hall Concerning the Jews*, London.

Jones, A. R., and P. Stallybrass (2000), *Renaissance Clothing and the Materials of Memory*, Cambridge: Cambridge University Press.

Jones, R. (2016), *Violent Borders: Refugees and the Right to Move*, London: Verso.

Jordan, T. (1663), *A Royal Arbor Of Loyal Poesie, Consisting of Poems and Songs. Digested into Triumph, Elegy, Satyr, Love & Drollery*, London.

Jordan, T. (1665), *Wit in a Wildernesse of Promiscuous Poesie*, London.

Jürs-Munby, K. (2013), 'Parasitic Politics: Elfriede Jelinek's "Secondary Dramas" *Abraumhalde* and *Faust In and Out*', in K. Jürs-Munby, J. Carroll and S. Giles (eds), *Postdramatic Theatre and the Political*, 209–31, London: Bloomsbury.

Kaplan, M. L. (ed.) (2002), *The Merchant of Venice: Texts and Contexts*, Boston: Bedford/St. Martin's.

Kaplan, M. L. (2007), 'Jessica's Mother: Medieval Constructions of Jewish Race and Gender in *The Merchant of Venice*', *Shakespeare Quarterly*, 58:1–30.

Kaplan, M. L. (2013), '"Who Drew the Jew that Shakespeare Knew?:" Misericords and Medieval Jews in *The Merchant of Venice*', *Shakespeare Survey*, 66: 298–315.

Kaplan, M. L. (2019a), '*The Merchant of Venice*, Jews and Christians', in H. Hamlin (ed.), *The Cambridge Companion to Shakespeare and Religion*, 168–83, Cambridge, Cambridge University Press.

Kaplan, M. L. (2019b), *Figuring Racism in Medieval Christianity*, Oxford: Oxford University.

Kasiske, A. (2015), 'A new play explores the myth behind *Mein Kampf*', *Deutsche Welle*, 4 September. Available online: http://www.dw.com/en/a-new-play-explores-the-myth-behind-mein-kampf/a-18693625 (accessed 15 August 2017).

Katz, D. S. (1982), *Philo-Semitism and the Readmission of the Jews to England, 1603–1655*, Oxford: Clarendon Press.

Katz, D. E. (2017), *The Jewish Ghetto and the Visual Imagination of Early Modern Venice*, Cambridge: Cambridge University Press.

Kaynar-Kissinger, G. (2017), '*The Merchant of Venice* on the German Stage and the 1995 'Buchenwald' Production in Weimar', in E. Nahshon and M. Shapiro (eds), *Wrestling with Shylock: Jewish Responses to The Merchant of Venice*, 291–316, Cambridge and New York: Cambridge University Press.

Keenan, S. (2016), 'Shakespeare and the Market in His Own Day', in D. Shellard and S. Keenan (eds), *Shakespeare's Cultural Capital*, 13–31, London: Palgrave Macmillan.

Kietzman, M. J. (2017), '*The Merchant of Venice*: Shylock and Covenantal Interplay', *ELH*, 84 (2): 423–52.

Kleinberg, S. (1983), '*The Merchant of Venice*: the Homosexual as Anti-Semite in Nascent Capitalism', in S. Kellogg (ed.), *Literary Visions of Homosexuality*, 113–26, New York: Haworth Press.

Knight, C. (1844), *London*, vol. 6, London.

Korda, N. (2009), 'Dame Usury: Gender, Credit, and Accounting in the Sonnets and *The Merchant of Venice*', *Shakespeare Quarterly*, 60 (2): 129–53.

Kruger, S. F. (1997), 'Medieval Christian (Dis)identifications: Muslims and Jews in Guibert of Nogent', *New Literary History*, 28 (2): 185–203

Kruger, S. F. (2006), *The Spectral Jew: Conversion and Embodiment in Medieval Europe*, Minneapolis: University of Minnesota.

Kümmel, P. (2015), 'Nein, sie bluten nicht', *Zeit Online*, 29 October. Available online: https://www.zeit.de/2015/42/matthias-lilienthal-muenchner-kammerspielen (accessed 15 August 2017).

Lampert, L. (2004), *Gender and Jewish Difference from Paul to Shakespeare*, Philadelphia: University of Pennsylvania.

Landau, A. (2006), 'Jews and Moors at the Crossroads: Female Conversion in *Don Quixote* and *The Merchant of Venice*', in C. Goodblatt and H. Kreisel (eds), *Tradition, Heterodoxy and Religious Culture: Judaism and Christianity in the Early Modern Period*, 391–403, Beersheba, Israel; Ben-Gurion University of the Negev.

Langis, U. (2011), 'Usury and Political Friendship in *The Merchant of Venice*', *Upstart Crow: A Shakespeare Journal*, 30: 18–41.

Levine, A-J. (1997), 'A Jewess, More and/or Less', in M. Peskowitz and L. Levitt (eds), *Judaism Since Gender*, 149–57, New York: Routledge.

Lewalski, B. (1962), 'Biblical Allusion and Allegory in *The Merchant of Venice*', *Shakespeare Quarterly*, 13 (3): 327–43.

Lewis, M. (2013), '"The Messiah promised in the Sacred Scripture came a long time ago": The Cambridge Platonists' Attitudes towards the Readmission of the Jews, 1655–56', *Jewish Historical Studies*, 45: 41–61.

Lilienthal, M. (2017), 'Citizens of Everywhere', Munich Kammerspiele 2017/18 season brochure. Available online: https://www.muenchner-kammerspiele.de/en/citizens-of-everywhere (accessed 15 August 2017).

Lim, W. (2010), 'Surety and Spiritual Commercialism in *The Merchant of Venice*', *Studies in English Literature*, 50 (2): 355–82.

Lindley, K. (2008), 'Packe, Christopher, appointed Lord Packe under the protectorate', *Oxford Dictionary of National Biography*, Oxford: Oxford University Press. Available online: http://www.oxforddnb.com.ezproxy.lib.uwf.edu/view/10.1093/ref:odnb/9780198614128.001.0001/odnb-9780198614128-e-15122 (accessed 6 June 2018).

Little, A. L., Jr. (2011), 'The Rites of Queer Marriage in *The Merchant of Venice*', in M. Menon (ed.), *Shakesqueer: A Queer Companion to the Complete Works of Shakespeare*, 216–24, Durham and London: Duke University.

Loomba, A. (2002), *Shakespeare, Race, and Colonialism*, Oxford: Oxford University.

Loomba, A. (2007), 'Periodization, Race, and Global Contact', *Journal of Medieval and Early Modern Studies*, 37 (3): 595–620.

Lupton, J. (2000), 'Exegesis, Mimesis, and the Future of Humanism in *The Merchant of Venice*', *Religion and Literature*, 32: 123–39.

Lupton, J. R. (2005), *Citizen-Saints: Shakespeare and Political Theology*, Chicago: University of Chicago.

Lupton, J. R. (2011), 'Job In Venice: Shakespeare and the Travails of Universalism', in L. Tosi and S. Bassi (eds), *Visions of Venice in Shakespeare*, 105–21, Surrey, England; Ashgate.

Luther, M. (1955–86), *Luther's Works*, ed. J. Pelikan and H. Lehmann, Philadelphia: Fortress.

Lutz, C. (2016), 'Lilienthal stellt die Kammerspiele auf den Kopf', *Süddeutsche Zeitung*, 20 November. Available online: http://www.sueddeutsche.de/muenchen/theater-besser-als-fernsehen-1.3256651 (accessed 15 August 2017).

MacInnes, I. (2008), '"Ill luck, Ill luck?" Risk and Hazard, *The Merchant of Venice*', in B. Sebek and S. Deng (eds), *Global Traffic: Discourses and Practices of Trade in English Literature and Culture from 1550–1700*, 39–55, Basingstoke: Palgrave Macmillan.

Markham, G. (1634), *The Art of Archerie*, London.

Masten, J. (1993), 'My Two Dads: Collaboration and the Reproduction of Beaumont and Fletcher', in J. Goldberg (ed.), *Queering the Renaissance*, 280–319, Durham and London: Duke University.

Masten, J. (1997). *Textual Intercourse: Collaboration, Authorship, and Sexualities in Renaissance Drama*, Cambridge: Cambridge University.

Matar, N. (1985), 'The Idea of the Restoration of the Jews in English Protestant Thought, 1661–1701', *The Harvard Theological Review*, 78 (1–2): 115–48.

Matar, N. (1990), 'George Herbert, Henry Vaughan, and the Conversion of the Jews', *Studies in English Literature, 1500–1900*, 30 (1): 79–92.

McAdam, I. (2015), 'Eucharistic Love in *The Merchant of Venice*', *Renaissance and Reformation / Renaissance et Réforme*, 38 (1): 83–116.

Metzger, M. J. (1998), '"Now by My Hood, a Gentle and No Jew": Jessica, *The Merchant of Venice*, and the Discourse of Early Modern English Identity', *PMLA*, 113 (1): 52–63.

Middleton, I. (2015), 'A Jew's Daughter and a Christian's Wife: Performing Jessica's Multiplicity in *The Merchant of Venice*', *Shakespeare Bulletin*, 33 (2): 293–317.

Midgley, G. (1960), '*The Merchant of Venice*: A Reconsideration', *Essays in Criticism*, 10: 119–33.

Miller, J. (1986), *Subsequent Performances*, London: Faber.

Mirrer, L. (1996), *Women, Jews, and Muslims in the Texts of Reconquest Castile*, Ann Arbor: University of Michigan.

Mokre, M. (2018), '"We Demand Our Rights!" The Refugee Protest Camp Vienna', in S. Rosenberger, V. Stern and N. Merhaut (eds), *Protest Movements in Asylum and Deportation*, 205–21, Springer: IMISCOE Research Series.

Montrose, L. (1983), 'Of Gentlemen and Shepherds: The Politics of Elizabethan Pastoral Form', *English Literary History*, 50 (3): 415–59.

Moore, K. (2012), 'Lessons on Risk from the Merchants of Venice: Is the World Really that Risky Today?' *Forbes*, 2

March. Available online: https://www.forbes.com/sites/karlmoore/2012/03/02/lessons-on-risk-from-the-merchants-of-venice-is-the-world-really-that-risky-today/#21c85ec4437b; (accessed 31 May 2019).

Muldrew, C. (1993), 'Interpreting the Market: The Ethics of Credit and Community Relations in Early Modern England', *Social History*, 18 (2): 163–83.

Muldrew, C. (1998), *The Economy of Obligation: The Culture of Credit and Social Relations in Early Modern England*, Basingstoke and New York: Macmillan; St. Martin's Press.

Muldrew, C. (2001), '"Hard Food for Midas": Cash and Its Social Value in Early Modern England', *Past & Present*, 170: 78–120.

Nachbar, T. B. (2005), 'Monopoly, Mercantilism, and the Politics of Regulation', *Virginia Law Review*, 91 (6): 1313–79.

Nachtkritik.de (2016), '#refugeeswelcome', 28 January. Available online: https://www.nachtkritik.de/index.php?option=com_content&view=article&id=11497:immer-mehr-theater-engagieren-sich-fuer-fluechtlinge&catid=1513:portraet-profil-die-neuen-deutschen&Itemid=85 (accessed 15 August 2017).

Nagel, A. (2017), *Kill All Normies: Online Culture Wars from 4chan and Tumblr to Trump and the Alt-Right*, Winchester: Zero Books.

Nahshon, E. (2017), 'New York City, 1947: A Season for Shylocks', in E. Nahshon and M. Shapiro (eds), *Wrestling with Shylock: Jewish Responses to* The Merchant of Venice, 140–67, Cambridge, UK: Cambridge University Press.

Nahshon, E. and M. Shapiro (eds) (2017), *Wrestling with Shylock: Jewish Responses to* The Merchant of Venice, Cambridge, UK: Cambridge University.

Neill, M. (2018), *Shakespeare's* The Merchant of Venice, Lacock, Wiltshire: Connell Publishing.

Nerlich, M. (1987), *Ideology of Adventure: Studies in Modern Consciousness, 1100–1750*, 2 vols, Minneapolis: University of Minnesota Press.

Newman, K. (1987), 'Portia's Ring: Unruly Women and Structures of Exchange in *The Merchant of Venice*', *Shakespeare Quarterly*, 38 (1): 19–33.

Nicholas, E. (1649), *An Apology for the Honorable Nation of the Jevvs*, London.

Nichols, J. (1824), 'London Pageants during the Commonwealth and Reign of Charles II', *Gentleman's Magazine*, 94 (2): 514–18.

Nirenberg, D. (2010), 'Shakespeare's Jewish Questions', *Renaissance Drama*, 38: 77–113.

O'Rourke, J. L. (2003), 'Racism and Homophobia in *The Merchant of Venice*', *ELH*, 70 (2): 375–97.

Odell, G. C. D. ([1920] 1966), *Shakespeare From Betterton to Irving*, New York: Dover.

Olivier, L. (1986), *On Acting*, London: Weidenfeld and Nicolson.

Orgel, S. (1996), *Impersonations: The Performance of Gender in Shakespeare's England*, Cambridge: Cambridge University Press.

Orgel, S. (2003), *Imagining Shakespeare*, London: Palgrave Macmillan.

Osterman, N. (1941), 'The Controversy over the proposed readmission of the Jews to England (1655)', *Jewish Social Studies*, 3: 301–28.

Owen, S. J. (1996), *Restoration Theatre and Crisis*, Oxford: Oxford University Press.

Oz, A. (2015), 'Disinheriting a Father: Shylock as Alien on the Hebrew Stage' [unpublished conference paper], The Shylock Project, Venice, 17 June.

Patinkin, Don (1946), 'Mercantilism and the Readmission of the Jews to England', *Jewish Social Studies*, 8 (3): 161–78.

Patterson, S. (1999), 'The Bankruptcy of Homoerotic Amity in Shakespeare's *Merchant of Venice*', *Shakespeare Quarterly*, 50 (1): 9–32.

Pequigney, J. (1992), 'The Two Antonios and Same-Sex Love in *Twelfth Night* and *The Merchant of Venice*', *ELR*, 22 (2): 201–21.

Peters, H. (1647), *A Word for the Armie. And Two Words to the Kingdome*, London.

Prynne, W. (1656), *Short Demurrer to the Jewes Long Discontinued Barred Remitter into England*, London.

Raber, K. (2013), *Animal Bodies, Renaissance Culture*, Philadelphia: University of Pennsylvania Press.

Remshardt, R. (2016), 'Fugitive Performance: Nicolas Stemann's *Die Schutzbefohlenen* and the Medial Matrix of Refugee Theatre', *Critical Stages/Scènes Critiques: The IATC Journal/Revue de l'AICT*, 14. Available online: http://www.critical-stages.org/14/fugitive-performance-nicolas-stemanns-die-schutzbefohlenen-and-the-medial-matrix-of-refugee-theatre/ (accessed 15 August 2017).

Rockas, L. (1973), '"A Dish of Doves": *The Merchant of Venice*', *ELH*, 40 (3): 339–51.

Rowe, N. (1709), 'Some Account of the Life & c. of Mr. William Shakespeare', in N. Rowe (ed.), *The Works of Mr. William Shakespear*, vol. 1, i–xl, London.

Sacerdoti, G. (2018), 'Jessica Cosmopolitan Dreams: Blood, Religion and Citizenship in *The Merchant of Venice*', in C. Caporicci (ed.), *Sicut Lilium inter Spinas. Literature and Religion in the Renaissance*, 141–65, Munich: Herbert Utz Verlag.

Samuel, E. (1988–1990), 'The readmission of the Jews to England in 1656, in the context of English economic policy', *Jewish Historical Studies*, 31: 153–69.

Schoenbaum, S. (1978), *William Shakespeare Compact Documentary Life*, Oxford: Oxford University Press.

Schorsch, J. (2004), *Jews and Blacks in the Early Modern World*, New York: Cambridge University.

Schülting, S. (2017), 'Evoking the Holocaust in George Tabori's Productions of *The Merchant of Venice*', in E. Nahshon and M. Shapiro (eds), *Wrestling with Shylock: Jewish Responses to The Merchant of Venice*, 291–316, Cambridge and New York: Cambridge University Press.

Schwartz, M. (1947), *Shylock and His Daughter: A Play Based on a Hebrew Novel by Ari Ibn Zahav*, trans. A. Regelson, New York: Yiddish Art Theatre.

Seccombe, T. (1892), 'Thomas Jordan', in S. Lee (ed.), *Dictionary of National Biography*, vol. 30, 198–200, London: Smith, Elder, & Co.

Sedgwick, E. K. (1985), *Between Men: English Literature and Male Homosocial Desire*, New York: Columbia University Press.

Sedgwick, E. K (1990), *Epistemology of the Closet*, Berkeley: University of California Press.

Sedgwick, E. K. (2008), *Epistemology of the Closet* (2nd edn.), Berkeley: University of California Press.

Shakespeare, W. ([1600] 2011), *The Merchant of Venice*, ed. J. Drakakis, Arden Shakespeare, Third Series, London: Bloomsbury.

Shakespeare, W. (1995), *Henry V*, ed. T. W. Craik, London: Bloomsbury.

Shakespeare, W. (1997), *King Lear*, ed. R. A. Foakes, London: Bloomsbury.

Shakespeare, W. (2000), *Henry VIII*, ed. G. McMullan, London: Bloomsbury.

Shakespeare, W. (2002), *1 Henry IV*, ed. D. S. Kastan, London: Bloomsbury.

Shakespeare, W. (2006a), *As You Like It*, ed. J. Dusinberre, London: Bloomsbury.

Shakespeare, W. (2006b), *The Merchant of Venice*, ed. L. Marcus, New York: W. W. Norton.

Shakespeare, W. (2010), *Shakespeare's Sonnets* (3rd edn.), ed. K. Duncan-Jones, London: Bloomsbury Arden.

Shakespeare, W. (2011), *The Tempest*, rev. ed., ed. V. M. Vaughan and A. T. Vaughan, London: Bloomsbury.

Shakespeare, W. (2015), *Troilus and Cressida*, rev. ed., ed. D. Bevington, London: Bloomsbury.

Shakespeare, W. (2016), *Hamlet*, rev. ed., ed. A. Thompson and N. Taylor, London: Bloomsbury.

Shannon, L. (2000), 'Nature's Bias: Renaissance Homonormativity and Elizabethan Comic Likeness', *Modern Philology*, 98 (2): 183–210.

Shannon, L. (2002), 'Likenings: Rhetorical Husbandries and Portia's "True Conceit" of Friendship', *Renaissance Drama*, 31: 3–26.

Shapiro, J. (1996), *Shakespeare and the Jews*, New York: Columbia University Press.

Shapiro, J. (2015), 'Shakespeare and the Jews' [unpublished conference paper], The Shylock Project, Venice, 3 July.

Shapiro, J. (2019), interview in *The Shylock Notebook*. Available online: http://shabegh.unive.it (accessed 10 April 2019).

Shell, M. (1982), *Money, Language, and Thought*, Baltimore: Johns Hopkins University Press.

Sher, A. (2002), *Beside Myself*, London: Arrow.

Shoulson, J. (2013), *Fictions of Conversion: Jews, Christians, and Cultures of Change in Early Modern England*, Philadelphia: University of Pennsylvania.

Sicher, E. (2017), *The Jew's Daughter: A Cultural History of a Conversion Narrative*, Lanham, MD: Lexington Books.

Silvayn, A. (1585), *The orator handling a hundred seuerall discourses, in forme of declamations: some of the arguments being drawne from Titus Liuius and other ancient vvriters, the rest of the authors owne inuention: part of which are of matters happened in our age*, Englished by L. P. London, 1585. Available online: http://quod.lib.umich.edu/e/eebo/A17337.0001.001/1:4.90?rgn=div2;view=fulltext

Sinfield, A. (1994), *Cultural Politics: Queer Reading*, Philadelphia: University of Pennsylvania Press.

Sinfield, A. (1996), 'How to Read *The Merchant of Venice* without being Heterosexist', in T. Hawkes and J Drakakis (eds), *Alternative Shakespeares 2*, 229–63, London, New York: Routledge.

Singh, J. (2000), 'Gendered 'Gifts' in Shakespeare's Belmont', in D. Callaghan (ed.), *A Feminist Companion to Shakespeare*, 2nd edn, 144–62, Malden, Oxford: Blackwell.

Skwire, D. (2007), 'How Actuarial is a Pound of Flesh? Risk Management and *The Merchant of Venice*', *Contingencies*: 24–6.

Slagman, T. (2015), 'Tanz der Vampire', *nachtkritik.de*, 9 October. Available online: https://www.nachtkritik.de/index.php?option=com_content&view=article&id=11616:der-kaufmann-von-venedig-nicolas-stemann-steuert-zum-intendanzauftakt-von-matthias-lilienthal-an-den-muenchner-kammerspielen-einen-karnevalesken-politischen-shakespeare-bei&catid=99:muenchner-kammerspiele&Itemid=100190 (accessed 15 August 2017).

Slater, T. (ed.) (2016), *Unsafe Space: The Crisis of Free Speech on Campus*, London: Palgrave Macmillan.

Smith, B. R. (1991), *Homosexual Desire in Shakespeare's England: A Cultural Poetics*, Chicago: University of Chicago Press.

Smith, E. (2013), 'Was Shylock Jewish?', *Shakespeare Quarterly*, 64 (2): 188–219.

Smith, I. (2016), 'The Textile Black Body: Race and "Shadowed Livery" in *The Merchant of Venice*', in V. Traub (ed.), *The Oxford Handbook of Shakespeare and Embodiment: Gender, Sexuality, and Race*, 170–85, Oxford: Oxford University Press.

Smith, I. (forthcoming), *Black Shakespeare*.

Smith, L. (2016), 'The Rise of the Far-Right in Poland: No More Eurovision, Vegetarians or Cyclists', *International Business Times*, 21 January. Available online: https://www.ibtimes.co.uk/rise-far-right-poland-no-more-eurovision-vegetarians-cyclists-1537735 (accessed 15 August 2017).

Smythe, R. (1808), *Historical Account of Charter-House*, London.

Spence, J. (1890), *Spence's Anecdotes*, John Underhill(ed.), London.

Spencer, C. (2011), *The Daily Telegraph*, 5 May.

Spiller, E. A. (1998), 'From Imagination to Miscengenation in Shakespeare's *The Merchant of Venice*', *Renaissance Drama*, n.s. 29: 137–64.

Stallybrass, P., and A. R. Jones (2001), 'Fetishizing the Glove in Renaissance Europe', *Critical Inquiry*, 28 (1): 114–32.

Stockton, W. (2017), *Members of His Body: Shakespeare, Paul, and a Theology of Nonmonogamy*, New York: Fordham University Press.

The Bible and Holy Scriptvres conteyned in the Olde and Newe Testament (1560), Geneva: Rouland Hall.

The Merchant of Venice (2004), [Film] dir. Michael Radford, UK, Italy, Luxembourg: Sony Pictures Classics.

The Mirrour of complements (1634), London.

Thurloe, J. (1742), *A Collection of the State Papers of John Thurloe, Esq.*, vol. 4, ed. Thomas Birch, London.

Topsell, E. (1607), *The Historie of Foure-Footed Beastes …*, London: William Jaggard.

Townshend, H. (1680), *Historical collections, or, An Exact Account of the Proceedings of the Four Last Parliaments of Q. Elizabeth of Famous Memory*, London.

UN Refugee Agency website (n.d.), 'Figures at a Glance'. Available online: http://www.unhcr.org/figures-at-a-glance.html (accessed 15 August 2017).

Veltri, G. (2009), *Renaissance Philosophy in Jewish Garb: Foundations and Challenges in Judaism on the Eve of Modernity*, Amsterdam: Brill.

Violet, T. (1661), *Petition Against the Jewes Presented to the Kings Majestie and the Parliament*, London.

Waldinger, R. (1988), 'Another Look at the International Ladies' Garment Workers' Union: Women, Industry Structure and Collective Action', in R. Milkman (ed.), *Women, Work & Protest: A Century of U.S. Women's Labor History*, 87–109, Boston: Routledge.

Watson, P. (1983), 'Bence, John (1622–88), of Bevis Marks, London', in B. D. Henning (ed.), *The History of Parliament: History of Commons, 1660-1690*, London: Secker & Warburg Limited. Available online: http://www.historyofparliamentonline.org/volume/1660-1690/member/bence-john-1622-88 (accessed 7 November 2017).

Weiss, B. (2017), 'I'm Glad the Dyke March Banned Jewish Stars', *The New York Times*, 27 June. Available online: https://www.nytimes.com/2017/06/27/opinion/im-glad-the-dyke-march-banned-jewishstars.html

Whittaker, D. (ed.) (2013), *Most Glorious & Peerless Venice: Observations of Thomas Coryate (1608)*, Charlbury: Wavestone Press.

Wildermann, P. (2015), 'Habt ihr einen Schaden?', *Der Tagesspiegel*, 29 April. Available online: https://www.tagesspiegel.de/kultur/nicolas-stemann-eroeffnet-theatertreffen-habt-ihr-einen-schaden/11703258.html (accessed 15 August 2017).

Williams, A. (1948), *The Common Expositor: An Account of the Commentaries on Genesis 1527–1633*, Chapel Hill: UNC Press.

Williams, G. (1994), 'Purse', in *A Dictionary of Sexual Language and Imagery in Shakespearean and Stuart Literature*, vol. 2, 1116–19, London: Althone.

Williams, R. (1643), *The Blovdy Tenent of Persecution*, London.

Wilson, L. (2003), 'Monetary Compensation for Injuries to the Body, A.D. 602–1697', in L. Woodbridge (ed.), *Money and the Age of Shakespeare: Essays in New Economic Criticism*, 19–37, New York: Palgrave Macmillan.

Witmore, M. (2001), *Culture of Accidents: Unexpected Knowledges in Early Modern England*, Stanford: Stanford University Press.

Wolf, L. (1901), *Menasseh Ben Israel's Mission to Oliver Cromwell*, London: Macmillan & Co.

Yaffe, M. D. (1998), *Shylock and the Jewish Question*, Baltimore: Johns Hopkins University Press.

Yates, J. (2017), *Of Sheep, Oranges, and Yeast: A Multispecies Impression*, Minnesota: University of Minnesota Press.

INDEX

Act Against Recusants. *See*
　Protestantism
Aeschylus 60, 63
Akkouch, Hassan 53–6, 58
Alexander, Bill 49
allosemitism 176–7
Al Qaeda 45
Alternative for Germany (AfD)
　46
antisemitism
　Equality and Human Rights
　　Commission (EHRC) 65
　Pittsburgh synagogue
　　shooting 65
　productions of *The*
　　Merchant of Venice (*see*
　　The Merchant of Venice,
　　antisemitism)
　Restoration 70, 83
Antonio
　antisemitism 208–9
　bond 83, 207, 224 (*see also*
　　economics; merchant)
　financial ruin 160
　homoeroticism (*see*
　　homoeroticism)
　in performance (*see*
　　individual actors)
　sadness (*see* sadness)
　self-sacrifice 124–6
　tainted 124–6, 128–9
　wealth 159–60, 211, 222
Arabic (language) 54–6
Aragon (Prince) 31
Ascham, Roger 162
Ashkenazic (German) 48, 173
Athens 189

Augustine (Aurelius Augustinus
　Hipponensis) 189
Austria 60

Balthazar
　and Bassanio 236–7
　cross-dressing 149, 232,
　　238–9
　homoeroticism (*see*
　　homoeroticism)
　Portia in disguise 221–2,
　　231, 233, 241
Barnfield, Richard 222–3
Barton, David 34
Barton, John 41
Bassanio
　agency 145
　debt 146–7, 159
　love-object 197–9, 205
　in performance (*see*
　　individual actors)
　prodigality 78, 204
　pursuit of Portia 148–9, 204
Beaumont, Francis 236–7
Bellario 57, 78, 238
Belmont
　commercialism, wealth 78,
　　80, 148–9, 204
　film productions 39
　stage productions 44, 56, 58
　venture 144–6, 160, 241
Bence, John 85
Bentham, Jeremy 12, 135–6
Berkshire Theatre Festival, *The*
　Merchant of Venice, dir.
　George Tabori (1996) 39
Blue, Lionel 41

Boccaccio, Giovanni 204–5
Bormann, Niels 44, 53–4, 58
Brexit 45, 65
British Broadcasting Company (BBC) 20, 34–5
Burton, Thomas 80

Cadman, Michael 27
Cain 6
Calder, David 23, 25–6
Calmo, Andrea 178–9
Calvin, John 122, 137
capitalism. *See* economics
Carlisle, John 27
Cartwright, Ebenezer and Joanna. *See* Protestantism
Caryll, Joseph 73
casket test
    Bassanio 79, 123, 143–6, 204
    deep play (*see* deep play)
    inheritance 127–8
    Morocco 31, 43, 163
    Portia 138, 144–5, 232, 233
    risk 124, 137, 144–5, 234
    virtue 160–1
cattle. *See* sheep
Cavendish, William 158
Cebà, Ansaldo 184–6
Chapman, George 150
Charles II 70, 88 n.19
Charlie Hebdo 45, 54
Christian Democrat Union (CDU) 66
Christian Hebraism 71
Christianity
    baptism 35, 39–40, 82 (*see also* Shylock, baptism)
    conversion (*see* conversion)
    economics 77, 83, 124 (*see also* economics)
    homosexuality 28
Church, Tony 26
Cleland, John 158
communism 91, 103
conversion
    Jessica 14, 85, 167, 180–1, 187–9
    Jews 71, 73, 81, 181, 184
    Shayloks tochter 90, 96–7, 99–100, 102
    Shylock 35–7, 39–40, 50, 55, 192
Copia Sulam, Sarra 14, 173–6, 179, 181, 183–7, 189–92. *See also Sareide*
Coryat, Thomas 177
credit
    agreements 77
    Christian 84–5
    culture 139–40
    insolvency 141
    risk 12
    system 142, 148, 150
    worthiness 164
Cromwell, Oliver 70–2, 74, 81, 83, 86 n.7
Cudworth, Ralph 73
Curry, Julian 27
Cush 188

Dachau 39
Daniel 238
debt
    burden 146
    debt-bond, bondage 78, 80, 141, 143, 150
    default 77, 203

INDEX

interest 78
language of 78, 159, 236
ownership 114
repayment 147, 206, 227
deep play
  casket test 136–7, 144
  Clifford Geertz 135–6, 138
  Jeremy Bentham 12, 135–6
  risk 137, 143, 149
Dekker, Thomas 150
Della Casa, Giovanni 165–6
Dennys, John 165
Deutsches Schauspielhaus 62
Die Schutzbefohlenen 60–2, 68 n.10
Disraeli, Benjamin 25
Doran, Gregory 27
Douglas, Alfred Bruce (Bosie) 26
Duke of Venice 170

economics
  agency
  capitalism 119, 140, 219
  crisis of the 1590s 77
  debt (*see* debt)
  deep play 135–8
  divine providence 11, 119–21, 140
  fortune 145–6
  gambling 138
  insurance 140–1, 147
  merchants 81, 139–41, 148
  monopolies 79–83, 87 n.13
  ownership 114, 119
  profit 122, 138, 142
  risk (*see* risk)
  self-interest 82
Edict of Expulsion 48, 71

Elias, Norbert 163
Elizabeth I 79, 85
enclosure 115
English (language) 55, 105
Erasmus, Desiderius 223, 227
Esau 118, 123, 131 n.8
eshet chayil 30, 34, 41, 184
European Union (EU) 45
Exodus 95

The Faerie Queene. *See* Spencer, Edmund
Farrell, Nicholas 27
fascism 91
feminism 7, 13–14, 103–5, 180–3
Fielding, Susannah 30–4
Fiorentino, Giovanni. *See Il Pecorone*
Fletcher, John 236–7
Friedan, Betty 103, 111 n.20
friendship
  homoerotic desire 15, 211
    (*see also* homoeroticism)
  Renaissance code 223–5
  sexual expression 220–1, 237

garment industry 91–2
Geertz, Clifford 135–6
Genesis 117, 132 n.9, 193 n.1
Genoa (Italy) 174
German (language) 55–6
Gesta Romanorum 144
Ghetto Nuovo. *See* Venice
Ghetto Vecchio. *See* Venice
Ginsburg, Ruth Bader 192
Goebbels, Joseph 50
Goldstein, Baruch 49
Goldstein, Charlotte 90

Goodman, Henry 34, 40–1
Goodwin, Thomas 72
Gorky Theatre 62
Graetz, Heinrich 185
Granville, George 69–70
Gratiano
   and Antonio 140, 199–200
   and Balthazar 236
   and Nerissa 36, 203
   and Shylock 19, 34–5, 57, 126, 170
Great Shirtwaist Strike 110 n.15
Greek Orthodox Church 48

Haggadah 41
Halakha 181
Ham 6, 188–9
Hamas 49
Hands, Terry 26
Handy, Scott 21, 27
Harrison, William 114
Haug, Helgard Kim and Daniel Wetzel (dirs), *Mein Kampf* (2015) 46–7
Hebrew Bible 18
Hebrew Immigrant Aid Society (HIAS) 65
Hebrew (language) 8, 30, 34, 37, 184
Hebrew prayer 23, 41, 183. *See also eshet chayil*; Haggadah; Kaddish
Heine, Heinrich 181–2
Hermanis, Alvin 68 n.10
Hess, Walter 58
Hitler, Adolf 46–7, 103
Holocaust
   The Merchant of Venice 1, 23, 50, 180

   post-Holocaust literature 8, 10, 90–1, 96 (*see also Merchant of Venice*)
   survivors 35, 47
homoeroticism
   class inequality 206–7, 221–2
   the closet 217–22
   critical tradition 34, 195, 198, 201–2, 210–11
   friendship (*see* friendship)
   homophobia 209, 218
   melancholy 222
   Renaissance 218–20, 223
   sodomy 15, 221
   stage productions 26–8, 34

Il Pecorone
   Ansaldo 15, 198, 202–3, 205–6, 210
   Belmonte 202, 204
   Giannetto 202–6
   as source-text 14–15, 195, 202–3, 208
Improvisations on Shakespeare's Shylock, dir. George Tabori (1978) 39
Inquisition. *See Shayloks tochter*, Inquisition
Institute for Contemporary History (IfZ) 47
Interregnum 75–6, 81
Irons, Jeremy 18, 198
Ishmael 6
Islamic State (ISIS/ISIL) 45
Islamophobia
   Equality and Human Rights Commission (EHRC) 65
   Muslim Council of Britain 65

Israel 41, 46, 49, 91, 96
Israel, Menasseh ben 71–3
Italy. *See individual city names*

Jacob 117–19, 121–3, 132 n.9, 132 n.17
Japheth 188
Jason 124, 189, 205
Jelinek, Elfriede 52, 59, 60, 63, 68 n.8
Jennings, Byron 26
Jessey, Henry 74, 81–2
Jessica
   beauty 174, 179–80
   conversion (*see* conversion)
   feminism 180, 182–3
   fictional (literary) character 175–6, 180, 182–3, 191–2
   miscegenation 56
   in performance (*see individual actors*)
   rape 39
   rebel 179–80
Jewish Ghetto
   Ghetto Nuovo 174
   Ghetto Vecchio 174
   liminal space 14, 176, 186
   Renaissance 177, 186
   as setting 48, 192 (*see also Shayloks tochter*)
Jew(s)
   Ashkenazic (*see* Ashkenazic)
   assimilated 26, 182
   comic villains 54, 76
   communism 103
   crucifiers of Christ 74
   crypto-Jews 86 n.2 (*see also* marranos)
   deceptive 83
   early modern concepts 2–8 (*see also* Jorndan, Thomas)
   expulsion (*see* Edict of Expulsion)
   factory work 92–3, 107 n.6
   figural 3
   identifying clothing 18, 19
   Jewess 56, 84, 177–80, 189 (*see also* Madonna Bellina)
   labour activism (*see* labour activism)
   in London 74, 83
   messianic passivism 91, 94, 101
   readmission to England 70–3, 81–2
   Sephardic (*see* Sephardic)
   sodomites 209
   tribe, 154–5, 166–7
   vampires 44, 55, 74
   in Venice (*see* Jewish Ghetto)
   violence 19, 21 (*see also* antisemitism)
Jonson, Ben 150
Jordan, Thomas
   boy actor in The King's Revels Company 75
   The Forfeiture 9–10, 70, 72, 75–7, 82–4
   London poet laureate 75–6
   'Player's Petition to the Long Parliament' 75
   A Royal Arbor of Loyal Poesy 70, 76, 85

Kaddish 29
Kammerspiele Theatre (Munich Kammerspiele) 44, 51, 62–6

Kiffin, William 81–2
Koohestani, Amir Reza 64
Kuljić, Jelena 53, 58
Küppers, Hans George 66
Kurski, Jacek 56

Laban 11, 113–14, 117–18,
    121–3, 130
labour activism
    Canada 106 n.5, 109–10
        n.15, 110 n.18, 111 n.20,
        111 n.22
    feminism 102
    industrial settings 92, 101
    Jewish participation 90–2
    Triangle Shirtwaist Fire (*see*
        Triangle Shirtwaist Fire)
    women's participation 10,
        90, 92, 103–5
Lambert, John 72
Lampedusa 60
Langhoff, Shermin 62
Las Vegas 21–33
Latin (language) 8, 36–7
Launcelot (Lancelot) Gobbo 32,
    44, 54, 93, 107 n.7, 180
Lawrence, Henry 72
Leah 95
Leake, William 70, 80, 82
Lilienthal, Matthias 62–6
limpieza de sangre 189
Lorenzo 29–30, 95–8, 101–2
Luther, Martin 120–2, 132
    n.14, 132 n.16–17
Lyly, John 150

Machiavelli, Niccolo 191
Madonna Bellina 178–9, 190
Magni, Alberto Dei 189–91
Malersaal Theatre 62

Manton, Thomas 73
Markham, Gervase 162
Marlowe, Christopher 208,
    222–3
marranos 181
Marston, John 150
Mason, Brewster 26
Massinger, Philip 150
McEnery, Peter 26
Medea 189
Melchiades 191
Merchant Adventurers 80, 87
    n.11
merchant(s). *See* economics
The Merchant of Venice
    antisemitism 9, 21–2, 48, 54,
        72, 209 (*see also* Jordan,
        Thomas)
    ballad adaptation (*see*
        Jordan, Thomas)
    Belmont in (*see* Belmont)
    bond plot 76, 136, 141–3,
        145, 221
    casket plot (*see* casket)
    as comedy 49, 53–4
    costumes 19–20, 23, 25–6,
        40, 44
    credit (*see* credit; debt;
        economics)
    dramatis personae (*see*
        individual characters)
    economics (*see* economics)
    film adaptation, dir. Michael
        Radford (2004), 18–19,
        21, 39, 198
    First Folio 49
    gambling (*see* economics)
    Holocaust (*see* Holocaust,
        and *The Merchant of
        Venice*)

homoeroticism,
  homosexuality (*see*
  homoeroticism)
The Jew of Venice 196
meta-theatre 59
novelistic adaptations 89
play-text
pound of flesh 142, 220–1
pre-shows 8, 20, 21
profit (*see* economics)
quality of mercy 57, 155,
  168–9
race (*see* race)
reviews 22
ring(s) 149, 221, 230–1,
  233–5, 239, 241
risk (*see* economics)
as romance 82–3, 123–4
sadness (*see* sadness)
as satire 44, 54
sheep (*see* sheep)
theatrical performances
  and adaptations (*see
  play-titles, theatres/
  companies and directors'
  names*)
Third Quarto edition 70,
  80, 82
as tragedy 69
Merkel, Angela 45, 66, 68 n.10
Middleton, Thomas 150
migration, migrants 9, 45,
  59–62, 65
Miller, Jonathan 53
Miltiades 191
The Mirror of Complements
  163
miscegenation. *See* race
Modena, Leon 191
Mogaji, Akim 49

Mogen Dovid. *See* Star of
  David
Montaigne, Michel (Michel
  Eqyquem de Montaigne)
  224–5, 237
Morocco (Prince) 13, 31, 43–4,
  155, 160–1, 241
Moses 95–6
Munby, Jonathan 19–21, 36,
  38–9
Muslim(s) 3, 5–7, 9, 13, 49, 53

National Theatre (London, UK),
  Merchant of Venice, dir.
  Jonathan Miller (1970)
  20–1, 25–6, 29, 53
Nazi(s) 44, 91, 96
Nehemiah, Benjamin (Benjamin
  Nehemiah ben Elnathan)
  100, 109 n.13
Nerissa 29, 203
*New World Lessons for Old
  World Peoples* 106 n.5
Nitzan, Omri 49
Noah 188
Notices from Parnassus 189
Nunn, Trevor 34
Nye, Christopher 72

Okada, Toshiki 64
Olivier, Laurence 25, 29, 34, 40
Ovid (Publius Ovidius Naso)
  60, 189
Owen, John 73

Pacino, Al 17, 26, 35
Pack, Christopher 80–2
Paluzzi, Numidio 185, 190
Passover (Pesach) 90, 95
pastoral 114–15, 222–3, 240

Patriotic Europeans Against the
   Islamisation of the
   Occident (PEGIDA) 45,
   47
Paul IV (Paolo IV) 93, 95,
   109 n.13
Peters, Hugh 73
philosemitism 71–3, 180
Phocion 191
Photius 191
Piscopia, Elena Lucrezia
   Cornaro 192
populism
Portia
   as Balthazar (*see* Balthazar)
   bourgeois subjectivity 219
   casket test (*see* casket test)
   choice 138, 144–5
   golden fleece 204–5
   heteronormativity 219
   inheritance 144–5
   malleability 166–7
   mercy 155, 168–70
   moot court trial 192
   in performance (*see*
      actors and individual
      productions)
   sacrifice 123–4
   wealth 149
Protection Orders. *See* Jelinek,
   Elfriede
Protestantism 75
   Millenarian Protestants
      71–2
   Quakerism, Quakers 82
Pryce, Jonathan 40
Pryce, Phoebe 38
Prynne, William 74
The Public Theatre (Manhattan,
   New York) 89

race
   class 155, 158, 162
   conduct 13, 154, 157–8,
      161–2, 167
   early modern concepts 6–7,
      13, 154, 158–9
   embodied difference 7
   hereditary servitude 4, 6, 7
   innate difference 154,
      161–2, 166–7, 180–1
   Jews 4–7
   kinship 159
   miscegenation 144
   Muslims 6
   racial politics 144
Red Bull Theatre 75
refugee(s). *See* migrant(s)
Restoration 75–6, 217
Riedler, Julia 53, 57–8
Rimini Protokoll 63
risk
   evolving attitudes 12, 137,
      139
   fatefulness 138, 148
   and gender 148–9
   insurance 140–1, 147
   management 113–14
   sacrificial gift 124–5
   theology 114, 119–21
Rome (Italy) 69, 95, 100–2
Rowe, Nicholas 69
Royal Africa Company 85
Royal Shakespeare Company
   (RSC)
   The Merchant of Venice, dir.
      Bill Alexander (1987)
      18–19, 21, 49
   The Merchant of Venice, dir.
      David Thacker (1993)
      20, 21, 25

The Merchant of Venice,
  dir. Gregory Doran
  (1997) 20
The Merchant of Venice,
  dir. John Barton (1978)
  20, 41
The Merchant of Venice,
  dir. Rupert Goold (2011)
  21–5, 30–4
Royal Shakespeare Theatre 21
Rüping, Christopher 66

sadness
  despair 197
  destined 200
  erotically motivated 198,
    222
  opening scene 78, 139, 143,
    196
  risk 140
Salerio (Salarino)
  Antonio's ships 139, 142–3,
    160, 197, 199
  bond 165, 226
  in performance 23, 27, 34–5,
    49
  on Shylock 160, 165, 170
Samuel Morro 95–7, 100–1
Sareide 186, 189. *See also*
  Copia Sulam, Sarra
Schmauser, Thomas 53, 58
School of San Rocco 192
Schwartz, Maurice 89, 94, 105,
  105–6 n.3
Sephardic 174, 189
Shakespeare's Globe Theatre
  19–20, 35–8, 40
Shakespeare, William
  As You Like It 156
  Hamlet 155–7

  Henry IV, Part 1 76, 156
  Henry V 156
  King Lear 156
  Macbeth 166
  Measure for Measure 210
  Othello 76
  Sonnets 196, 201, 207,
    210–11
  The Tempest 156
  Timon of Athens 206
  Troilus and Cressida 156
  Twelfth Night 210
  Two Noble Kinsmen (with
    John Fletcher) 157
Shayloks tochter
  activism (*see* labour
    activism)
  antisemitism 99
  conversion (*see* conversion,
    Shayloks tochter)
  Inquisition 90–1, 95–7,
    99–100
  Jessica 10, 90, 94–101, 104
  Jewish Ghetto 94–5, 98–102
  Jewish identity 97, 99–101,
    104–5
  materialism 96–8
  patriarchal authority 98
  religious martyrdom 100–2
  religious study 94–6, 98,
    100–1
  Shylock 92–6
  Venice 90, 94–5, 98–9
sheep
  breeding 11, 116, 121–3,
    125, 130
  moral qualities 116
  pastoral (*see* pastoral)
  as property 115, 118, 123,
    126, 129

'tainted wether' 114, 123–4,
    126–9, 198, 200, 213 n.7,
    214 n.10
  and wolves 126
Shem 188
Shepheardes Calender. *See*
    Spenser, Edmund
Sher, Antony 34, 49
shofar 28
Sholem Aleichem 94, 108 n.10
Shylock
  anti semitism 19, 22, 23,
    155, 170
  assimilated Jew 22, 26, 41
  baptism 39–40
  clothing 20, 25, 26, 36 (*see
    also Merchant of Venice*,
    costumes)
  comic villain 76
  conversion (*see* conversion)
  and Jessica, 30, 37
  money 20–2, 25–6, 77–8,
    117 (*see also* economics)
  observant Jew 23, 25, 34, 41
  in performance (*see
    individual actors*)
  and Portia 32
  usurer 76, 77, 133, 159,
    225–6 (*see also* usury)
  vengeance 55, 82, 137, 165,
    170, 226, 228
  as wolf 125–6
The Shylock Project 48, 53
Silvayn, Alexander 208, 214 n.13
slavery, slave trade 4, 82, 85,
    189, 232–3
socialism 91
Solanio (Salanio)
  on Antonio's ships 139, 142,
    160, 197, 199
  on Jews 166–7, 226
  in performance 20, 23, 27,
    35, 93
Spain
  Barcelona 45
  Cambrils 45
  expulsion of Jews 189
Spenser, Edmund 145, 222–3
Star of David 19
Stemann, Nicholas 9, 43–4, 51,
    53–61, 63
Stewart, Patrick 22–4, 26, 34–5,
    40–1
Suchet, David 26, 34, 40–1
Sullivan, Daniel 39

Tabori, George 39
Talmud 94, 100–1, 175
Thalia Theatre 61, 68 n.10
Tintoretto 192
Topsell, Edward 116, 121, 125,
    128, 130
Tourneur, Cyril 150
Triangle Shirtwaist Fire 101,
    109 n.14
Trump, Donald 44, 65
Tubal 25, 36, 95, 166, 188

United Poland Party. *See*
    Kurski, Jacek
United States
  Charlottesville, VA 46
  New York City 101
  US-Mexico border 44
usury
  commerce 210
  early modern attitudes 11,
    114
  Jews 83
  justification of 117, 127

in performances of *Merchant*
17–18
theology 119–21, 123, 208,
225

Venice
Jewish Ghetto (*see* Jewish
Ghetto)
setting for *The Merchant
of Venice* 21, 39, 90,
148–9, 176, 207 (*see also
Shayloks tochter*)
Victorian era 25–6
Violet, Thomas 83
Virgil (Publius Vergilius Maro)
222–3
Voss, Philip 20

Whichcote, Benjamin 73
Whitehall Conference 71–4,
80–2, 86 n.2
Wilde, Oscar 26
Williams, Clifford 26
Wissenschaft des Judentums
185
Wurst, Conchita 56

Yiddish (language) 8, 11, 40,
89, 93–4, 105
Yiddish Art Theatre 96

Zahav, Ari ibn 89
Zionism 91, 96
Christian Zionism 74